Beyond JACOB'S LADDER

By
Lois Carscallen

TEACH Services, Inc.
P U B L I S H I N G
www.TEACHServices.com • (800) 367-1844

World rights reserved. This book or any portion thereof may not be copied or reproduced in any form or manner whatever, except as provided by law, without the written permission of the publisher, except by a reviewer who may quote brief passages in a review.

This book was written to provide truthful information in regard to the subject matter covered. The author assumes full responsibility for the accuracy of all facts and quotations as cited in this book. The opinions expressed in this book are the author's personal views and interpretation of the Bible, Spirit of Prophecy, and/or contemporary authors and do not necessarily reflect those of TEACH Services, Inc.

This book is sold with the understanding that the publisher is not engaged in giving spiritual, legal, medical, or other professional advice. If authoritative advice is needed, the reader should seek the counsel of a competent professional.

Copyright © 2013 TEACH Services, Inc.
ISBN-13: 978-1-4796-0152-3 (Paperback)
ISBN-13: 978-1-4796-0153-0 (ePub)
ISBN-13: 978-1-4796-0154-7 (Kindle/Mobi)
Library of Congress Control Number: 2013943722

Published by

www.TEACHServices.com • (800) 367-1844

Scriptures in this book, unless otherwise noted, are taken from the New King James Version.

Scripture quotations marked "NIV" are taken from the HOLY BIBLE, NEW INTERNATIONAL VERSION®. NIV®. Copyright © 1973, 1978, 1984 by International Bible Society. Used by permission of Zondervan. All rights reserved.

Scripture quotations marked "NASB" are taken from the New American Standard Bible®, Copyright © 1960, 1962, 1963, 1968, 1971, 1972, 1973, 1975, 1977, 1995 by The Lockman Foundation. Used by permission. (www.Lockman.org)

Scripture quotations marked "ESV" are taken from The Holy Bible, English Standard Version®, Copyright © 2001 by Crossway Bibles, a publishing ministry of Good News Publishers. ESV® Text Edition: 2007. Reproduced in cooperation with and by permission of Good News Publishers. All rights reserved.

Scripture quotations marked "NCV" are taken from the New Century Version of the Bible. Copyright © 2005 by Thomas Nelson, Inc. Used by permission. All rights reserved.

Scripture quotations marked "ASV" are taken from the American Standard Version of the Bible.

Scripture quotations marked "AMP" are taken from the Amplified® Bible. Copyright © 1954, 1958, 1962, 1964, 1965, 1987 by The Lockman Foundation. Used by permission.

Portions of this book were previously published at http://www.everlastingcovenant.com.

Contents

Acknowledgments vii

Prologue 9

Chapter One - Jacob's Ladder: Jacob's Dream 17

Chapter Two - Peter's Ladder: Love 29

Chapter Three - God's Ten Commandments 57

Chapter Four - Jesus' Ladder 91

Chapter Five - Paul's Ladder: The Fruit of the Spirit 117

Chapter Six - God's Creation Ladder 136

Chapter Seven - Moses/John's Ladder: The Sanctuary 159

Epilogue 204

Acknowledgments

To the memory of my father, Charles Koth, and my mother, Effie Bishop Koth, a devoted Christian whose desire was for her children to walk in the way of the Lord.

To the memory of my siblings, Charlie, Elise, Mable, Lennie, J.M., and Lucile, who made footprints for me to follow.

To the memory of my husband, Vern, who taught me to love and encouraged, as well as financed, me in all my educational endeavors.

To my children, Vern Jr., Nelle Ann, Jane, and Carey, along with their spouses; my grandchildren, great-grandchildren, siblings, nieces, and nephews who greatly influenced my thinking as I considered writing this book.

To friends in my Bible study group who helped me find answers to many questions as we studied together. Also, to the pastors and other church members who encouraged me.

To those who took the time to read and endorse this book for publication:

- Rhonda Backman, Health and Evangelism Director, Sandpoint Adventist Church
- John Stanton, Personal Evangelism and Discipleship Director, Upper Columbia Conference
- Sue Patzer, Women's Ministries Director, North Pacific Union Conference
- Max Torkelsen II, President, North Pacific Union Conference

I would also like to thank my son Carey Carscallen, Dean of Architecture and Design, Andrews University, and Ben Jepson, Vagabond Graphics, Sandpoint, Idaho, for the ladder design.

Prologue

Fitting the story of salvation on the ladder that God revealed to Jacob in a dream captures my experience. It is an experience I do not want to forget—one continuous path of God's leading. This experience can become reality to all who are willing to follow God's directions and allow the Holy Spirit to do the work needed in their lives. His leading takes us from the kingdom of grace, where we now live, to the kingdom of glory, where we shall live forever with Jesus, our Savior.

> " ... Behold, a ladder was set up on the earth, and its top reached to heaven; and there the angels of God were ascending and descending on it. And behold, The LORD stood above it and said: "I am the LORD God of Abraham your father and the God of Isaac; the land on which you will lie I will give to you and your descendants" (Gen. 28:12, 13).

Through inspiration, Ellen White, one of my favorite authors, elaborated on this text:

> "Christ is the ladder that Jacob saw, the base resting on the earth, and the topmost round reaching to the gate of heaven, to the very threshold of glory. If that ladder had failed by a single step of reaching the earth, we should have been lost. But Christ reaches us where we are. He took our nature and overcame, that we through taking His nature might overcome."
> *The Desire of Ages*, pp. 311, 312

Ellen White states that Christ not only said that He could reach Jacob, but that He could reach us, too. Angels will guard the edges of the ladder to keep us from falling if we choose to mount it and ascend with Jesus to the top.

"And this is the will of Him who sent Me, that everyone who sees the Son and believes in Him may have everlasting life; and I will raise him up at the last day" (John 6:40).

"I will raise him up at the last day." This is also a promise to us today. And God always keeps His promises; however, His promises are conditional.

This book is about how God has worked in the circumstances in my life, which taught me to trust in His promises. This is the opportunity God gives to everyone.

We make the choices that determine our destiny, either life or death, by our response to these promises. Abraham, Isaac, Jacob, Moses, Peter, Paul, John, and all of Jesus' faithful witnesses believed God's promises, and we should believe in them during this day and age as well.

When I learned about Jacob's dream of the ladder which reached from earth, the kingdom of grace, to heaven, the kingdom of glory, scripture began to fit the pattern of an orderly progression. As I placed the texts on the steps of the ladder God revealed to Jacob in his dream, the Bible became easier for me to understand.

I had begun taking college classes when my youngest of four children was five years old. The theories I learned while I was in college regarding mental, physical, and social sequential development, helped me to realize that it was God's plan for us to learn and spiritually grow in an orderly sequential manner, too. However, most of the sociology and psychology teachers only included mental, physical, and social development while promoting secular humanism. They did not factor in God. While they did not help me directly in my spiritual pursuit, they were helpful when I began to design the path I was to follow spiritually.

As I saw how they perceived we develop sequentially, when I read the parable of the growing seed, the light finally came on. "And He said, 'The kingdom of God is as if a man should scatter seed on the ground, and should sleep by night and rise by day, and the seed should sprout and grow, he himself does not know how. For the earth yields crops by itself: first the blade, then the head, after that the full grain in the head" (Mark 4:26–28).

Just as the plant develops and produces beautiful flowers or delicious fruit, He leads us to maturity, step-by-step. Generally, we are not able to ascend to the next step until we have understood and incorporated the prior level in our lives. This concept came alive to me when I placed the texts on each step of the ladder Jacob dreamed about.

It was as though I were ascending or descending a ladder in my journey to becoming a complete Christian. Jesus was the ladder lifting me up. All I had to do was choose to let Him do the work. God was very patient with me–He never gives up on His children. However, He does expect us to respond when he draws us by His power. We must seek to know the Lord. " ... And those who seek me diligently will find me" (Prov. 8:17). "Seek the LORD while He may be found, Call upon him while He is near. Let the wicked forsake his way, And the unrighteous man his thoughts; Let him return to the LORD, and He will have mercy on him; And to our God, for He will abundantly pardon" (Isa. 55:6–8).

> "Not by painful struggles or wearisome toil, not by gift or sacrifice, is righteousness obtained; but it is freely given to every soul who hungers and thirsts to receive it."
> *Thoughts from the Mount of Blessing*, p. 18

Circumstances in my childhood instilled a fear that has remained with me most of my life. It was a fear that I might do something wrong, but I didn't know what that "wrong thing" might be. Finally, I learned that God does not want me to be afraid. The Bible tells us not to fear many times. These verses assure us that He will be with us, and He will cast out our fear. There are still times when I fear that I might unknowingly offend others, but I am aware of and believe His promises.

Prologue

"Fear not, for I am with you; Be not dismayed, for I am your God. I will strengthen you, Yes, I will help you, I will uphold you with My righteous right hand" (Isa. 41:10).

" ... Perfect love casts out fear ... " (1 John 4:18). There is only One who has that perfect love: God, the Father, God, the Son, and God, the Holy Spirit. But He is teaching me to love more perfectly and to not be afraid of doing wrong.

"We have nothing to fear for the future, except as we shall forget the way the Lord has led us, and His teaching in past history" (*Testimonies for the Church*, vol. 9, p. 10).

God assures me that He will neither leave me nor forsake me. "... I will never leave you nor forsake you" (Heb. 13:5).

Although I learned little Bible doctrine while I was growing up, my mother taught me moral behavior. I always wanted to do what was right, and most of the time, I followed her instructions. She quoted two Bible verses that remain in my memory even though I did not understand their meaning. One verse was 1 Peter 5:8, "Be sober, be vigilant; because your adversary the devil walks about like a roaring lion, seeking whom he may devour."

Perhaps this contributed to my tendency to be fearful, but if she had continued with the next verse, maybe I would have understood. "Resist him, steadfast in the faith, knowing that the same sufferings are experienced by your brotherhood in the world" (1 Peter 5:9).

The other verse that I retained and quote often is: "I can do all things through Christ who strengthens me" (Phil. 4:13).

But somehow the "through Christ" had no meaning for me until recent years. I thought I was doing the work. I did not know Jesus, but I am thankful that He knew me. I believe God chose me to be His child before I was born like He did Jeremiah. In the same way He chooses all of us, but we must respond to Him. "Before I formed you in the womb I knew you; Before you were born I sanctified you ... " (Jer. 1:5).

My mother was a godly woman, but she almost died when I was born. She was in the hospital for a long time while our neighbor, Mrs. Smith, took care of me. It was a miracle that I lived, but Mrs. Smith had two old-maid daughters living at home, and I'm sure they gave me around-the-clock care. However, I missed that early bonding of love with my mother.

I can remember going to Mrs. Smith's house when I was five or six years old so one of the old-maids could cut my hair. Once when it was extremely hot outside, I fainted and fell off the stool while she was cutting my hair! My sister, Lucile, and I loved to go there and play in the attic while the others visited. There were a lot of dolls and toys, and we did not have many at our house. The older children would go down to the river and catch crabs while we played. Mr. Smith was what my mother called a "Hardshell Baptist" and believed in the ordinance of foot-washing, which Jesus taught in the Bible. Interestingly, I keep that ordinance now.

Mama never really was "well" after I was born, but my oldest sister by ten years helped her, along with the two hired black ladies we called Auntie Lizzie and Auntie Jane. They did most of the cooking and cleaning. We took the laundry to another lady we called Auntie Flora.

When I was twelve years old, I learned to drive by taking the laundry on Monday morning and picking it up on Wednesday. No one taught me how to drive. My father just handed me the keys, showed me the gas pedal, the clutch, and how to shift gears, and I took off. I was terrified, but I obeyed. It was sandy soil near a river in South Carolina and the ruts were so deep, there was no way I could get out of them and run off the road! It seems that everything I have learned in life, I learned the hard way, mostly without a teacher.

In spite of her illnesses, my mother had to work very hard later in life, and I worried about her. Having seven children in twelve years had taken its toll on her health, which was fragile to begin with. She always had a nap after dinner at noon, and after all my siblings had left home, I can remember listening at the door when I got home from school to hear her snoring. If I didn't hear a sound, I quietly cracked open the door and peeped in to make sure she was still breathing. Thankfully, she always was. I would then go to the dining room and eat what I wanted, clear the table, and wash the dirty dishes. As children, we were taught to work; there was little time for frivolity in our home as I was growing up. My mother taught me to attend Sunday School and church, and I was happy for that because it meant that I didn't have to work on Sundays!

I kept hearing about "surrender" when I went to church, but I did not know what surrendering to God meant. I didn't realize that my works counted for nothing, and that if I did anything good, it was Christ in me and not myself that did it. Even while I was teaching parenting classes and seminars for pastors and teachers later in life, self and pride ruled. It took years of His love and some disappointments in life to bring me to the knowledge of the truth that is in Christ, and the wisdom to heed it. However, God patiently waited while I slowly learned. "Therefore the LORD will wait, that He may be gracious to you; And therefore He will be exalted, that He may have mercy on you. For the LORD is a God of justice; Blessed are all those who wait for Him" (Isa. 30:18).

I am still learning and waiting to see many of my prayers answered, and I am certain that He will answer. He is blessing me in my old age as He has promised. I am an octogenarian now, and He has never let me down. I cling to this promise from Isaiah: "But those who wait on the LORD Shall renew their strength; They shall mount up with wings like eagles, They shall run and not be weary, They shall walk and not faint" (Isa. 40:31).

I am thankful that He waited for me and revealed His grace toward me. "For by grace you have been saved through faith, and that not of yourselves; it is the gift of God, not of works, lest anyone should boast. For we are His workmanship, created in Christ Jesus for good works, which God prepared beforehand that we should walk in them" (Eph. 2:8–10).

I was like those who fit the following description:

> There are those who profess to serve God, while they rely upon their own efforts to obey His law, to form a right character, and secure salvation. Their hearts are not moved by any deep sense of the love of Christ, but they seek to perform the duties of the Christian life as that which God requires of them in order to gain heaven. Such religion is worth nothing. When Christ dwells in the heart, the soul will be so filled with His love, with the joy of communion with Him, that it will cleave to Him; and in the contemplation of Him, self will be forgotten. Love to Christ will be the spring of action. Those who feel the constraining love of God, do not ask how little may be given to meet the requirements of God; they do not ask for the lowest standard, but aim at perfect conformity to the will of their Redeemer. With earnest desire they yield all and manifest an interest proportionate to the value of the object

which they seek. A profession of Christ without this deep love is mere talk, dry formality, and heavy drudgery. (*Steps to Christ*, pp. 44, 45)

This quotation is from the writings of Ellen White (1827–1915), who had visions from God. She did not claim to be a prophet, only "a messenger of the Lord." However, she met Bible criteria for prophets. God promised through the prophet Joel long ago that He would send other prophets: "And it shall come to pass afterward That I will pour out My Spirit on all flesh; Your sons and your daughters shall prophesy, Your old men shall dream dreams, Your young men shall see visions. And also on My menservants and on My maidservants I will pour out My Spirit in those days" (Joel 2:28, 29).

Ellen White described herself as a "lesser light" to lead us to Bible truth, "the greater light." "Little heed is given to the Bible, and the Lord has given a lesser light to lead men and women to the greater light" (*Colporteur Ministry*, p. 125).

She gave practical counsel and was a positive influence during her lifetime. Some of her contributions are:

- Accepting the Bible as the final authority for all faith and practice.
- Confirming biblical truth and guiding understanding to new light.
- Understanding the great controversy between Christ and Satan.
- Anchoring the central message of justification by faith by confirming the emphasis on righteousness by faith at the 1888 General Conference session.
- Presenting a holistic health message and promoting a healthy lifestyle.
- Promoting Christian education. She pointed out the significance of early childhood training.
- Building a worldwide publishing ministry to promote and distribute Christian literature and values.
- Establishing an effective worldwide organization and structure which enables the church to maintain a worldwide mission that is currently in more than 200 countries.

Ellen White's writings are not a replacement for the Bible; instead, she lifts up the Bible and helps me understand and take the Word of God seriously. Her ministry was God's gift to the remnant church in the end time.

I have not had a vision, and I do not claim to be a prophet; however, I believe there are both true and false prophets working today, and we are admonished to test them. "To the law and to the testimony! If they do not speak according to this word, it is because there is no light in them" (Isa. 8:20).

Prophecy in the Bible has become of great interest to me, and I am learning more and more about end-time prophecies. It is as though I "hunger and thirst after righteousness" and God continues to teach me, and He will as long as I am willing to obey. I pray that God will help me distinguish between the true and the false. Since I believe in the Lord, I am certain that He will guide me to what is true. "... Believe in the LORD your God, and you shall be established; believe His prophets, and you shall prosper" (2 Chron. 20:20).

There are still many things I do not understand. However, God keeps revealing more and more of the mysteries that have been hard to perceive even by the clergy. "The mystery which has been hidden from ages and from generations, but now has been revealed to His saints. To them God willed to make known what are the riches of the glory of this mystery among the Gentiles: which is Christ in you, the hope of glory" (Col. 1:26, 27).

"Christ in me" —that is my desire. Now, I want God's will to be my will, and I know that the only way to allow the Holy Spirit to work is to stay in the Word. Yet, no matter how much I learn, there is more beyond. I am told that we will still be learning throughout eternity. I shall have many questions to ask Jesus when I get to heaven.

> "The cross of Christ will be the science and the song of the redeemed through all eternity."
> *The Faith I Live By*, p. 361

I believe there may be others who, like me, have not understood God's plan of salvation, and it is my desire that they might realize that God has made it easy for us if we seek Him with all our heart. He has promised salvation to spiritual Israel, the name given Jacob after he "passed the test" and was blessed by God. "And so all Israel will be saved, as it is written: 'The Deliverer will come out of Zion, And He will turn away ungodliness from Jacob; For this is My covenant with them, When I take away their sins" (Rom. 11:26, 27).

Putting the steps on the ladder has taken out much of the mystery of salvation for me. I have heard scores of exegetical sermons that were far beyond my level of learning. I am still trying to understand and apply the information that has been given to me. Because a lot of pastors preach at the analytical and evaluation levels, and I simply needed to understand, the sermons resulted in little meaning for me.

I discovered many places in the Bible to which Jacob's ladder was referred, and I began to pursue them. I discovered seven ladders (I'm sure there are many more) that revealed God's plan of salvation. All had knowledge that I needed, and it was presented to me in a way I could understand. Now, as I ascend each round on Jacob's ladder, which is Jesus, He knows what I need next. He led me to construct the following ladders.

- Jacob's ladder taught me faith and how other scripture led to our salvation.
- Peter's ladder gave me a list of God's character traits we must add to our faith.
- God's ladder taught me that the Ten Commandments are our guide for living.
- Jesus' ladder assured me of His blessings if I meet His conditions.
- Paul's ladder taught me that we all have spiritual gifts, which we must use to bless others.
- God's Creation ladder tells the story of beginnings, and God's plan for our lives.
- Moses/John's ladder taught me how God gave Moses the plan to build an earthly sanctuary where He could be worshipped, and John revealed the vision God gave him of Jesus in the heavenly sanctuary and beyond where we can live for an eternity with Him.

After ascending these seven ladders, I know for sure that God is guiding me. Seven is a symbol of spiritual perfection. It is significant in the symbolism of the Spirit. For example, a prophecy of the Holy Spirit upon Jesus emphasizes seven aspects of the Spirit's power on Him. "The Spirit of the LORD shall rest upon Him, The Spirit of wisdom and understanding, The Spirit of counsel and might, The Spirit of knowledge and of the fear of the LORD" (Isa. 11:2).

Prologue

If we choose, this power is also available to us:

- Spirit of the LORD (Holy Spirit)
- Wisdom
- Understanding
- Counsel
- Might
- Knowledge
- Fear of the Lord

Seven is a perfect number, but I know I am not perfect. However, I have asked God to "free me from every entanglement," so that I might share with you how easy God makes obedience through the power of the Holy Spirit. Thus, I have titled this book "Beyond Jacob's Ladder: The Simplicity of Salvation."

Chapter One
JACOB'S LADDER: JACOB'S DREAM

Families often have children who do not get along well when they are growing up. My family was no exception. There were three brothers who shared a large bedroom and usually cooperated with each other, but every now and then, the rest of the family would become aware of quarrels they had between them. I remember one day my father came home with a pair of boxing gloves. He showed them to all the family and the next time there was a dispute between the boys, he made them don the boxing gloves and fight until they were willing to give in and be at peace with each other. It was a great lesson for me at the age of five; I never wanted to be in a fight. I tried my best to please everyone! And it must have worked for my brothers because later in life they became business partners.

It was not that simple with Isaac's sons, Jacob and Esau. Jacob had deceived his brother Esau into selling his birthright, due him as the first-born, for a bowl of lentil stew. Later, he deceived Isaac, their father, and also received the blessing which should have gone to Esau.

Esau had sworn to kill Jacob after their father died, so in order to protect him, his mother, Rebecca, who had been instrumental in convincing him to deceive his father, helped to hasten his departure. She did not live to see him again, but I am certain that she never forgot him and the events that led to his escape. Jacob left home with the blessings of his father to go to his uncle's home and find a wife, rather than marry one of the daughters of Ishmael as Esau had.

Tired and weary from travel, Jacob laid down to rest, troubled with the fear of his brother's wrath. God, in His mercy, gave him the dream which is beautifully recorded in the Bible.

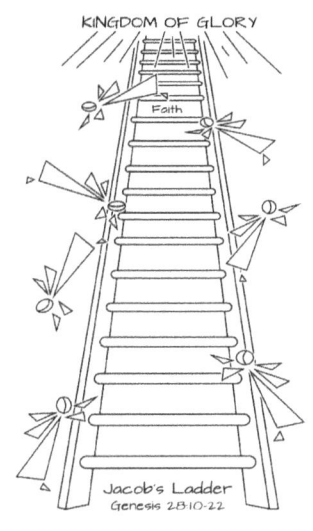

Now Jacob went out from Beersheba and went toward Haran. So he came to a certain place and stayed there all night, because the sun had set. And he took one of the stones of that place and put it at his head, and he lay down in that place to sleep. Then he dreamed, and behold, a ladder was set up on the earth, and its top reached to heaven; and there the angels of God were ascending and descending on it. And behold, the LORD stood above it and said: "I am the LORD God of Abraham your father and the God of Isaac; the land on which you lie I will give to you and your descendants. Also your descendants shall be as the dust of the earth; you shall spread abroad to the west and the east, to the north and the south; and in you and in your seed all the families of the earth shall be blessed. Behold, I am with you and will keep you wherever you go, and will bring you back to this land; for I will not leave you until I have done what I have spoken to you." Then Jacob awoke from his sleep and said, "Surely the LORD is in this place, and I did not know it." And he was afraid and said, "How awesome is this place! This is none other than the house of God, and this is the gate of heaven!" Then Jacob rose early in the morning, and took the stone that he had put at his head, set it up as a pillar, and poured oil on top of it. And he called the name of that place Bethel; but the name of that city had been Luz previously. Then Jacob made a vow, saying, "If God will be with me, and keep me in this way that I am going, and give me bread to eat and clothing to put on, so that I come back to my father's house in peace, then the LORD shall be my God. And this stone which I have set as a pillar shall be God's house, and of all that You give me I will surely give a tenth to You." (Gen. 28:10–22)

When I learned that the ladder is God's glorious light, Jesus, reaching down to us so that we might rise up higher to Him, and that Christ Himself actually brings us up the ladder, it became an inspiration to me. Ellen White talks in detail about Jacob's dream.

> Jacob in the night vision saw earth connected with heaven by a ladder reaching to the throne of God. He saw the angels of God, clothed with garments of heavenly brightness, passing down from heaven and up to heaven upon this shining ladder. The bottom of this ladder rested upon the earth, while the top of it reached to the highest heavens and rested upon the throne of Jehovah. The brightness from the throne of God beamed down upon this ladder and reflected a light of inexpressible glory upon the earth. This ladder represented Christ, who had opened the communication between earth and heaven. In Christ's humiliation He descended to the very depths of human woe in sympathy and pity for fallen man, which was represented to Jacob by one end of the ladder resting upon the earth, while the top of the ladder, reaching unto heaven, represents the divine power of Christ grasping the Infinite and thus linking earth to heaven and finite man to the infinite God. Through Christ the communication is opened between God and man. Angels may pass to and fro from heaven to earth with messages of love to fallen man, and to minister unto those who shall be heirs of salvation. It is through Christ alone that the heavenly messengers minister to men. (*Confrontation*, p. 46)

Jacob must have remembered this dream many times as he dealt with his Uncle Laban. He had to go through many trials before he really understood the meaning of the ladder that God had given him in his dream on the way to find a bride. Once Laban came to think unfavorably of Jacob, Jacob ran away with his children, wives, and flocks, but Laban decided to chase after him. Jacob grew in frustration toward Laban, and ultimately, toward God. "Then Jacob was angry and rebuked Laban, and Jacob answered and said to Laban: 'What is my trespass? What is my sin, that you have so hotly pursued me? Although you have searched all my things, what part of your household things have you found? Set it here before my brethren and your brethren, that they may judge between us both" (Gen. 31:36, 37).

Even though God made His care of Jacob a sure promise, Jacob's vow to God was conditional. God had told Jacob that He would not leave him, but Jacob counted on God's visibility in his life. When it seemed God wasn't there for him, Jacob, like most of us, came to doubt God's word. But in the end, God was the one to be trusted and I am assured that God will do what He promises if we obey.

One way that we can obey God is in regards to tithing. Jacob knew what God's Word said about tithing, for he said, " … I will surely give a tenth to You" (Gen. 28:22). His grandfather paid tithe. Moses wrote of Abraham: "And he gave him a tithe of all" (Gen. 14:20).

And we are told to give a tithe of our increase to God. "'Bring all the tithes into the storehouse, That there may be food in My house, And try Me now in this,' Says the LORD of hosts, 'If I will not open for you the windows of heaven And pour out for you such blessing That there will not be room enough to receive it'" (Mal. 3:10).

My mother paid tithe, which I am sure was like the widow's mite because she had little money, so I should have known that was what God wanted me to do. I did learn, but it was many years later. I can still remember that she had a box containing a year's supply of tithe envelopes which the Baptist church provided. She kept it on the mantle above the fireplace in her bedroom, and when we went to church, she would put some money in one of the envelopes and put it in the offering plate when it was passed. It made me feel proud that she was doing what the other adults did. Usually, I was given a nickel or dime to put in. As children, we were not given allowances for doing chores like most parents give their children today. We had to ask for whatever we wanted, and if my mother could, she would provide it for us.

God really loved Jacob; He loves everyone. But He said He hated Esau. "As it is written, 'Jacob I have loved, but Esau I have hated.' What shall we say then? Is there unrighteousness with God? Certainly not! For he says to Moses, 'I will have mercy on whomever I will have mercy, and I will have compassion on whomever I will have compassion'" (Rom. 9:13–15).

Does God really hate anyone? This strong expression does not imply positive hatred, as the term is used today, but that God had preferred Jacob above Esau to be the progenitor of the chosen race. It seems to have been common in Bible times to use the term hate in this sense. Jacob's preference for Rachel is compared with his hatred for Leah. In the New Testament, Jesus speaks about hating one's father and mother and hating one's life. "He who loves his life will lose it, and he who hates his life in this world will keep it for eternal life" (John 12:25). The idea is that Christ takes special care of those that give Him their devotion. I, myself, had to learn that my love for God must be first in my life.

> "Christ never forces His company upon anyone. He interests Himself in those who need Him … But if men are too indifferent to think of the heavenly Guest, or ask Him to abide with them, He passes on. Thus many meet with great loss."
>
> *The Desire of Ages,* p. 800

Jacob realized that God had given him the dream, and he set up an altar as was the custom when something significant happened in a certain place. It would be remembered when he returned and saw it again. However, it was a dream that God wanted Jacob to take with him, a promise which was intended for him to cling to. God was pointing the way for Jacob to save the nation so they in turn would save others. He never forgot the dream.

Jacob was deceived by his Uncle Laban many times, and he was not free from his own practice of deception himself, but he finally made his escape. He had bargained with Laban and gained his wealth by God's blessings. However, it was not until God met with him the second time that he became an honest man. Jacob had received a vision of Jesus in the dream of the ladder when he was fleeing from his brother Esau. Now, he was fleeing from Laban. When they finally confronted each other, Jacob said:

> These twenty years I have been with you; your ewes and your female goats have not miscarried their young, and I have not eaten the rams of your flock. That which was torn by beasts I did not bring to you; I bore the loss of it. You required it from my hand, whether stolen day or stolen by night. There I was! In the day the drought consumed me, and the frost by night, and my sleep departed from my eyes. Thus I have been in your house twenty years; I served you fourteen years for your two daughters, and six years for your flock, and you have changed my wages ten times. Unless the God of my father, the God of Abraham and the Fear of Isaac, had been with me, surely now you would have sent me away empty-handed. God has seen my affliction and the labor of my hands, and rebuked you last night. (Gen. 31: 36–42)

"For twenty years Jacob remained in Mesopotamia, laboring in the service of Laban, who, disregarding the ties of kinship, was bent upon securing to himself all the benefits of their connection. Fourteen years of toil he demanded for his two daughters; and during the remaining period, Jacob's wages were ten times changed. Yet Jacob's service was diligent and faithful."

Patriarchs and Prophets, p. 190

In a dream God had sent an angel to warn Laban not to harm Jacob, so they departed in peace. In spite of his spending twenty years as a servant of Laban and being deceived many times, Jacob kept his word and was always faithful. Now his worry was for Esau.

> Then Jacob said, "O God of my father Abraham and God of my father Isaac, the LORD who said to me, 'Return to your country and to your family, and I will deal well with you': I am not worthy of the least of all the mercies and of all the truth which You have shown Your servant; for I crossed over this Jordan with my staff, and now I have become two companies. Deliver me, I pray, from the hand of my brother, from the hand of Esau; for I fear him, lest he come and attack me and the mother with the children. For You said, 'I will surely treat you well, and make your descendants as the sand of the sea, which cannot be numbered for multitude.' ... And he arose that night and took his two wives, his two female servants, and his eleven sons, and crossed over the ford of Jabbok. He took them, sent them over the brook, and sent over what he had. Then Jacob was left alone; and a Man wrestled with him until the breaking of day. Now when He saw that He did not prevail against him, He touched the socket of his hip; and the socket of Jacob's hip was out of joint as He wrestled with him. And He said, "Let Me go, for the day breaks." But he said, 'I will not let you go unless You bless me!" So He said

to him, "What is your name?" He said, "Jacob." And He said, 'Your name shall no longer be called Jacob, but Israel; for you have struggled with God and with men, and have prevailed." Then Jacob asked, saying, 'Tell me Your name, I pray.' And He said, "Why is it that you ask about My name?" And He blessed him there. So Jacob called the name of the place Peniel: "For I have seen God face to face, and my life is preserved." Just as he crossed over Penuel the sun rose on him, and he limped on his hip." (Gen. 32:9-12, 22-31)

Jacob was willing to continue in battle unto death in defense of his family. So must we. He received a name change when he refused to let go, and the angel knew that his repentance was heartfelt. He held fast to Jesus, and so must we.

> Through humiliation, repentance, and self-surrender, this sinful, erring mortal [Jacob] prevailed with the Majesty of heaven. He had fastened his trembling grasp upon the promises of God, and the heart of Infinite Love could not turn away the sinner's plea. As an evidence of his triumph and an encouragement to others to imitate his example, his name was changed from one which was a reminder of his sin, to one that commemorated his victory. (*The Great Controversy*, p. 617)

We are told that we will receive a new name as well. I wonder what my new name will be. I didn't like my name when I was growing up. But when I learned that it means faithful, it became special to me—what better name could I have? My desire is to be faithful. But no matter what my new name is, I am sure I will like it because it will come from God. "... To him who overcomes ... I will give him a white stone, and on the stone a new name written which no one knows except him who receives it" (Rev. 2:17).

It took the second meeting with God on his return trip home to enable Jacob's true conversion. Jacob's Pentecost came when he would not let go of the angel until he received the blessing. He was broken in the process and suffered from this wound the remainder of his life. But God honored his true repentance, and changed his name to Israel—the nation that would lead the world in the direction God would have them go.

This was not the first time Jacob had a wrestling match. Before he was born, he wrestled with Esau in the womb, but he did not win the battle and come out first. It took God many years to teach him the lesson he needed to learn. Hosea refers to Jacob's struggle before his birth.

> He took his brother by the heel in the womb, And in his strength he struggled with God. Yes, he struggled with the Angel and prevailed; He wept, and sought favor from Him. He found Him in Bethel, And there He spoke to us—That is, the LORD God of hosts. The LORD is His memorable name. So you, by the help of your God, return; Observe mercy and justice, And wait on your God continually. (Hosea 12:3-6)

After wrestling with the angel, Jacob had experienced enough deception. His mother had favored him above Esau because of Esau's defiance of God. And even though Jacob did not want to leave home, he honored his mother by being obedient.

Before he died, my oldest brother told me that I was favored by my mother; however, I was anxious to leave home when I graduated from high school. Although my father told others how much he loved his children, I did not feel that love, but I was obedient.

It was through the love of the man God sent to be my husband that I began to get a glimpse of what God's love was really like. As I look back, he reminds me of Jacob. I saw resemblances in my husband's experience to compare with Jacob's. He left his home, not of his choosing, but of a call to be drafted into the army during World War II. Neither did Jacob leave home by his own choice. He was fleeing from the wrath of his brother, Esau. Jacob had gone in search of a wife, and that, too, was the hope of my future husband.

When Jacob saw Rachel at the well, it was love at first sight. My future husband and I were invited on a blind date by a couple we both knew individually. The wife worked with me, and her husband was in the same Air Force unit with my future husband. It was love at first sight also or perhaps, at least, infatuation, which grew into love. He was the kind of person that was easy for me to relate to, and he made for a good, kind husband.

I can identify with Rachel also. She did not know God, but her father's idol worship meant so much to her that she stole his idols when she and Jacob were leaving. As a child, my mother taught me to sing Jesus Loves Me, to be "good" and say my nightly prayer by rote, "Now I lay me down to sleep, etc.," and go to church, but I didn't know Jesus. It was much later in life when I was wounded and broken from failing to receive the expectations I had that God opened my eyes to His leading by the power of the Holy Spirit. It took a lot of searching for me.

After having four children, my husband and I were baptized together in the Palouse River and accepted into the Seventh-day Adventist Church. Years later, three of our grandchildren chose to be baptized in the same place. What a blessing!

When our children reached the ages five to twelve, we began to wonder how we would ever finance their education. God helped me through many trials, so I enrolled in college. I finally realized that He was the source of my help, but I still did not have that relationship of really knowing Jesus.

Now I enjoy studying my Bible more and more. It is as though I "hunger and thirst after righteousness." God continues to teach me, and He will as long as I am willing to obey. There are still many things I do not understand. However, He keeps revealing more and more of the mysteries that have been hard to understand, even by the clergy.

I felt like the chickens must have when they had to scratch for their feed among the straw. I had a lot of scratching to do! You see, when I was a very young child, one of my chores was to feed the chickens. My father grew the corn we fed them, but there was a lot of work to do to get the corn ready for the chickens to eat it, and that was part of my job.

First of all, I had to go to the barn and get the ears of dried corn out of the corn crib. Then I had to shuck them. We had a corn grinder that separated the corn from the cob, so that came next. To operate the grinder, I had to hold the ear of corn with my left hand and push down on it while I turned the handle of the grinder with my right hand. Actually, watching the corn fly off the cob was sort of fun. After I had ground enough corn for the day's feed, I took it out to the chicken yard and scattered it in the straw. The chickens had to do a lot of scratching to find enough grains of corn to satisfy their hunger for the day. But the scratching gave them the exercise they needed, so it was a good thing that I made it a little hard for them to get food.

It was different for the baby chicks which my mother hatched in an incubator every spring. Their first food was mash, which I put into a small feeder easily within their reach. Then when they grew older, the mash was replaced with cracked corn—just the size they could handle. After they became pullets, they joined the hens in the chicken yard and had to scratch for their own food among the straw.

That is the way God led me—one step at a time as I was ready. When I saw the dream that Jacob had of the ladder reaching from earth to heaven, I began to understand what I was lacking. My spiritual growth had been stunted.

I came to learn that we are utterly dependent upon God dispensing His grace to us through the heavenly hosts. I must remember this, and I must also remember that while I am ascending that ladder, I must invite others to come with me. But I found that I had a problem. I became critical of others if they were not living by my standards.

As the Holy Spirit began to help me fit certain scriptures into my life, salvation began to appear simple, yet sometimes I made it hard for myself. My critical spirit turned to bitterness, but I learned that "the heart knows its own bitterness" (Prov. 14:10).

Criticism and bitterness do not come from God. They are the fool's simplicity. God does not want us to have this kind of simplicity, but I'm afraid I was in that category. The following verse explains the idea of simplicity. I believe it can most certainly be in reference to those who like to sit on the sidelines and criticize other's actions or the efforts of their fellow church members. And many times this leads them to pluck away at the foundational doctrines of the Christian faith itself. I was guilty of this, but God gave me a wake-up call.

> "Then set your mark high, and step by step, even though it be by painful effort, by self denial and sacrifice, ascend the whole length of the ladder of progress. Let nothing hinder you. ... A character formed according to the divine likeness is the only treasure that we can take from this world to the next. ... The heavenly intelligences will work with the human agent who seeks with determined faith that perfection of character which will reach out to perfection in action. To everyone engaged in this work Christ says, I am at your right hand to help you. As the will of man cooperates with the will of God, it becomes omnipotent. Whatever is to be done at His command may be accomplished in His strength. All His biddings are enabling."
>
> *Christ's Object Lessons*, pp. 331-333

"How long, you simple ones, will you love simplicity? For scorners delight in their scorning, And fools hate knowledge" (Prov. 1:22).

God says, "And let us consider one another to provoke unto love and to good works" (Heb. 10:24, KJV).

The idea of provoking others unto love and good works, without being considered critical or judgmental, eludes me most of the time, but God reminds me to let Him take control through Ellen White's counsel. "In matters of conscience the soul must be left untrammeled. No one is to control another's mind, to judge for another, or to prescribe his duty. God gives to every soul freedom to think, and to follow his own convictions" (*The Desire of Ages*, p. 550).

My problem is that I try to tell people what to do, instead of pointing to Jesus, and letting Him be the one to draw them to the ladder through the power of the Holy Spirit. I have been like Rebecca and Jacob, trying to make things happen with others, especially my children. Rebecca wanted so badly for her children to follow the God of Israel that she led Jacob into deceiving his father. I wanted my children to follow Jesus; and like Rebecca, I tried to do it in my own way. The sad part for me is that, like Paul, I thought I was doing things God's way.

There were times when I was told "You never listen to me." But that is not like Jesus.

He listened and reasoned with the people as He directs us to do. "'Come now, and let us reason together,' says the LORD ... " (Isa. 1:18).

In spite of all my mistakes, I know my children love me, and God has promised to save them even if they should rebel for a period of time. Thankfully, God forgives when we ask, even in our ignorance, and I'm holding Him accountable to this promise!

"Truly, these times of ignorance God overlooked, but now commands all men everywhere to repent" (Acts 17:30).

When Jesus was choosing the twelve disciples who would be His companions and students, He referred to angels ascending and descending. Look at what He said when He was speaking to Nathanael: "Jesus answered and said to him, 'Because I said to you, I saw you under the fig tree, do you believe? You will see greater things than these.' And He said to him, 'Most assuredly, I say to you, hereafter you shall see heaven open, and the angels of God ascending and descending upon the Son of Man'" (John 1:50, 51).

When God spoke to Jacob about the ladder, His words were: "The angels of God were ascending and descending on it" (Gen. 29:12).

God did not have to give Nathanael a vision as He did Jacob. He was present to tell him in person. Jesus, the Son of man, is the ladder. It is His power, through the Holy Spirit; we have no power of our own. But there is another power which intrudes—the power of Satan. We choose which one we want to operate within us. If we choose Jesus, we have the power we need to lift us up the ladder. God did not give me a dream like He gave Jacob, and He did not speak to me like He did Nathanael. He speaks to me through the knowledge I get from the Word of God, the Bible. And it is my responsibility to study it daily and always be in an attitude of prayer. God has given us the gift of repentance. Even when we don't have godly sorrow, God will provide it if we open ourselves to receive it. "He was clothed with a robe dipped in blood, and His name is called The Word of God" (Rev. 19:13).

> "The angels of God are ascending, bearing the prayers of the needy and distressed to the Father above, and descending, bringing blessing and hope, courage, help, and life, to the children of men. The angels of God are ever passing from earth to heaven, and from heaven to earth.... And it is through Christ, by the ministration of His heavenly messengers, that every blessing comes from God to us. ... Christ is the medium of communication of men with God, and of God with men."
>
> *The Desire of Ages*, p. 143

Jacob's Ladder: Jacob's Dream

Some Bible translations use stair-steps instead of a ladder. In our day of a mechanized society, Jacob's ladder might best be described as an escalator. An escalator fits the description of Jesus' angels, constantly propelling us upward toward the heavenly city. Whatever we call it, we must take the journey on it, for Jesus is that ladder.

When I learned about the ladder, I wondered how I would ever reach the top. I had not been a Bible student before I was married. After we joined the church, we faithfully took the children to Sabbath School and church. We read Bible stories to them at bedtime and had prayer, but we didn't really study the Bible with them.

I knew that I could not teach my children as they should be taught, so we enrolled them in church school and depended on the teachers to teach them the Bible. I hoped that as they learned, they would help me understand more, but that didn't happen because I really didn't let them know how little I understood.

I was so busy with the duties of home; I was taking care of four children, keeping books for the partnership we were in with my husband's three brothers, and later, attending college myself, so I spent my time in general busyness and studying college textbooks. Thankfully, I had a husband who had been taught when he was a child, and even though he had not always followed the Lord, all I had to do was ask him a question of whether something was right according to the Bible.

I had never realized exactly what Pentecost was all about, but God has revealed at least a tiny picture to me. I know that if we are to have the experience of Pentecost, we must first meet the requirements of Pentecost, and the work of Pentecost will follow. At Pentecost, the believers were all of one accord and spent their time in prayer. I knew I must do the same, and I knew Jesus would help me. Ellen White makes an interesting point.

> We are living in the perils of the last days. All heaven is interested in the characters you are forming. Every provision has been made for you, that you should be a partaker of the divine nature, having escaped the corruption that is in the world through lust. Man is not left alone to conquer the powers of evil by his own feeble efforts. Help is at hand, and will be given every soul who really desires it. Angels of God, that ascend and descend the ladder that Jacob saw in vision, will help every soul who wills to climb even to the highest heaven. (*Fundamentals of Christian Education*, p. 86)

I have learned that I need only be concerned for my own salvation, not anyone else's, especially my children's. He has promised to save them even if they resist Him for a while. "The love of God still yearns over the one who has chosen to separate from Him, and He sets in operation influences to bring him back to the Father's house" (*Christ's Object Lessons*, p. 202).

He even tells me how He does it. "Angels are rearranging environments, changing circumstances, weaving about disinterested souls a network of influences which will some day lead to a surrender. God never forces Himself on a single life, but

> "It is not the fear of punishment, or the hope of everlasting reward, that leads the disciples of Christ to follow Him. They behold the Saviour's matchless love, revealed throughout His pilgrimage on earth, from the manger of Bethlehem to Calvary's cross, and the sight of Him attracts, it softens and subdues the soul. Love awakens in the heart of the beholders. They hear His voice, and they follow Him."
>
> *The Desire of Ages*, p. 480

there is one way to connect a man to heaven in spite of himself and that way is through prayer" (*The Story of the Seer of Patmos,* p. 147).

God gives encouraging words to parents. "Thus says the LORD: 'Refrain your voice from weeping, and your eyes from tears; For your work shall be rewarded,' says the LORD, 'And they shall come back from the land of the enemy. There is hope in your future,' says the LORD, 'That your children shall come back to their own border'" (Jer. 31:16, 17).

We are given the true motive for children or anyone to follow Christ.

We are told to share our own experience with others when we have opportunity, and we are given specific instructions regarding our children. "Train up a child in the way he should go, And when he is old he will not depart from it" (Prov. 22:6).

This was Jacob's experience. His father had taught him to worship the true God, but it took the wrestling match with the angel when he was older to bring about his true conversion.

I am thankful that over the years, God has taught me many things; and many of His lessons have made their impression as I placed the gospel of salvation on the steps of Jacob's ladder. When I first saw the significance of the ladder God let down for Jacob to see, what joy I experienced! As a sinner, separated from God, most of us see His law from below, and it seems impossible to be kept. Perhaps, like me, you have repeatedly tried to please God, only to realize that you have selfish motives. Or perhaps you feel that He is not interested in your desires, and you don't even try. In either case, what relief you will feel when you see Jesus with open arms offering to lift you above the ladder; He wants to take you directly to God! Once Jesus lifts you into God's presence, you are free to obey–out of love, not fear, through God's power. You know that if you stumble, you will not fall back to the ground. Instead, you will be caught and held in Christ's loving arms, for He is the ladder, and I believe the Holy Spirit is the safety net that will keep you from falling. "But when the Helper comes, whom I shall send to you from the Father, the Spirit of truth who proceeds from the Father, He will testify of Me" (John 15:26). "He will glorify Me, for He will take of what is Mine and declare it to you" (John 16:14).

We must never forget how much God loves us. "For God so loved the world that He gave His only begotten Son, that whoever believes in Him should not perish but have everlasting life. For God did not send His Son into the world to condemn the world, but that the world through Him might be saved" (John 3:16, 17).

God is love–that is His essence, His character. He was willing to die for sinners. There are records of others besides Jacob who were willing to die to save another soul. Moses was one of those people. He was trying to lead God's people out of Egypt to inhabit the land God had promised them, but they were rebellious. While he was away communing with God, the children of Israel under Aaron's leadership, made a golden calf to worship. Moses was so angry when he saw them sinning, he broke the tablets of commandments God had given him. But despite their betrayal, he was still willing to plead for them with his life.

"Then Moses returned to the LORD and said, 'Oh, these people have committed a great sin, and have made for themselves a god of gold! Yet now, if You will forgive their sin–but if not, I pray, blot me out of Your book which You have written'" (Exod. 32:31, 32).

God inflicted death upon many, but out of His infinite love and mercy gave Moses another copy of the Ten

Commandments. Most of us, I believe, would be willing to die for our children, or our spouse, or someone we love dearly in order for them to be saved. There was a time when I thought if I were truly willing to die for my children, it would give me the assurance that they would be in heaven with their dad, and I prayed as Moses did. But God does not accept the death of anyone to save another except His Son, Jesus. Then I discovered this verse: "He who loves father or mother more than Me is not worthy of Me. And he who loves son or daughter more than Me is not worthy of Me" (Matt. 10:37).

Jesus died for you just as He did for me and my family. He is the one who will save everyone who is willing to love, trust, and serve Him through obedience; for He has promised: "For when we were still without strength, in due time Christ died for the ungodly. For scarcely for a righteous man will one die; yet perhaps for a good man someone would even dare to die. But God demonstrates His own love toward us, in that while we were still sinners, Christ died for us" (Rom. 5:6–8).

I learned that each must have his own relationship with Jesus. He has the power to save all who come to him in faith. He has shown us what the necessary steps are to go from the kingdom of grace at the bottom of the ladder to the kingdom of glory at the top.

These three words described my condition: weak, ignorant, and unworthy. Thus I set out to do just what He invited me to do: to seek to join myself to Jesus and unite my weakness to His strength, my ignorance to His wisdom, my unworthiness to His merits.

Jacob wrestled with the angel until he prevailed, but he was injured in the process and limped for the rest of his life, but he never gave up on God. The apostle Paul received a wound, which he called a "thorn in the flesh," when he met Jesus on the road to Damascus, and he became God's servant. I am often wounded by the words of others.

God has mercifully answered my prayers and given me the desire of my heart—that I might have a living relationship with Jesus, share that relationship with others, and trust in Him to do the saving of all those whom I love and pray for each day. King Solomon said, "Trust in the Lord with all your heart, And lean not on your own understanding; In all your ways acknowledge Him, And He shall direct your paths" (Prov. 3:5, 6).

Now, I trust Him to lead me every day and to give me the strength to follow Jesus.

> "It is in this life that we are to separate sin from us, through faith in the atoning blood of Christ. Our precious Saviour invites us to join ourselves to Him, to unite our weakness to His strength, our ignorance to his wisdom, our unworthiness to His merits."
> *The Great Controversy*, p. 623

> Christ does not weigh character in scales of human judgment. He says, "I, if I be lifted up from the earth, will draw all men unto me" (John 12:32). Every soul who responds to this drawing will turn from iniquity. Christ is able to save to the uttermost all who come unto Him. He who comes to Jesus is setting his feet upon a ladder that reaches from earth to heaven. Teach it by pen, by voice that God is above the ladder; the bright rays of His glory are shining upon every round of the ladder. He is

looking graciously upon all who are climbing painfully upward, that He may send them divine help, when the hand seems to be relaxing and the foot trembling. Yes, tell it, tell it in words that will melt the heart, that no one who shall perseveringly climb the ladder will fail of an entrance into the everlasting kingdom of our Lord and Saviour Jesus Christ; those who believe in Christ shall never perish, neither shall any pluck them out of His hand.... If we reach heaven it must be by binding the soul to the Mediator. (*Selected Messages*, book 1, pp. 181, 182)

I am still unworthy, but my Savior, Jesus, is worthy. And His love draws us to Him. "Behold what manner of love the Father has bestowed on us, that we should be called children of God! Therefore the world does not know us, because it did not know Him" (1 John 3:1).

In spite of this, God had mercy and Jacob experienced the victory of faith after God showed him the shining ladder. I have ascended the ladder with him, and my faith is strengthened. Now, my desire is to help others learn about the ladder that God provided for all to have the opportunity to reach the top. We can ascend if we accept the gift of His Righteousness.

"For every soul struggling to rise from a life of sin to a life of purity, the great element of power abides in the only 'name under heaven given among men, whereby we must be saved'" (*The Ministry of Healing*, p. 179).

Will I be wounded when I meet Jesus on His ladder? I'm willing to take the risk just as Jacob did. "Not until he fell crippled and helpless upon the breast of the covenant angel did Jacob know the victory of conquering faith and receive the title of a prince with God" (*Thoughts from the Mount of Blessing*, p. 62).

> Who may ascend into the hill of the LORD? Or who may stand in His holy place? He who has clean hands and a pure heart, Who has not lifted up his soul to an idol, Nor sworn deceitfully. He shall receive blessing from the LORD, And righteousness from the God of his salvation. This is Jacob, the generation of those who seek Him, Who seek Your face. Lift up your heads, O you gates! And be lifted up, you everlasting doors! And the King of glory shall come in. Who is this King of glory? The LORD strong and mighty, The LORD mighty in battle. Lift up your heads, O you gates! Lift up you everlasting doors! And the King of glory shall come in. Who is this King of Glory? The LORD of hosts, He is the KING of glory. (Ps. 24:3–10)

Jacob knew the victory of conquering faith when he fell helpless upon the breast of the covenant angel, so I have placed faith at the top of Jacob's Ladder. If we surrender our will to God, He will bestow upon us that same faith through which we are saved.

The foundation of our next ladder is faith. Let's go to Peter's ladder now and learn what he tells us that we must do with our faith.

Chapter Two
PETER'S LADDER: LOVE

After learning about Jacob's ladder, which God sent down from heaven to represent Jesus, it seemed easy to see how other Bible passages fit on that ladder from earth where Jesus lived as a human, to the top of the ladder where He lives with His Father as the Son of God. Peter makes clear the steps we must take to enter the kingdom of glory, but he was speaking to those that needed love, despite having already found faith. So I shall put faith on the first rung of the ladder and start ascending.

> To those who have obtained like precious faith with us by the righteousness of our God and Savior Jesus Christ: Grace and peace be multiplied to you in the knowledge of God and of Jesus our Lord, as His divine power has given to us all things that pertain to life and godliness, through the knowledge of Him who called us by glory and virtue, by which have been given to us exceedingly great and precious promises, that through these you may be partakers of the divine nature, having escaped the corruption that is in the world through lust. (2 Peter 1:1–4)

We have seven steps to ascend to reach the top of Peter's ladder. I think of his ladder as being just like Jacob's. It is the link between earth and heaven that represents Jesus. He not only draws us to it; He takes us to the top. All we have to do is come to Him in faith.

"Planted firmly upon the earth, and reaching heavenward to the throne of God, is a ladder of shining brightness. God is above the ladder, and His light is shining along its whole length. This ladder is Christ. Every round that you climb, you are coming step after step into fellowship with the sufferings of Christ, and are becoming fashioned after His divine similitude. The angels of God are constantly ascending and descending this glorious ladder. They will not let you fall, if you keep your eye fixed upon the glory of God which is at the top of the ladder."

The Upward Look, p. 256

> But also for this very reason, giving all diligence, add to your faith virtue, to virtue knowledge, to knowledge self-control, to self-control perseverance, to perseverance godliness, to godliness brotherly kindness, and to brotherly kindness love. For if these things are yours and abound, you will be neither barren nor unfruitful in the knowledge of our Lord Jesus Christ. (2 Peter 1:5–8)

I had to keep focused upon Jesus and what he was trying to teach me. First of all, I needed to know what faith obtained by the righteousness of Christ was. I needed to know what Peter and other Bible authors have said about faith and how I could obtain it. Paul said, "So then faith comes by hearing, and hearing by the word of God" (Rom. 10:17).

But what exactly is faith? Some say it is belief, or trust, but I must know what the Bible says. Paul also said, "Now faith is the substance of things hoped for, the evidence of things not seen" (Heb. 11:1).

How could I implement something in my life that I hoped for even though I had not seen it? I really did not understand the meaning of faith. And I was always too proud to ask questions when an opportunity arose because I didn't want people to know how ignorant I was. They judged me by my behavior, I thought. Now I realize how legalistic I was; yet, I feel certain that none of my friends questioned the motive for my actions. However, I came to the conclusion that I needed to look past my pride; I became determined to know the truth.

God gave Adam and Eve the freedom to choose, and they made a bad choice. Today, in spite of all the consequences of our wrong choices, He still gives us that freedom, and He will keep us on the ladder unless we choose to get off. Even then, His love is so strong that if we fall, He forgives us and puts us back on the ladder if we ask.

"If we confess our sins, He is faithful and just to forgive us our sins and to cleanse us from all unrighteousness" (1 John 1:9).

The act of cleansing did not make practical sense to me, but I had to learn. I knew what Paul had written to the Hebrews when he was recounting all the acts that were accomplished by Abel, Enoch, Noah, Abraham, Isaac, Jacob, Moses, etc., because of their faith. Paul said, "But without faith it is impossible to please Him, for he who comes to God must believe that He is, And that He is a rewarder of those who diligently seek Him" (Heb. 11:6).

Perhaps there are others, like me, to whom the following quotation has applied at some time. It is the key to our salvation.

> "Faith is the first round in the ladder of advancement. Without faith it is impossible to please God. But many stop on this round, and never ascend higher. They seem to think that when they have professed Christ, when their names are on the church record, their work is completed."
> "The Path of Progress," *The Review and Herald,* February 21, 1888

I had not even thought about "advancement" past faith because I thought we were saved by faith. I thought God had given me faith, but now I realized that what I had was a "form of godliness" for which I took the credit. I was doing "good things" for others and was proud of the praise I received. But now I was determined to understand how I could mount and ascend this ladder. Not surprisingly, my knowledge increased as I searched for answers. I joined a Bible study prayer group and began my journey. Finally, two definitions were brought to my attention that I found I could use to make a practical application.

First, the following

> What is faith? ... It is an assent of the understanding to God's words which binds the heart in willing consecration and service to God, who gave the understanding, who moved on the heart, who first drew the mind to view Christ on the cross of Calvary. Faith is rendering to God the intellectual powers, abandonment of the mind and will to God, and making Christ the only door to enter into the kingdom of heaven. (*The Ellen G. White 1888 Materials*, p. 818)

Sometime later as I met with my prayer group of sisters in Christ, one statement from the book we were reading gave me a simple working definition of faith I could understand and apply personally. Jesus was drawing me into a relationship with Him. I am thankful for His faithfulness to me. Now, my practical working definition of faith is:

> "... faith is the knowing that in the Word of God there is this power, the expecting the Word itself to do the thing spoken, and the depending upon that Word itself to do that which the Word speaks."
>
> *Lessons on Faith*, p. 9

The book, *Lessons on Faith*, helped me to learn that faith is knowing what God's Word, the Bible, says, believing what God's Word says, expecting God's Word to do what it says, and depending on God's Word to do what it says.

I learned that it is "all about Jesus and His faith." I had heard the expression "all about Jesus" many times, but now it began to make sense. "In the beginning was the Word, and the Word was with God, and the Word was God" (John 1:1). I had to surrender my will for His will. I learned that Jesus was the Word from the beginning. Jacob taught me that Jesus is the ladder connecting me with Heaven.

Knowing the power of God through the Word, believing in what He said and did, and expecting and depending on Him to do what he promised me, I can ascend the ladder. Faith is simply turning my mind over to God, letting Him fill it as I study His Word, and letting His power control it. The verse my mother often quoted, Philippians 4:13, came back to my mind: "I can do all things through Christ who strengthens me."

Somehow, I had missed the "through Christ" part and just thought I could do anything if I tried hard enough. God was merciful. He did do some work through me, even though I thought I was doing what was needed to be done all by myself. It all sounds like a two-year-old! I should have understood because even Jesus could do nothing except through God, His Father, and nothing is impossible with God. "For with God nothing will be impossible" (Luke 1:37). "... Most assuredly, I say to you, the Son can do nothing of Himself, but what He sees the Father do; for whatever He does, The Son also does in like manner" (John 5:19).

From Genesis, where I learned of Jacob's ladder, man's sins, and God's rescue plan, there has been hope— "And I will put enmity Between you and the woman, And between your seed and her Seed; He shall bruise your head, And you shall bruise His heel" (Gen. 3:15).

And that hope continues all the way to Revelation where John describes those who will be saved. Faith is involved from beginning to end. " ... here are those who keep the commandments of God, and the faith of Jesus." (Rev. 14:12).

I came to see that it is not really faith that saves me, but I must have faith in order to be saved. Neither do my works save me, but I must do good works if I am to be saved. I am saved by God's grace, the power that enables me to ascend the ladder. "For by grace you have been saved through faith, and that not of yourselves; it is the gift of God, not of works, lest any man should boast ... for good works, which God prepared beforehand that we should walk in them" (Eph. 2: 8–10).

Peter gives us the progression of transitions on the ladder until the top is reached, as well as the one-word description of the character of God—love—which must be within the heart of those who seek Him. Jesus taught this in many lessons through nature. He said, "For the earth yields crops by itself; first the blade, then the head, after that the full grain in the head" (Mark 4:28).

Just as the grain grows, there is a steady progression on the ladder from a lower to a higher level. We cannot skip any steps; all are necessary to reach the top. Each rung on the ladder is a gift from God.

As babies, we were a gift to our parents. First we learned to sit up, next we learned to crawl, then walk, then run. God first meets the need upon which the next is dependent before He can take us to the next level. We have to start on the bottom rung and grow daily in our knowledge of Christ. Once we ask, we will receive.

"Ask, and it will be given to you; seek, and you will find ... " (Matt. 7:7).

Through reading the writings of one of my favorite authors I learned:

> We must believe the naked promise, and not accept feeling for faith. When we trust God fully, when we rely upon the merits of Jesus as a sin-pardoning Savior, we shall receive all the help that we can desire. (*Faith and Works*, p. 36)

We are saved by grace, and faith is the medium of connection. Now, how do I fit grace into the ladder I am ascending? My faith must have grace passing through it. And, it is not a feeling; it is believing.

"Many have an idea that they must do some part of the work alone. They have trusted in Christ for the forgiveness of sin, but now they seek by their own efforts to live aright. But every such effort must fail. Jesus says, 'Without Me ye can do nothing.' Our growth in grace, our joy, our usefulness,—all depend upon our union with Christ. It is by communion with Him, daily, hourly,—by abiding in Him,—that we are to grow in grace."

Steps to Christ, p. 69

"Faith is the medium of connection between human weakness and divine power."

In Heavenly Places, p. 107

As I learned that each step on the ladder represented one of the attributes of God's character, it all began to make sense to me. They are in ascending order. God does things in an orderly way. Often in our ordinary actions of life we can't move to the next level until we understand

and accomplish what is given at a lower level. God has given to each of us "a measure of faith," just the amount we each need. "For I say, through the grace given to me, to everyone who is among you, not to think of himself more highly than he ought to think, but to think soberly, as God has dealt to each one a measure of faith" (Rom. 12:3).

We are saved by grace with faith being the medium of connection. "For whatever is born of God overcomes the world. And this is the victory that has overcome the world— our faith. Who is he who overcomes the world, but he who believes that Jesus is the Son of God?" (1 John 5:4, 5).

Now, how do I fit grace and faith into the ladder I am ascending? My faith must have grace passing through it, if I understand correctly. From there, Peter tells us that the next step is virtue, and we are told we cannot stop on the first round, so let's keep moving forward.

VIRTUE

"... add to your faith virtue..." (2 Peter 1:5).

Now I know that faith is the gift of God, and we are justified by faith, and we become righteous by faith, but what about virtue? Is it also a gift?

According to Strong's Concordance, using the King James Version, the word virtue appears seven times in the Bible. However, in the New King James Version, virtue is changed to power.

- "And Jesus, immediately knowing in Himself that power had gone out of Him, turned around in the crowd and said, 'Who touched My clothes?'" (Mark 5:30).
- "And the whole multitude sought to touch Him, for power went out from Him and healed them all" (Luke 6:19).
- "But Jesus said, 'Somebody touched Me, for I perceived power going out from Me'" (Luke 8:46).

The word originally translated virtue in each of these three passages is from the Greek word *dunamis* meaning "miraculous power."

Newer Bible translations have not helped in understanding because they imply "self-effort."

- NIV: "add to faith goodness"
- NRSV: "support your faith with goodness"

My mind must be controlled by virtue, the power of Jesus. Is part of our problem that we do not wait for that power? Do we run ahead of the Lord? Peter did; he was ever so zealous. Paul did, probably more so than anyone. In the name of religion, he was responsible for the death of many Christians. But when they were really converted and received the power of the Holy Spirit, what a work they did for the Lord. We can receive that same power. Like Enoch, we can walk with God. "And

> "Enoch's walk with God was not in a trance or a vision, but in all the duties of his daily life. He did not become a hermit shutting himself entirely from the world; for he had a work to do for God in the world. In the family and in his intercourse with men, as a husband and father, a friend, a citizen, he was the steadfast, unwavering servant of the Lord."
>
> *Patriarchs and Prophets*, p. 85

Enoch walked with God, and he was no more, for God took him" (Gen. 5:24).

We receive Christ's healing power through faith in what Christ did at the cross. "For when we were still without strength (power), in due time Christ died for the ungodly.... God demonstrates His own love toward us, in that while we were still sinners, Christ died for us" (Rom. 5:6, 8)

We must recognize that Jesus died on the cross between two criminals who deserved death in order to save us from the death we deserve. He was perfect, but he died for our sins.

> "As the sinner, drawn by the POWER of Christ, approaches the uplifted cross, and prostrates himself before it, there is a new creation. A new heart is given him. He becomes a new creature in Christ Jesus. Holiness finds that it has nothing more to require. God Himself is 'the justifier of him which believeth in Jesus.' Romans 3:26. And 'whom He justified, them He also glorified.' Romans 8:30"
>
> *Christ's Object Lessons,* p. 163, emphasis added

I believe this is the place in our lives where we "abandon our mind and will" and make the choice to receive the power of the Holy Spirit. We need to let it become the active agent to direct our mind to the point where there is grace in our lives. Our humanity is joined to His divinity. We make the choice as Peter directed. But are we really converted?

> "Communion with God imparts to the soul an intimate knowledge of His will. But many who profess the faith know not what true conversion is."
>
> *Testimonies for the Church,* vol. 4, p. 534

I was one who did not know what conversion really was. I vividly remember the altar call from the evangelist in the Beaufort Baptist Church when I was eleven years old. Without any prompting by my parents, my heart was touched, and I went forward to signify that I wanted to be baptized. No one studied the Bible with me to be sure I understood what I was committing to, but I was baptized the following night. I knew that I needed to be baptized, but I didn't know why. God was calling, but I was not converted yet.

About thirty years later, after having four children, I learned about the Seventh-day Sabbath. My heart was again touched when the pastor preached a sermon on the Sower and the kinds of soil. My husband and I both decided to be baptized—he for the first time, and I, re-baptized. Again, no one gave us Bible studies or checked about our knowledge of the plan of salvation, but God was leading step-by-step.

Peter is a prime example of one who was not converted when he thought he was. He became a model for us to follow. He was naturally forward and impulsive. When Jesus was trying to get the message of humility across to them at the Last Supper, Peter voiced words that might lead one to believe that he was truly converted.

> After that, He poured water into a basin and began to wash the disciples' feet, and to wipe them with the towel with which He was girded. Then He came to Simon Peter. And Peter said to Him, 'Lord, are You washing my feet?' Jesus answered and said to him, 'What I am doing you do not understand now,

but you will know after this.' Peter said to Him, 'You shall never wash my feet!' Jesus answered him, "If I do not wash you, you have not part with Me." Simon Peter said to Him, "Lord, not my feet only, but also my hands and my head!" Jesus said to him, 'He who is bathed needs only to wash his feet, but is completely clean; and you are clean, but not all of you.' For He knew who would betray Him; therefore He said, "You are not all clean." So when He had washed their feet, taken His garments, and sat down again, He said to them, 'Do you know what I have done to you?' (John 13:5–12)

> "In these words Christ was not merely enjoining the practice of hospitality. More was meant than the washing of the feet of guests to remove the dust of travel. Christ was here instituting a religious service. By the act of our Lord this humiliating ceremony was made a consecrated ordinance. It was to be observed by the disciples, that they might ever keep in mind His lessons of humility and service."
>
> *The Desire of Ages*, p. 650

Now each time I partake of the ordinance of foot-washing, I am reminded that Jesus wants me to renew my baptismal vows to Him and let the Holy Spirit lead me in His Service.

My sister, Mabel, did not think washing dirty feet was much fun when she was growing up. At one time, she had the chore of washing four pairs of dirty feet. My brother, just younger than she was, broke his arm, so she had to wash his feet plus the feet of my older sister, my feet, and, of course, her own feet. We did not have a bathroom, so we lined up on the steps of the back-porch while she pumped a basin full of water to wash our feet. The hand pump was on the porch, so she didn't have to carry the water far. That was the extent of the bath we got before going to bed each night.

It's different when you wash your own children's feet.

I remember one morning, just after I finished bathing and helping Vern Jr. and Nelle get dressed and let them go in the yard to play, I went out to check on them, and they were in the dusty road that went by our house. Vern was making roads in the road with his truck even though he knew he should stay in the yard and make his roads in the sand box. He usually did, but this day was different. Nelle, not quite two years old, was throwing the dust in the air above her head and squealing delightedly as it sifted down on her hair, face, and all over the clean clothes I had just put on her. I couldn't get angry; it was too amusing! I would have just stood there and watched them enjoy themselves, but it was dangerous for them to be playing in the road. Logging trucks frequently went by, and they didn't slow down.

As I was musing on how Jesus washed the disciples' feet in order to give them, and us, the example of serving others, I realized that I should be just as happy to serve others who need help as I am my own family. Vern and Nelle were too young to clean themselves, so I did it for them. That is what Jesus does for us; He puts His Spirit within us to do the spiritual work for us. Parents can keep their children clean physically, but only Jesus can make them clean spiritually by taking their dirty, filthy rags and giving them His robe of righteousness. Both of them were baptized when they were older and made that exchange.

However, neither of them is afraid of getting dirty seeing as they have chosen to do commercial fishing in Alaska during the salmon run. Nelle often has to wade through knee-deep mud to get to her cabin, yet students at the college where she works would never know this because they only see her immaculately clean and dressed in her professional garb as she counsels them at the Career Center.

From my childhood, I wanted to be like Jesus, but I didn't know Him even when I was baptized the second time. I learned that it takes a full surrender to be converted and conversion never ends. We must be converted and continue to grow daily. As some have said "let go and let God." My full surrender occurred while I was driving to work one morning. Troubled by some things that were causing grief in the family, my heart was broken, and I sang my prayer of total surrender. I wrote the words in the song down after I got to my desk at school because they tell the story of my desire. Now I knew I only wanted the mind of Christ to be my mind and to control my thoughts and actions. "Let this mind be in you which was also in Christ Jesus" (Phil. 2:5).

> "Mental power alone is not a guarantee of virtuous superiority.... If this intelligence were controlled by virtue and rectitude, it would be powerful for good...."
>
> *Testimonies for the Church*, vol. 2, p. 407

There is no way that we can do any good thing on our own. Our efforts can avail nothing without the power of Christ. That power is our great need today, and it is available to us if we are willing to receive it. "And the whole multitude sought to touch Him, for power went out from Him and healed them all" (Luke 6:19). Like Peter, we can be restored. Peter had only been baptized by John's baptism, but he needed the baptism of the Holy Spirit. The disciples all had faith that Jesus was the Son of God, but there was more that they needed.

"And, being assembled together with them, He commanded them not to depart from Jerusalem, but to wait for the Promise of the Father, 'which,' He said, 'you have heard from Me; for John truly baptized with water, but you shall be baptized with the Holy Spirit not many days from now'" (Acts 1:4, 5).

It was at this point that Jesus left them. The power was given at Pentecost when Peter preached the sermon that resulted in 120 people being baptized by the Holy Spirit. God had promised them the power they needed.

"But you shall receive power when the Holy Spirit has come upon you; and you shall be witnesses to Me in Jerusalem, and in all Judea and Samaria, and to the end of the earth" (Acts 1:8).

Finally, the disciples received the power of the Holy Spirit. Like me, many today are baptized with water, but receive the baptism of the Holy Spirit much later in life.

We have climbed the round of virtue and learned that virtue means power and grace. John Wesley was convicted that grace and power are synonymous. He called the grace available previous to conversion, "prevenient grace." This is a part of God's grace that draws us by His power and leads us to conversion. We have faith, we believe, we have accepted the power of the Holy Spirit, so we must now continue on the ladder and continue on to be higher than angels who have never fallen.

"Great as is the shame and degradation through sin, even greater will be the honor and exaltation through redeeming love. To human beings striving for conformity to the divine image there is imparted an outlay of

> "Having received the faith of the gospel, the next work of the believer is to add to his character virtue, and thus cleanse the heart and prepare the mind for the reception of the knowledge of God. This knowledge is the foundation of all true education and of all true service. It is the only real safeguard against temptation; and it is this alone that can make one like God in character. Through the knowledge of God and of His Son Jesus Christ, are given to the believer 'all things that pertain unto life and godliness.' No good gift is withheld from him who sincerely desires to obtain the righteousness of God."
>
> *The Acts of the Apostles*, p. 530, 531

heaven's treasure, an excellency of POWER, that will place them higher than even the angels who have never fallen" (*Christ's Object Lessons*, p. 163, emphasis added). I cling to that promise. "For the grace of God that brings salvation has appeared to all men, teaching us that, denying ungodliness and worldly lusts, we should live soberly, righteously, and godly in the present age" (Titus 2:11, 12).

Jesus is at the top of the ladder in His glory, and we must always give Him the glory for all the things He does through His grace. The righteousness we gained by faith through virtue/power, given by God's grace, is what takes us to the top of the ladder. I was searching for that same righteousness that Abraham had, and I have obtained it by believing as he did. "... Abraham believed God, and it was accounted to him for righteousness" (Rom. 4:3).

Peter tells us we must continue to grow in grace and knowledge. "But grow in the grace and knowledge of our Lord and Savior Jesus Christ. To Him be the glory both now and forever. Amen" (2 Peter 3:18).

Over and over the words grace, faith, and virtue impressed me as I read my Bible. I knew I needed more knowledge.

His virtue/power/grace is drawing me to advance to the next higher level. So, now I must move up the round of knowledge and learn more about Jesus.

KNOWLEDGE

"Add ... to virtue knowledge" (2 Peter 1:5).

> ... to those who have obtained like precious faith with us by the righteousness of our God and Savior Jesus Christ: Grace and peace be multiplied to you in the knowledge of God and of Jesus our Lord, as His divine power has given to us all things that pertain to life and godliness, through the knowledge of Him who called us by glory and virtue, by which have been given to us exceedingly great and precious promises, that through these you may be partakers of the divine nature, having escaped the corruption that is in the world through lust. (2 Peter 1:1–4)

The Greek word for knowledge in 2 Peter 1:5 is *epignosis*, which means more perfect knowledge that comes from contemplation of the object studied.

Of the seven character traits on Peter's ladder, knowledge is the only one that is intellectual. The others are experiential. We do not get it by reasoning. It is not religion, but it is essential for us to be like Jesus and to know deception.

It is knowledge of the truth as well as knowledge of the great plan of salvation. To be ignorant of God's commandments and laws will not excuse anyone. No one will dare to plead around the throne of God, "I did not know the truth. I was ignorant." The Lord has given His Word to be our guide, our instructor. With this heavenly enlightening, there is no excuse for ignorance. We must know what truth is and what is error or false doctrine. Only by studying the Bible can we be sure. We learn His will for us in His Word. "If anyone wills to do His will, he shall know concerning the doctrine, whether it is from God or whether I speak on My own authority" (John 7:17).

> "Man's advantages for obtaining a knowledge of the truth, however great these may be, will prove of no benefit to him unless the heart is open to receive the truth, and there is a conscientious surrender of every habit and practice that is opposed to its principles."
>
> *The Desire of Ages*, p. 455, 456

We will know the truth if we are His disciples. "Then Jesus said to those Jews who believed Him, 'If you abide in My word, you are My disciples indeed. And you shall know the truth, and the truth shall make you free'" (John 8:31, 32).

At Jesus' trial His conversation with Pilate was convincing, but Pilate did not have the courage to stand for truth.

> Pilate therefore said to Him, 'Are You a king then?' Jesus answered, 'You say rightly that I am a king. For this cause I was born, and for this cause I have come into the world, that I should bear witness to the truth. Everyone who is of the truth hears My voice.' Pilate said to Him, 'What is truth?' And when he had said this, he went out again to the Jews, and said to them, 'I find no fault in Him at all.' (John 18:37, 38)

When Thomas questioned Jesus after His resurrection, He replied: "...I am the way, the truth, and the life. No one comes to the Father except through Me" (John 14:6).

> Truth is an active, working principle, molding heart and life so that there is a constant upward movement.... In every step of climbing, the will is obtaining a new spring of action. The moral tone is becoming more like the mind and character of Christ. The progressive Christian has grace and love which passes knowledge, for divine insight into the character of Christ takes a deep hold upon his affections. The glory of God revealed above the ladder can only be appreciated by the progressive climber, who is ever attracted higher, to nobler aims which Christ reveals. All the faculties of mind and body must be enlisted. (*Our High Calling*, p. 68)

"All the faculties of mind and body must be enlisted." This means that we must take very seriously the counsel regarding our body as the temple in which the Holy Spirit must dwell.

I beseech you therefore, brethren, by the mercies of God, that you present your bodies a living sacrifice, holy, acceptable to God, which is your reasonable service. And do not be conformed to this world, but be transformed by the renewing of your mind, that you may prove what is that good and acceptable and perfect will of God. (Rom. 12:1)

> "Any habit or practice that would lead into sin, and bring dishonor upon Christ, would better be put away, whatever the sacrifice. That which dishonors God cannot benefit the soul. The blessing of heaven cannot attend any man in violating the eternal principles of right. And one sin cherished is sufficient to work the degradation of the character, and to mislead others."
> *The Desire of Ages*, p. 439

God is waiting to give us a new heart. He promises: "I will give you a new heart and put a new spirit within you; I will take the heart of stone out of your flesh and give you a heart of flesh" (Ezek. 36:26).

So, the knowledge we advance to on this round is insight into the character of Christ and knowledge about ourselves to be fit vessels for His Spirit to dwell in. And, what else does this knowledge do for us? Grace and peace are ours. "Grace and peace be multiplied to you in the knowledge of God and of Jesus our Lord, as His divine power has given to us all things that pertain to life and godliness, through knowledge of Him who called us by glory and virtue" (2 Peter 1:2, 3).

> "In the whole Satanic force there is not power to overcome one soul who in simple trust casts himself on Christ.... But we must have knowledge of ourselves, a knowledge that will result in contrition, before we find pardon and peace.... It is only he who knows himself to be a sinner that Christ can save."
> *Christ's Object Lessons*, pp. 157, 158

> "God intends that even in this life the truths of His word shall be ever unfolding to His people. There is only one way in which this knowledge can be obtained. We can attain to an understanding of God's word only through the illumination of that Spirit by which the word was given."
> *Steps to Christ*, p. 109

Through the knowledge of God, by His virtue/power, we have grace and peace. Next, Peter says to add self-control to virtue, so now we can move up to the next round on Peter's ladder.

Self-Control

"... to knowledge self-control ..." (2 Peter 1:6).

I prefer to think of self-control as God-control through the power of the Holy Spirit. I have learned that I cannot control another person, and the more I allow God to control me, the less need I have to try to control others. It takes a lot of power to keep from trying to control or change others. We must have received that power on the round of "virtue."

When I think about controlling myself, my thoughts, my words, my actions, it seems impossible. But when I think of adding Jesus-control, I know I can do it through His power. Getting to know Jesus brings self-control.

> "Into the city of God there will enter nothing that defiles. All who are to be dwellers there will here have become pure in heart. In one who is learning of Jesus, there will be manifest a growing distaste for careless manners, unseemly language, and course thought. When Christ abides in the heart, there will be purity and refinement of thought and manner."
>
> *Thoughts from the Mount of Blessings*, pp. 24, 25

Peter tells us what some of the things we need to control are. "Therefore, laying aside all malice, all deceit, hypocrisy, envy, and all evil speaking, as newborn babes, desire the pure milk of the word, that you may grow thereby, if indeed you have tasted that the Lord is gracious" (1 Peter 2:1–3).

James, another of Christ's disciples, gives sound counsel to which we all need to listen. "So then, my beloved brethren, let every man be swift to hear, slow to speak, slow to wrath; for the wrath of man does not produce the righteousness of God.... If anyone among you thinks he is religious, and does not bridle his tongue but deceives his own heart, this one's religion is useless" (James 1:19, 20, 26).

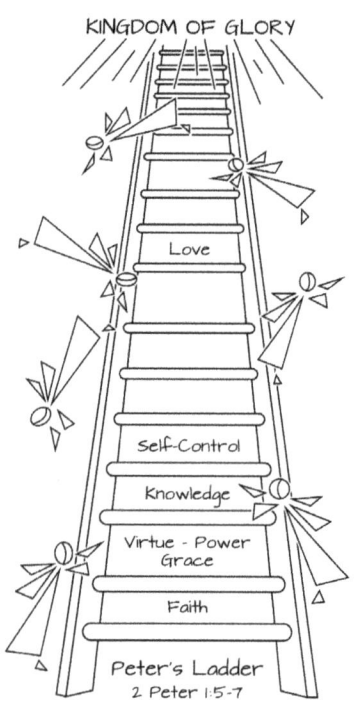

Even so the tongue is a little member and boasts great things. See how great a forest a little fire kindles! And the tongue is a fire, a world of iniquity. The tongue is so set among our members that it defiles the whole body.... But no man can tame the tongue. It is an unruly evil, full of deadly poison. With it we bless our God and Father, and with it we curse men, who have been made in the similitude of God. Out of the same mouth proceed blessing and cursing. My brethren, these things ought not to be so.... But if you have bitter envy and self-seeking in your hearts, do not boast and lie against the truth. This wisdom does not descend from above, but is earthly, sensual, demonic. For where envy and self-seeking exist, confusion and every evil thing are there. (James 3:5, 6, 8–10, 14–16)

Athletes in training are a good example of self-control.

Athletes cheerfully comply with the conditions in order to be trained for the highest taxation of their physical strength. They do not indulge appetite, but put a constant restraint upon themselves, refraining from food which would weaken or lessen the full power of any of their organs. Yet they fight 'as one that beateth the air,' while Christians are in a real contest. Combatants in the games seek for mere perishable laurels. Christians have before them a glorious crown of immortality, incorruptible. And in this heavenly race there is plenty of room for all to obtain the prize. Not one will fail if he runs well, if he does according to the light which shines upon him, exercising his abilities which, to the best of his knowledge, he has kept in a healthful condition.... (*Our High Calling*, p. 69)

My son-in-law, Jim, is a runner. He has disciplined himself to get up early and run before he goes to work each day. He reads magazines about running to gain more knowledge about the best foods to eat, the best practice methods, the best shoes to wear, etc. It is like a runner's Bible. He runs marathons periodically, and his goal is to run one in all fifty states. His exercise room's walls are lined with the ribbons he has won and shelves full of trophies. Recently, he had pains in his hip, and his doctor suggested that he stop running. Jim's reply to him was that is was not an option. So, he keeps on running. He has the needed self-control to pace himself.

During the 17th and 18th centuries, scientists who studied the mind discovered that there are many faculties involved in the operation of the brain. There are four faculties that are primary: the will, conscience, reason, and the heart's desire. These different sections determine what we choose to do.

> "The will is the governing power in the nature of man. ... If you cannot control your impulses, your emotions, as you may desire, you can control the will, and thus an entire change will be wrought in your life."
>
> *My Life Today,* p. 318

The will is the most important mind faculty. The other faculties respond to it.

- The will answers the question: "What shall I choose to do?"
- The conscience answers the question: "Is it the right thing to do?"
- Reason answers the question: "Is it the best thing to do?"
- The heart's desire answers the question: "Do I want to do it?"

If the conscience and reason say, "It's the right thing and the best thing to do," then the heart's desire must also say, "Yes, I want to do it." This works when making spiritual decisions. "Every emotion and desire must be held in subjection to reason and conscience. Every unholy thought must be instantly repelled" (*Testimonies for the Church*, vol. 5, p. 177). "So let each one give as he purposes in his heart, not grudgingly or of necessity; for God loves a cheerful giver" (2 Cor. 9:7).

The motive for our actions must always be love for God and a desire to do His will. "Whenever man accomplishes anything, whether in spiritual or in temporal lines, he should bear in mind that he does it through co-operation with his Maker. There is great necessity for us to realize our dependence on God" (*Christ's Object Lessons*, p. 82).

Satan took control when man sinned. Our mind must become strong when we take it back from His control. We may need to change some habits and, thankfully, change is possible. One of our problems when we decide to change is that we want to do everything all at once. But we need to start with one thing at the time to be successful. It takes approximately six hours to really process your decision to change before you act. If you try to make two changes at once, you don't do either well.

I realized I needed to change some habits that had been with me since childhood. I learned that I must put forth some effort to improve myself. I attended a twenty-eight-day wellness program at Weimar in California where I learned eight "free remedies" that anyone can implement at home. The acronym is NEWSTART; each letter being a reminder of its principle:

N = Nutrition: eat a balanced diet of fruits, herbs, grains, and nuts

E = Exercise: check with your doctor for level recommended

W = Water: drink at least 8 glasses daily; eliminate caffeine

S = Sunshine: spend a minimum of twenty minutes daily in the sun

T = Temperance: Use self-control

A = Air: get plenty of fresh air outdoors and sleep in well-ventilated room

R = Rest periods daily; Eight hours sleep at night; Sabbath days rest from work

T = Trust in God

Implementing these principles has improved my health, but I'm still working on them. I learned that I cannot change my habits. I must depend of Christ, and I must consent for Him to change me. It is necessary to put forth the effort to learn how the changes need to be made.

> "Man's great danger is in being self-deceived, indulging self-sufficiency, and thus separating from God, the source of his strength. Our natural tendencies, unless corrected by the Holy Spirit of God, have in them the seeds of moral death.... In order to receive help from Christ, we must realize our need. We must have a true knowledge of ourselves. It is only he who knows himself to be a sinner that Christ can save. Only as we see our utter helplessness and renounce all self-trust, shall we lay hold on divine power. It is not only at the beginning of the Christian life that this renunciation of self is to be made. At every advance step heavenward it is to be renewed. All our good works are dependent on a power outside of ourselves; therefore there needs to be a continual reaching out of the heart after God, a constant, earnest confession of sin and humbling of the soul before Him."
> *Testimonies for the Church*, vol. 8, p. 315, 316

Allowing anyone to do things for me has always been hard. I want to be in control. As I have gotten older, I realize that it cannot remain that way, even in the daily events of life. Even though we abide by all the natural laws of health, illness comes, and death is the enemy. It is ironic that when our children were born, they were helpless and dependent on their father and me to meet their every need. Now I realize that soon I shall be depending on them to see that I am well-cared-for. I must be prepared to give the control of my care over to someone whose mind is still alert and able to plan what is best for me. Am I prepared to give that responsibility to my children—or to anyone else? I would need to trust that they would give me the very best care possible, but I don't want to lay that burden upon them. Again, is that my self-sufficiency and pride? I pray that God will direct me when the time comes. But in the meantime, I need to remember to have my full trust in Jesus. Then there will be no question of whether I am doing His will. My desire is for Him to be in control.

> "... temperance is a round of the ladder upon which we must plant our feet before we can add the grace of patience. In food, in raiment, in work, in regular hours, in healthful exercise, we must be regulated by the knowledge which it is our duty to obtain that we may, through earnest endeavor, place ourselves in right relation to life and health."
>
> *Our High Calling*, p. 69

How did Peter know that self-control must come before patience and perseverance? Perhaps it was his life experiences that taught him that. Either way, I have also come to understand that this order is true. We cannot be patient people unless we are controlled by the Holy Spirit. With self-control in mind, let's move up to the round of perseverance on the ladder.

PERSEVERANCE (PATIENCE)
"... to self-control perseverance [patience]" (2 Peter 1:6).

> Therefore we also, since we are surrounded by so great a cloud of witnesses, let us lay aside every weight, and the sin which so easily ensnares us, and let us run with endurance (patience) the race that is set before us, looking unto Jesus, the author and finisher of our faith, who for the joy that was set before Him endured the cross, despising the shame, and has sat down at the right hand of the throne of God. (Heb. 12:1, 2)

Before I was converted, when in the midst of some trying situation, it seemed as though my concern was the only thing I could think about. Now I try to follow Paul's counsel:

> Rejoice in the Lord always. Again I will say, rejoice! ... Be anxious for nothing, but in everything by prayer and supplication, with thanksgiving, let your requests be made known to God; and the peace of God, which surpasses all understanding, will guard your hearts and minds through Christ Jesus. Finally, brethren, whatever things are true, whatever things are noble, whatever things are just,

whatever things are pure, whatever things are lovely, whatever things are of good report, if there is any virtue and if there is anything praiseworthy—meditate on these things. (Phil. 4:4, 6–8)

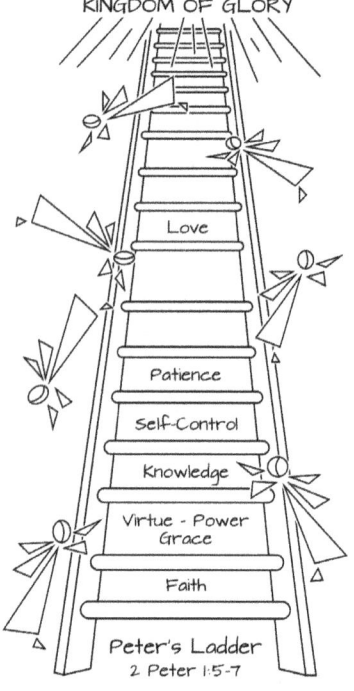

Focusing on the positive things in life supplants concern for the negative thinking. And still, I find myself falling back into my old habit at times; however, I often recall one particular time when we were having business and financial problems. I quoted a Bible verse that was meaningful to me at the moment: "... 'Fear not, for I have redeemed you.... When you pass through the waters, I will be with you; And through the rivers, they shall not overflow you. When you walk through the fire, you shall not be burned, Nor shall the flame scorch you. For I am the LORD your God...." (Isa. 43:1–3).

My son took the words literally, and I am still not sure he understands the true meaning today. He asked, "Why is it that when we are having the most problems, you seem to be happiest?" At the time, I wasn't aware that was how he perceived me, and I really didn't know Jesus. I knew about Him and believed in scripture, but I couldn't explain what made me seem happy. I did not know it was Christ, the Word, which activated it in my life. But I was growing spiritually, and God was patient with me. I can't remember how I responded, but most likely quoted "All things work together for good, etc." God has given me another promise through Isaiah which I claim:

Fear not, for I am with you; I will bring your descendants form the east, And gather you from the west; I will say to the north, 'Give them up!' And to the South, 'Do not keep them back!' Bring My sons from afar, And My daughters from the ends of the earth—Everyone who is called by My name, Whom I have created for My Glory; I have formed him, yes, I have made him. (Isa. 43:5–7)

> "The creative energy that called the worlds into existence is in the word of God. This word imparts power; it begets life. Every command is a promise; accepted by the will, received into the soul, it brings with it the life of the infinite One. It transforms the nature and re-creates the soul in the image of God."
>
> *Education*, p. 126

We are all God's sons and daughters, and God always keeps His promises in His timing. I have many relatives who have not realized their need "to keep the commandments of God and the faith of Jesus" (see Rev. 14:12). Sometimes I think He keeps me waiting for answers so that I will develop more patience.

David's son, Solomon, the king of wisdom, said: "The end of a thing is better than its beginning; The patient in spirit is better than the proud in spirit. Do not hasten in your spirit to be angry, For anger rests in the bosom of fools. Do not say 'Why were the former days better than these?' For you do not inquire wisely concerning this" (Eccles. 7:8–10).

We need to have far less confidence in what man can do and far more confidence in what God can do for every believing soul. He longs to have you reach after Him by faith. He longs to have you expect great things from Him. He longs to give you understanding in temporal as well as in spiritual matters. He can sharpen the intellect. He can give tact and skill. Put your talents into the work. Ask God for wisdom, and it will be given you. (*Christ's Object Lessons,* p. 146)

My brethren, count it all joy when you fall into various trials, knowing that the testing of your faith produces patience. But let patience have its perfect work, that you may be perfect and complete, lacking nothing. If any of you lacks wisdom, let him ask of God, who gives all men liberally and without reproach, and it will be given to him. But let him ask in faith, with no doubting, for he who doubts is like a wave of the sea driven and tossed by the wind. (James 1:2–6)

I remember my mother telling me two things after I was married and had children: "Ask yourself: what would Jesus do? And pray for wisdom." This advice has helped me through many trials.

When I began studying the Bible for myself, I realized how important her advice was. We succeed in the grace of self-control to become patient and persevere under trials. Patience will keep us from saying and doing those things that will injure our own souls and injure those with whom we associate. Everyone has trials, but nothing can seriously injure you if you exercise perseverance. Let God take control and do not let go of His promises, no matter how rough the road may seem.

> "We can see the wisdom of Peter in placing self-control to be added to knowledge before patience.... There will need to be firm principle and fixedness of purpose not to offend in word or action either our own conscience or the feelings of others. There must be a rising above the customs of the world in order to bear reproach, disappointment, losses and crosses without one murmur, but with uncomplaining dignity.... A petulant, ill-natured man or woman really knows not what it is to be happy. Every cup which he puts to his lips seems to be bitter as wormwood and his path seems strewn with rough stones, with briars and thorns; but he must add to self-control, patience and he will not see or feel slights."
>
> *Our High Calling,* p. 70

Christ is working patiently with us now. He gives us the patience we need in any situation. This promise will be ours just before Jesus returns: "Here is the patience of the saints; here are those who keep the commandments of God and the faith of Jesus" (Rev. 14:12).

To those who have heard and listened and received the gift of faith, the foundation of Peter's ladder, will develop Christ's character. Christ's faith in His Father will be our faith.

According to Paul, patience goes beyond its round on Peter's ladder to our hope in Christ's return. But before we get to that point, we must obtain the character of God.

" ... We also glory in tribulations, knowing that tribulation produces perseverance, and perseverance, character; and character, hope" (Rom. 5:3, 4). I have that hope, the hope that Christ will return to take those who love Him to heaven. "Therefore be patient, brethren, until the coming of the Lord. See how the farmer waits for the precious fruit of the earth, waiting patiently for it until it receives the early and latter rain. You also be patient. Establish your hearts, for the coming of the Lord is at hand" (James 5:7, 8).

And so I wait patiently! But why do I have to wait? It is a mystery. "Oh, the depth of the riches both of the wisdom and knowledge of God! How unsearchable are His judgments and His ways past finding out" (Rom. 11:33).

> "The word of God, like the character of its divine Author, presents mysteries that can never be fully comprehended by finite beings.... But we have no reason to doubt God's word because we cannot understand the mysteries of His providence.... God has given us in the Scriptures sufficient evidence of their divine character, and we are not to doubt His word because we cannot understand all the mysteries of His providence."
>
> *Steps to Christ,* pp. 106, 107

Godliness is the next step on the ladder, so let's keep ascending with the angels.

GODLINESS

"... to perseverance godliness ..." (2 Peter 1:6).

From Paul, I learned that I could only ascend to godliness if I had obtained patience. Grace, again is used synonymously with virtue, which is the power that God bestows upon those who are seeking to do His will and must be obtained before we can move up to knowledge–the pre-requisite for godliness. Godliness is "to have the spirit and likeness of the character of Jesus Christ."

I have no virtue of my own, so I must accept the gift of His power to bestow His character in me. Fortunately, like Paul, I knew that God was faithful, and I could depend on Him.

> I thank God–through Jesus Christ our Lord! So then, with the mind I myself serve the law of God, but with the flesh the law of sin.... There is therefore now no condemnation to those who are in Christ Jesus, who do not walk according to the flesh, but according to the Spirit. For the law of the Spirit of life in Christ Jesus has made me free from the law of sin and death. For what the law could not do in that it was weak through the flesh, God did by sending His own Son in the likeness of sinful flesh, on account of sin: He condemned sin in the flesh, that

the righteous requirement of the law might be fulfilled in us who do not walk according to the flesh but according to the Spirit. For those who live according to the flesh set their minds on the things of the flesh, but those who live according to the Spirit, the things of the Spirit. (Rom. 7:25; 8:1–5)

> "Here, then, is an advance grace, godliness which is to have the spirit and likeness of the character of Jesus Christ. To raise us to His divine ideal is the one end of all the dealings of God with us, and of the whole plan of salvation."
>
> *Our High Calling*, p. 71

I wanted to know that I was "free from the law of sin and death." However, a discussion of the law will have to be my next topic because I shall continue my ascent on Peter's ladder right now.

Godliness is still a mystery to me, and it must have been to Paul as he wrote to Timothy: "And without controversy great is the mystery of godliness: God was manifested in the flesh, justified in the Spirit, seen by angels, preached among the Gentiles, believed on in the word, received up in glory" (1 Tim. 3:16).

But God did not leave us to speculate about the mystery; He gave us His Word.

> The Bible was designed to be a guide to all who wish to become acquainted with the will of their Maker. God gave to men the sure word of prophecy; angels and even Christ Himself came to make known to Daniel and John the things that must shortly come to pass. Those important matters that concern our salvation were not left involved in mystery. They were not revealed in such a way as to perplex and mislead the honest seeker after truth. (*The Great Controversy*, p. 521)

> "While the Christian's life will be characterized by humility, it should not be marked with sadness and self-depreciation. It is the privilege of everyone so to live that God will approve and bless him. It is not the will of our heavenly Father that we should be ever under condemnation and darkness.... We may go to Jesus and be cleansed, and stand before the law without shame and remorse."
> *The Great Controversy*, p. 477

I shall investigate those things "that must shortly come to pass," which "Christ Himself came to make known to Daniel and John;" however, that will have to wait until a later chapter.

As for now, it is important to recognize that Paul gave a warning to Timothy regarding godliness:

> But know this, that in the last days perilous times will come: For men will be lovers of themselves, lovers of money, boasters, proud, blasphemers, disobedient to parents, unthankful, unholy, unloving, unforgiving, slanderers, without self-control, brutal, despisers of good, traitors, headstrong, haughty, lovers of pleasure rather than lovers of God, having a form of godliness but denying its power. And from such people turn away! (2 Tim. 3:1–5)

Whatever I try to do without His power is only "a form of godliness," and I am told to turn away from others who display this kind of "godliness."

I realized that I have been guilty of several of these character traits, and I determined to allow the Holy Spirit to bring about change. I am not there yet, but He is constantly showing me where I need to make changes in my life. I also recognize that I need to follow his counsel to "turn away" from other people who manifest these unacceptable behaviors.

> "How often, in our own day, is the love of pleasure disguised by a 'form of godliness!' A religion that permits men, while observing the rites of worship, to devote themselves to selfish or sensual gratification, is as pleasing to the multitudes now as in the days of Israel. And there are still pliant Aarons, who, while holding positions of authority in the church, will yield to the desires of the unconsecrated, and thus encourage them in sin."
>
> *Patriarchs and Prophets*, p. 317

I thought I could depend on church leaders to support me when I pointed out an ignored problem in the church. I thought some would even encourage me, but instead of support, I was ridiculed.

Thankfully, with new administration, the problem was resolved. Now I know that my only dependable source of help is Jesus, the Word. I learned that when I discovered the true definition of faith, so I shall continue to study and pray because I know there is still much more for me to learn. I do want to attain godliness, so I can continue up the ladder to the top. Even though I might suffer persecution through my desire to live godly, I shall persevere.

"Yes, and all who desire to live godly in Christ Jesus will suffer persecution" (2 Tim. 3:12).

> "So it will be with all who will live godly in Christ Jesus. Persecution and reproach await all who are imbued with the Spirit of Christ. The character of the persecution changes with the times, but the principle—the spirit that underlies it—is the same that has slain the chosen of the Lord ever since the days of Abel."
>
> *The Acts of the Apostles*, p. 576

But persecution and reproach can lead one to examine oneself. I decided that God had allowed my trials to lead me to humility. There is a song "Humble Yourself in the Sight of the Lord," and I knew this was what I needed to do. I needed to do a self-examination!

"Examine yourself as to whether you are in the faith. Test yourselves. Do you not know yourselves, that Jesus Christ is in you?–unless indeed you are disqualified" (2 Cor. 13:5).

To know whether or not I am "disqualified," I had to go back to my definition of faith and study my Bible more to know, believe, expect, and depend on God's Word to do what it says. I prayed, "Create in me a clean heart, O God, And renew a steadfast spirit within me" (Ps. 51:10).

Many accept an intellectual religion, a form of godliness, when the heart is not cleansed. Let it be your prayer, 'Create in me a clean heart, God; and renew a right (steadfast) spirit within me.' Psalm 51:10. Deal truly with your own soul. Be as earnest, as persistent, as you would be if your mortal life were at stake. This is a matter to be settled between God and your own soul, settled for eternity. A supposed hope, and nothing more, will prove your ruin. (*Steps to Christ*, p. 35)

I was eventually able to see why it is imperative to have obtained a measure of faith, virtue, knowledge, self-control, and patience before being able to reach the "godliness" step on the ladder. Peter had failed to be true to Jesus at one time, but he was converted, and I can listen to his counsel now.

"We must live, every one of us, by the simplicity of true Godliness. It brings such a power, for the angels of God are right around us. We are not left to our own dispositions" ("Talk by Sister White," *The Wisconsin Reporter*, August 25, 1909).

> "Who then is a faithful and wise servant, whom his Lord hath made ruler over His household? Can we answer? Am I the steward, faithful to the sacred trust which is committed to me? To every man is given an individual responsibility. The watchmen have their specific work to discern the approach of danger and sound the note of warning. The soldiers of the cross of Christ are to have ears keen to hear. In their position of responsibility they are to give the trumpet a certain sound, that everyone may gird on the armor for action."
>
> *Testimonies to Ministers and Gospel Workers*, p. 236

Thankfully, God does not leave me to my own sinful disposition. "Let no one say when he is tempted, 'I am tempted by God'; for God cannot be tempted by evil, nor does He Himself tempt anyone. But each one is tempted when he is drawn away by his own desires and enticed" (James 1:13, 14).

All around us are influences working to hold us to a low, earthly level of behavior, but Jesus is always near, and if we invite him, He will lift us up. However, we must remember that we must be fully surrendered to Him in order to have the assurance that Jesus is with us. Our part is to keep our eyes fixed on Jesus. Jesus is the ladder; He is there with us, and if we waver and start to fall, He catches us and keeps us on the ladder.

I have added to faith and virtue (the power of the Holy Spirit through grace). I have gained more knowledge about myself and Jesus as well as learned more about self-control, patience, and godliness. Now, I will take you up to the next step on the ladder—brotherly kindness.

BROTHERLY KINDNESS

"... to godliness brotherly kindness ..." (2 Peter 1:7).

We can show courtesy or kindness without having put on godliness. Unfortunately, this is only a "form of godliness" and is not what God expects of us. It is godliness which denies the power from which it comes. I have turned away from this form, and now my love of God and desire to be like Jesus is my motive for attaining His character.

> "Love is the basis for godliness. Whatever the profession, no man has pure love to God unless he has unselfish love for his brother. But we can never come into possession of this spirit by trying to love others. What is needed is the love of Christ in the heart. When self is merged in Christ, true love springs forth spontaneously. The completeness of Christian character is attained when the impulse to help and bless others springs constantly from within."
>
> *Christ's Object Lessons,* p. 384

Without true godliness we cannot show brotherly kindness. We must learn how Jesus was able to do this regardless of what kind of person He encountered. "Finally, all of you be of one mind, having compassion for one another; love as brothers, be tenderhearted, be courteous not returning evil for evil or reviling for reviling, But on the contrary blessing, knowing that you were called to this, that you may inherit a blessing" (1 Peter 3:8).

God has a blessing waiting for us if we show kindness to everyone, not only our close friends and family. He tells us to "Be kindly affectionate to one another with brotherly love, in honor giving preference to one another; not lagging in diligence, fervent in spirit, serving the Lord" (Rom. 12:10).

> "The reason there are so many differences existing between brethren is that they have failed to add brotherly kindness."
>
> "The Path of Progress," *The Review and Herald,* February 21, 1888

Being kind to each other is the way the Lord wants us to serve Him. The problem is that we are often looking at the actions of our brothers and sisters, or our pastor and church leaders, rather than the example Jesus gave us.

"The heart of the true minister is filled with an intense longing to save souls. Time and strength are spent, toilsome effort is not shunned; for others must hear the truths that brought to his own soul such gladness and peace and joy.... With invitations and pleadings, mingled with the assurances of God's love, he seeks to win souls to Jesus ..." (*The Acts of the Apostles,* p. 371).

All of us are ministers, or at least, we should be. We can share God's love by following in the footsteps of Jesus and working for souls as He did. "He was never rude, never needlessly spoke a severe word, never gave needless pain to a sensitive soul. He did not censure human weakness. He fearlessly denounced hypocrisy, unbelief, and iniquity, but tears were in His voice as He uttered His scathing rebukes" (*The Desire of Ages*, p. 353).

I have made a decision to do God's will. My conscience tells me it is the right thing to do; my reason tells me it is the best thing to do; and it is my heart's desire. To do His will is His desire for us, and to be successful, we must use His method. However, sometimes it is difficult for me to see that the actions of others are human weaknesses. I now realize that I must get to know them first.

> "Christ's method alone will give true success in reaching the people. The Saviour mingled with men as one who desired their good. He showed His sympathy for them, ministered to their needs, and won their confidence. Then He bade them, 'Follow Me.'"
>
> *The Ministry of Healing*, p. 143

I am thankful that I made the decision to put away my pride and selfishness and now recognize others as precious in God's sight regardless of their character traits. He paid the infinite price for each of us, and when we value ourselves as God's property, we will be able to show brotherly kindness to everyone.

> "The religion of Jesus Christ is a system of the true heavenly politeness and leads to a practical exhibition of habitual tenderness of feeling, kindness of deportment. He who possesses godliness will also add this grace, taking a step higher on the ladder. The higher he mounts the ladder, the more of the grace of God is revealed in his life, his sentiments, his principles. He is learning, ever learning the terms of his acceptance with God, and the only way to obtain an inheritance in the heavens is to become like Christ in character. The whole scheme of mercy is to soften down what is harsh in temper, and refine whatever is rugged in the deportment. The internal change reveals itself in the external actions. The graces of the Spirit of God work with hidden power in the transformation of character. The religion of Christ never will reveal a sour, coarse, and uncourteous action. Courtesy is a Bible virtue. The virtue of the grace of brotherly kindness characterized the life of Christ. Never was such courtesy exhibited upon the earth as Christ revealed, and we cannot overestimate its value.... Growing in grace is an earnest working out of what God works in. It is an earnest of future glory, the working out here upon the earth of the spirit that is cherished in heaven."
>
> *Our High Calling*, p. 72

"Let brotherly love continue. Do not forget to entertain strangers, for by so doing some have unwittingly entertained angels" (Heb. 13:1, 2).

I praise God for continual guidance. We cannot have true brotherly kindness from our hearts, unless we first travel the ladder of godliness. So, when I find that I am having a problem with really caring about other people and making an attempt to be kind to them, I go down one rung on the ladder to godliness and examine myself some more to find out what is keeping me from showing the kindness of Jesus to others.

> "Love is the basis for godliness. Whatever the profession, no man has pure love to God unless he has unselfish love for his brother. But we can never come into possession of this spirit by trying to love others. What is needed is the love of Christ in the heart. When self is merged in Christ, love springs forth spontaneously. The completeness of Christian character is attained when the impulse to help and bless others springs constantly from within."
>
> *Christ's Object Lessons*, p. 384

There are still people who do not realize this; therefore, that is a desire God puts in the hearts of those who have learned about His truth—to share that knowledge with them. "The truth is to be planted in the heart. It is to control the mind and regulate the affections. The whole character must be stamped with the divine utterances. Every jot and tittle of the word of God is to be brought into the daily practice" (*Christ's Object Lessons*, p. 314).

Sometimes I realize I am trying too hard to please others. I have a tendency to do that, but I am finding that God is giving me self-control to have patience with myself and with others. I want others to know Jesus and the love He has shown me. He has given me the burden to work for those who have left the faith of the church as well as those who are in the church but struggling to hold on to their faith. When Jesus sent the disciples out, He told them to go first to the household of faith, and He encourages us to do the same.

"Therefore, as we have opportunity, let us do good to all, especially to those who are of the household of faith" (Gal. 6:10).

God's word is sure. Solomon said, " ... And there is nothing new under the sun" (Eccles. 1:9).

God has been and always will be the same. We may change, but He does not. We have " ... one Lord, one faith, one baptism; one God and Father of all, who is above all, and through all, and in you all" (Eph. 4:4–6).

He was one God then, is so now, and will be for all eternity. God the Father, God the Son, and God the Holy Spirit gave the people of Israel answers when they had faith in God's word, and the same Trinity gives people today the same promises. When we pray, we pray in the name of Jesus.

> But to pray in Christ's name means much. It means that we are to accept His character, manifest His Spirit, and work His works. The Saviour's promise is given on condition. 'If ye love me,' He says, 'keep my commandments.' He saves men, not in sin, but from sin; and those who love Him will show their love by obedience.... Through an appreciation of the character of Christ, through communion with God, sin will become hateful to us. (*The Desire of Ages*, p. 668)

He is always the same. We now know how much God wants us to serve Him. We shall go to the next rung on the ladder. Love is the only acceptable way to reach the top and enter the kingdom of glory.

Love

"… and to brotherly kindness love" (2 Peter 1:7).

"But above all these things put on love, which is the bond of perfection" (Col. 3:14).

"… love your neighbor as yourself" (Lev. 19:18)

"Love to God and love to our neighbor constitute the whole duty of man. Without brotherly kindness we cannot exhibit the grace of love to God or to our fellow men" (*Our High Calling*, p. 73).

My daughter, Jane, demonstrated this concept to me when some friends were visiting. She had a little suitcase full of doll clothes that her grandmother had made to fit her favorite doll. Our friend's youngest child's favorite thing to do when they visited was to dress the doll in one outfit, then another. When it was time for them to leave, she packed the clothes in the suitcase and started out the door with them. Her mother told her she could not take them home, and she started to cry. Immediately, Jane told her she could have the suitcase with the clothes, and I objected; however, she insisted, and not wanting to thwart her generosity, I allowed it. She has continued to show generosity to others in need. Our older daughter, Nelle, has always shown that same kind of caring for others. In academy, she had a friend she was concerned about. I remember one night after we had gone to bed, she came into our room to tell us the problem, and we gave her some suggestions and prayed about it together. She later chose to go into Career Counseling and now works with students in college.

Brotherly kindness is necessary to be put into action before one can truly love. By our deeds of kindness to others, we show that we love them. I don't believe that we can show brotherly kindness until we have ascended the step of godlinesss and acquired the goodness of God in our hearts. And that can only come after we have acquired the graces of patience, self-control, and knowledge, all which we attain through the power of the Holy Spirit.

I have only acquired this knowledge since I began my search to determine what love really is.

I thought I was kind to others, but now I realize my motive for some of my actions were not pure. My actions were not true kindness; they were self-serving. Love for others must come from the heart. I have learned to pray, "Lord, I know you love this person, so please help me to love them, too." Ellen White frequently talks about how Christ's love is our example.

> We are to love our brethren as Christ has loved us. We are to be patient and kind, and yet there is something lacking–we must love. Christ tells us that we must forgive the erring even seventy times seven…. When there is much forgiven, the heart loves much. Love is a tender plant. It needs to be constantly cultured or it will wither and die. All these graces we must have. We must climb the whole length of the ladder. (*Our High Calling*, p. 73)

> "This last step in the ladder gives to the will a new spring of action. Christ offers a love that passeth knowledge. This love is not something kept apart from our life, but it takes hold of the entire being. The heaven to which the Christian is climbing will be attained only by those who have this crowning grace. This is the new affection which pervades the soul. The old is left behind. Love is the great controlling power. When love leads, all the faculties of mind and spirit are enlisted. Love to God and love to man will give the clear title to heaven. No one can love God supremely and transgress one of His commandments. The heart softened and subdued with the beauty of Christ's character and bridled by the pure and lofty rules which He has given us will put into practice what it has learned of love, and will follow Jesus forthwith in humble obedience. The living power of faith will reveal itself in loving acts."
>
> *Our High Calling*, p. 73

We love because God first loved us, gave the ultimate sacrifice for us, and is continually drawing us to Him. Another promise about love has meant a lot to me: "There is no fear in love; but perfect love casts out fear ..." (1 John 4:18).

There was a time when Peter denied Jesus because of fear, but Jesus forgave him and later told him what work needed to be done. That same work is ours today.

"He said to him the third time, 'Simon, son of Jonah, do you love me?' Peter was grieved because He said to him the third time, 'Do you love Me?' And he said to Him, 'Lord, You know all things; You know that I love You.' Jesus said to him, 'Feed My sheep'" (John 21:17).

One of the things I feared was snakes, and growing up in rural South Carolina, we had many snakes. Our house was four feet off the ground, not enclosed, and the space beneath was used for storage of many things. Often I was sent to get something, and I was terrified until I got out from under the house and back into the open yard. Fortunately, they were mostly black snakes and would run away if they saw me first.

There were many times when I went to feed the chickens that I would encounter a snake. It was scary to reach into the nest boxes for the eggs. Sometimes I saw snakes in the chicken coops. What was even more scary was feeding the pigeons in their pen. Momma raised pigeons and sold the squabs to one of the up-scale resorts for her spending money. Sometimes I saw a snake with a big bump a few inches from its throat, and I knew it had just swallowed one of the squabs. I would run and get momma and she would come with the hoe and kill the snake before it disappeared in the woods nearby.

Even after I was married, my fear of snakes remained with me. My husband was in the Army Air Force at Myrtle Beach. This was before the days of beach development with lines of hotels and condos; it was mostly wooded area above the beach. We spent many hot summer days in the cool ocean water and lying on the beach. One day to avoid the sun, we moved our blanket up under the shade of a tree with a little brush and grass growing under it. We were almost asleep when I heard a rustle in the brush and opened my eyes and saw a snake headed directly for me. I screamed and jumped on top of my husband. With all the commotion, the snake slithered off in the other direction. There are many texts about fear I did not know then (that I shall include later); however, I'm not sure they would have abated my fear of snakes.

My husband eventually got out of the service, and we moved to an area in Idaho where the only snakes seen were little garter snakes. I was very grateful, but even today they still startle me when I come upon one in my garden. I have no real fear of them though because I know they are harmless.

What really helped me overcome my fear of snakes was studying my Bible and learning that when the children of Israel were going through the wilderness, they were told to look to the snake on the pole in order to live. That snake represented Jesus. And we show that we love God by keeping His Commandments. That was my husband's favorite verse:

> Whoever believes that Jesus is the Christ is born of God, and everyone who loves Him who begot also loves him who is begotten of Him. By this we know that we love the children of God, when we love God and keep His commandments. For this is the love of God, that we keep His commandments. And His commandments are not burdensome. (1 John 5:1–3)

The last line really impressed me. "And His commandments are not burdensome." I may slip, but He will catch me, unless I choose otherwise. I have the assurance that Jesus is the ladder that lifts me up when I fall and will carry me to the top. "I will heal their backsliding, I will love them freely, For my anger has turned away from him" (Hosea 14:4).

"He who does not climb the ladder of progress and add grace to grace 'is blind, and cannot see afar off.' He fails to discern that without taking these successive steps in ascending the ladder round after round, in growing in grace and the knowledge of our Lord Jesus Christ, he is not placing himself in a position where the light of God above the ladder is reflected upon him. As he does not add grace to grace, he has forgotten the claims of God upon him, and that he was to receive the forgiveness of sins through obedience to the requirements of God....

"We ascend to heaven by climbing the ladder—the whole height of Christ's work—step by step. There must be a holding fast to Christ, a climbing up by the merits of Christ. To let go is to cease to climb, is to fall, to perish. We are to mount by the Mediator and all the while to keep hold on the Mediator, ascending by successive steps, round above round, stretching the hand from one round to the next above.... There is fearful peril in relaxing our efforts in spiritual diligence for a moment, for we are hanging, as it were, between heaven and earth. We must keep the eye directed upward to God above the ladder. The question with men and women gazing heavenward is, How can I obtain the mansions for the blessed? It is by being a partaker of the divine nature. It is by escaping the 'corruption that is in the world through lust.' It is by entering into the holiest by the blood of Jesus, laying hold of the hope set before you in the gospel. It is by fastening yourself to Christ and straining every nerve to leave the world

> behind.... It is by being in Christ and yet led by Christ; by believing and working, ...holding onto Christ and constantly mounting upward toward God.... Plant your feet on the ladder. Forsake your sins. Climb step by step and you will reach God above the ladder, and the Holy City of God. When all the successive steps have all been mounted, when the graces have been added one after another, the crowning grace is the perfect love of God—supreme love to God and love to our fellow men. And then the abundant entrance into the kingdom of God."
>
> *Our High Calling,* pp. 74, 75

It is then that I will have reached my goal—the top round on the ladder: love.

I must remember that reaching the top is a process. "The Scriptures plainly show that the work of sanctification is progressive. When in conversion the sinner finds peace with God through the blood of the atonement, the Christian's life has but just begun. ... Peter sets before us the steps by which Bible sanctification is to be attained ... (2 Peter 1:5–10)" (*The Great Controversy*, p. 470).

I believe I was justified when by faith I accepted Jesus' calling and received His grace; I am being sanctified as I travel up this ladder. I am gaining knowledge, self-control, patience, godliness, brotherly kindness, and then at the top, love that only God can bestow; and I can't wait to be glorified when Jesus comes. Each day I try to remember to pray the prayer of David. "Create in me a clean heart, O God, And renew a steadfast Spirit within me" (Ps. 51:10).

Paul gave us a wonderful picture of what love is like. "Love suffers long and is kind; love does not envy; love does not parade itself, is not puffed up; does not behave rudely, does not seek its own, is not provoked, thinks no evil; does not rejoice in iniquity, but rejoices in the truth; bears all things, believes all things, hopes all things, endures all things. Love never fails ..." (1 Cor. 13:4–8).

We must keep that love in our hearts while we wait for Jesus to return, but while we wait, we must also work because the Bible tells us: "Thus also faith by itself, if it does not have works, is dead" (James 2:17).

We have reached the top round on Peter's ladder of love. Peter accepted Jesus' instructions to feed His sheep. So must we. He has work for all who believe in Him. With God's love in our hearts, our greatest desire will be to keep loving, obeying, and serving Him. So we must remember to "... add to your faith virtue, to virtue knowledge, to knowledge self-control, to self-control perseverance, to perseverance godliness, to godliness brotherly kindness, and to brotherly kindness love" (2 Peter 1:5–7).

Now, let's go to God's ladder and learn more about His law of love.

Chapter Three
GOD'S TEN COMMANDMENTS

After I reached the top of Peter's ladder, and realized how much God loved me, I had to keep studying to find out how I could return that love. I had to have love before I could start up God's ladder. Peter also said to add knowledge, so I had to know what the Ten Commandments were really saying. Peter's ladder took us to the entrance to heaven: love. This is where our love merges with God's love. No one can enter heaven without the pure love of God in their heart; for God is love, and His love will be perfected in us. "... God is Love" (1 John 4:8).

I saw that when I reached the top I would be content with my status and not covet or desire another's blessings. It looked like an impossible task. He gave the Ten Commandments for us to follow, and He said, "If you love Me, keep My commandments" (John 14:15).

I began to realize how much searching I need to do in order to know and do God's will. I had already learned that His Word is His will. I thought I had made a complete surrender, but I really didn't know what surrender meant. However, God was providing for my growth. He has always known what I needed to learn and has kept leading me and giving me spiritual food I can digest. More and more, I am thinking, "Salvation is simple!" With Jesus being the ladder that Jacob saw in his dream, it should be easy to go up the commandment ladder, just as I did Peter's ladder. But in reading them as is, they simply tell me what I should not do.

And God spoke all these words, saying: 'I am the LORD your God, who brought you out of Egypt, out of the house of bondage.

I. You shall have no other gods before Me.

II. You shall not make for yourself a carved image—any likeness of anything that is in heaven above, or that is in the earth beneath, or that is in the water under the earth; you shall not bow down to them nor serve them. For I, the LORD your God, am a jealous God, visiting the iniquity of the fathers upon the children of the third and fourth generations of those who hate Me, but showing mercy to thousands, to those who love Me and keep My commandments.

III. You shall not take the name of the LORD your God in vain, for the LORD will not hold him guiltless, who takes His name in vain.

IV. Remember the Sabbath day, to keep it holy. Six days you shall labor and do all your work, but the seventh day is the Sabbath of the LORD your God. In it you shall do no work: you, nor your son, nor your daughter, nor your male servant, nor your female servant, nor your cattle, nor your stranger who is within your gates. For in six days the LORD made the heavens and the earth, the sea, and all that is in them, and rested the seventh day. Therefore the LORD blessed the Sabbath day and hallowed it.

V. Honor your father and your mother, that your days may be long upon the land which the LORD your God is giving you.

VI. You shall not murder.

VII. You shall not commit adultery.

VIII. You shall not steal.

IX. You shall not bear false witness against your neighbor.

X. You shall not covet your neighbor's house; you shall not covet your neighbor's wife, nor his male servant, nor his female servant, nor his ox, nor his donkey, nor anything that is your neighbor's.' (Exod. 20:1–17)

When put this way, they seem so negative. I do not have a lot of desire for all the "do-nots" without some positive instructions of what I should do. In order for me to love the commandments, I need to think of them in positive form. As God gave them at Mount Sinai, all are negative except two.

I believe we might more readily obey them if we learned them in positive form. Changing the meaning is not my intent.

I believe that God originally gave the laws in positive form. Adam and Eve were given their instructions in the positive. Only one negative—not to eat of the tree in the midst of the garden—and their disobedience is what caused all the problems. They were to dress the garden and care for all God's creation. He told them which trees they could eat fruit from and which one to exclude.

"And the LORD God commanded the man, saying, 'Of every tree of the garden you may freely eat; but of the tree of the knowledge of good and evil you shall not eat, for in the day that you eat of it you shall surely die'" (Gen. 2:16, 17).

God does not change, and neither do His laws. They are promises to us.

> The ten commandments, Thou shalt, and Thou shalt not, are ten promises ... The ten holy precepts spoken by Christ upon Sinai's mount were the revelation of the character of God, and made known to the world the fact that He had jurisdiction over the whole human heritage. That law of ten precepts of the greatest love that can be presented to man is the voice of God from heaven speaking to the soul in promise, 'This do and you will not come under the dominion and control of Satan.'

There is not a negative in that law, although it may appear thus. It is DO and Live.'(*Seventh-day Adventist Bible Commentary*, vol. 1, p. 105)

I try to obey the civil laws, but even if I don't He still loves me and understands my weaknesses. During years of captivity, the pharaohs robbed Israel of the privilege to practice all of God's law as handed down by their ancestors. After Moses led them out of Egypt, God said, " ... Behold, I will rain bread from heaven for you. And the people shall go out and gather a certain quota every day, that I may test them, whether they will walk in My law or not" (Exod. 16:4).

If they collected more than "a certain quota every day," the manna spoiled, and they failed the test. Yet, they were still able to collect enough on Friday for their Sabbath meals with it still fresh and sweet on Sabbath morning. This makes it evident that the commandments were in effect from before Sinai when God wrote them with His own finger in stone.

In the beginning God made an eternal covenant of salvation by grace through faith with Abraham. He confirmed the covenant with Isaac, his son, and now we are following the ladder given to Jacob, Isaac's son. "And I will make your descendants multiply as the stars of heaven; I will give to your descendants all these lands; and in your seed all the nations of the earth shall be blessed; because Abraham obeyed My voice and kept My charge, My commandments, My statutes, and My laws" (Gen. 26:4, 5).

> "Still the great leader was filled with fear that the people would depart from God. In a most sublime and thrilling address he set before them the blessings that would be theirs on condition of obedience, and the curses that would follow upon transgression."
> *Patriarchs and Prophets*, p. 466

Joshua, who became the leader after Moses died, read the commandments to the people every seven years to remind them. We need to study them daily.

> The writings of Moses were taught by Joshua to all Israel. ... This was in harmony with the express command of Jehovah providing for a public rehearsal of the words of the book of the law every seven years, during the Feast of Tabernacles. ... Had this counsel been heeded through the centuries that followed, how different would have been Israel's history! (*Prophets and Kings*, p. 465)

King Josiah is a favorite king of mine. He became king when he was just a young boy. When the temple was being cleaned, the scrolls on which God's law was written were found. He realized that the people needed to hear them since the scroll has been lost for many years. "Then the king stood by a pillar and made a covenant before the LORD, to follow the LORD and to keep His commandments and His testimonies and His statutes, with all his heart and all his soul, to perform the words of this covenant that were written in this book. And all the people took a stand for the covenant" (2 Kings 23:3).

But they needed more than knowledge; they needed the law of love in their hearts. The destruction that was prophesied would take place, but Josiah was spared because of his loyalty to God. "Through Huldah the Lord sent Josiah word that Jerusalem's ruin could not be averted. Even should the people now humble themselves before God, they could not escape their punishment. So long had their senses been deadened by wrongdoing that, if judgment should not come upon them, they would soon return to the same sinful course" (*Prophets and Kings*, p. 399).

"Now he who keeps His commandments abides in Him, and He in him. And by this we know that He abides in us, by the Spirit whom He has given us. Beloved, do not believe every spirit, but test the spirits, whether they are of God; because many false prophets have gone out into the world" (1 John 3:24; 4:1).

God's word is the final standard that God has given to us. God revealed His glory to Moses, and His words are recorded:

> And the Lord passed before him and proclaimed, 'The LORD, the LORD God, merciful and gracious, longsuffering, and abounding in goodness and truth, keeping mercy for thousands, forgiving iniquity and transgression and sin, by no means clearing the guilty, visiting the iniquity of the fathers upon the children and the children's children to the third and fourth generation ... (Exod. 34:6, 7)

I have converted the commandments to positive actions and have shared my understanding of them below. As previously stated, I have no intention of changing the meaning—I only want to see His laws as what I should be doing rather than what I should not be doing.

"Because You loved me so much, You gave Your Son, Jesus Christ, who died for my sins. You gave me directions to follow in order to live a happy life; therefore, by the power of God, the great I AM: Father, Son, and Holy Spirit, which You also gave me:

1. I will worship and serve You, the true God, the great I AM: Father, Son, and Holy Spirit

2. I will worship You only; I will disregard all earthly gods.

3. I will reverence Your name and speak of You lovingly.

4. I will remember You as Creator and keep the Sabbath day holy.

5. I will honor my parents by my obedience in the Lord.

> "Since it was the Spirit of God that inspired the Bible, it is impossible that the teaching of the Spirit should ever be contrary to that of the Word. The Spirit was not given—nor can it ever be bestowed—to supersede the Bible; for the Scriptures explicitly state that the Word of God is the standard by which all teaching and experience must be tested. Says the apostle John, 'Believe not every spirit, but try the spirits whether they are of God: because many false prophets are gone out into the world' (1 John 4:1)."
>
> *The Great Controversy,* pp. iv, v

6. I will respect the life of all God's children regardless of their beliefs or behaviors.

7. I will keep myself sexually pure.

8. I will respect the property of others.

9. I will only speak the truth and do so in a loving manner..

10. I will be happy for the blessings of others and be thankful for my own.

> "Not one command has been annulled, not a jot or tittle has been changed. Those principles that were made known to man in Paradise as the great law of life will exist unchanged in Paradise restored. When Eden shall bloom on earth again, God's law of love will be obeyed by all beneath the sun."
>
> *Thoughts from the Mount of Blessings,* pp. 50, 51

"[God] does not ask if we are worthy of His love, but He pours upon us the riches of His love, to make us worthy. He is not vindictive. He seeks not to punish, but to redeem. ... It is true that God 'will by no means clear the guilty' (Exodus 34:7), but He would take away the guilt" (*Thoughts from the Mount of Blessing*, p. 22). I wondered how I could ever know if I really loved God or if I obeyed His Commandments just to receive the rewards they bring. I eventually found the answer.

"Now by this we know that we know Him, if we keep His commandments. He who says, 'I know Him,' and does not keep His commandments, is a liar, and the truth is not in him. But whoever keeps His word, truly the love of God is perfected in him.... He who says he abides in Him ought himself also to walk just as He walked" (1 John 2:3–6).

He has given me His love, so I know He will take me to the top of the ladder.

> "The law requires righteousness,—a righteous life, a perfect character; and this man has not to give. He cannot meet the claims of God's holy law. But Christ, coming to the earth as man, lived a holy life, and developed a perfect character. These He offers as a free gift to all who will receive them. His life stands for the life of men. Thus they have remission of sins that are past, through the forbearance of God. More than this, Christ imbues men with the attributes of God. He builds up the human character after the similitude of the divine character, a goodly fabric of spiritual strength and beauty. Thus the very righteousness of the law is fulfilled in the believer in Christ. God can 'be just, and the justifier of him which believeth in Jesus'. Romans 3:26"
>
> *The Desire of Ages,* p. 762

I read a survey that was done regarding knowledge of the Ten Commandments, and I was surprised at the small percent of people who knew all ten from memory. Even among some church clergy, only thirty-four percent could repeat them verbatim. I wondered about myself; do I know all of the Ten Commandments? I had memorized them in Sunday School as a child but without an understanding of what they really meant. I realized some had been lost from memory, so I began to commit them to memory again, and this time I learned what each one entailed if it were to be kept.

> "Man's advantage for obtaining a knowledge of the truth, however great these may be, will prove of no benefit to him unless the heart is open to receive the truth, and there is a conscientious surrender of every habit and practice that is opposed to its principles."
> *The Desire of Ages*, pp. 455, 456

I had reached the place where I was not only willing, but anxious to know the truth. And I knew that God's word was truth. I knew Jesus had said, "... I am the way, the truth, and the life. No one comes to the Father except through me" (John 14:6).

God is jealous for His Law; He said so in the second commandment, and we must not take it lightly. His law and His love are everlasting. Both will be renewed before He returns.

> In the last days of this earth's history, God's covenant with His commandment-keeping people is to be renewed.... They will free themselves from every entanglement and will stand before the world as monuments of God's mercy. Obedient to the divine requirements, they will be recognized by angels and by men as those that have kept 'the commandments of God, and the faith of Jesus' (Revelation 14:6, 7, 12).... In the time of trouble just before the coming of Christ, the righteous will be preserved through the ministration of heavenly angels; but there will be no security for the transgressor of God's Law. Angels cannot then protect those who are disregarding one of the divine precepts. (*Prophets and Kings*, pp. 299, 300; *Patriarchs and Prophets*, p. 256)

His purpose for giving the law when He revealed it to Israel was to make a holy people. However, their professed obedience was often only forms or ceremonies rather than a surrender of their hearts in response to God's love. " ... you shall be holy men to Me ... " (Exod. 22:31).

Some people think that the law was done away with when Jesus died on the cross, but that is not true. It was the ordinances that God gave Moses, and Moses wrote them down himself that some confuse with the Ten Commandments.

> Do not think that I came to destroy the Law or the Prophets. I did not come to destroy but to fulfill. For assuredly, I say to you, till heaven and earth pass away, one jot or one tittle will by no means pass from the law till all is fulfilled. Whoever therefore breaks one of the least of these commandments, and teaches men so, shall be called least in the kingdom of heaven. For I say to you, that unless your righteousness exceeds the righteousness of the scribes and Pharisees, you will by no means enter the kingdom of heaven. (Matt. 5:17–20)

God divided the commandments into two distinct categories, love for God and love for humanity. He emphasized this when He was later asked which the greatest commandment was. "... 'You shall love the LORD your God with all your heart, with all your soul, and with all your mind.' This is the first and great commandment.

God's Ten Commandments

And the second is like it: 'You shall love your neighbor as yourself.' On these two commandments hang all the Law and the Prophets" (Matt. 22:37–40).

Go with me now up God's ladder, step-by-step, and think of them as they could have been said in positive form. My prayer is that looking at them in a positive mode will open a new understanding to you, as they have to me. Our goal is to reach the top round and be happy for the blessings God bestows upon others. It is then that we will have the peace and contentment we are seeking.

The first four enlarge on the command to love God with all our heart.

THE FIRST COMMANDMENT

"I am the LORD your God, who brought you out of Egypt, out of the house of bondage. You shall have no other gods before Me" (Exod. 20:2, 3).

"I will worship and serve You, the true God, the great I AM: Father, Son, and Holy Spirit" (Carscallen version).

God gives us many opportunities to fix His laws in our mind so that we are able to overcome sin. He will do the work if we consent. I do now have His laws in my mind, The Word, Jesus, put them there. By His grace, I plan to keep them there even though I may offend some or forget sometimes.

" ... I will put My laws in their mind and write them on their hearts; and I will be their God, and they shall be My people" (Heb. 8:10).

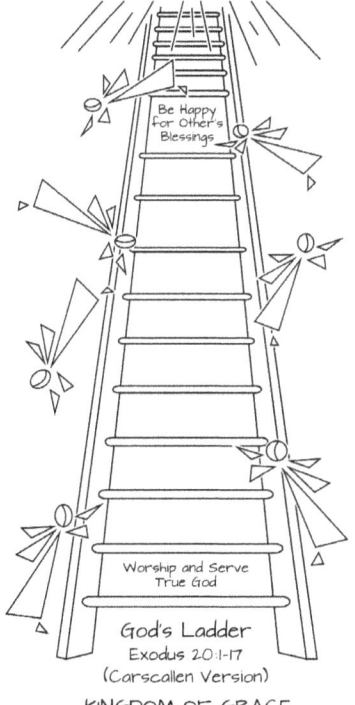

> "And if we consent, He will so identify Himself with our thoughts and aims, so blend our hearts and minds into conformity to His will, that when obeying Him we shall be but carrying out our own impulses.... When we know God as it is our privilege to know Him, our life will be a life of continual obedience. Through an appreciation of the character of Christ, through communion with God, sin will become hateful to us."
> *The Desire of Ages*, p. 668

I prayed the prayer of David, and God is answering. "Create in me a clean heart, O God, And renew a right spirit within me" (Ps. 51:10).

And like David, I pray that God will keep His law alive in my heart. I love Psalm 1. "Blessed is the man Who walks not in the counsel of the ungodly, Nor stands in the path of sinners, Nor sits in the seat of the scornful; But his delight is in the law of the LORD, And in His law he meditates day and night" (Ps. 1:1, 2).

> "You are just as dependent upon Christ, in order to live a holy life, as is the branch upon the parent stock for growth and fruitfulness. Apart from Him you have no life. You have no power to resist temptation or to grow in grace and holiness. Abiding in Him, you may flourish. Drawing your life from Him, you will not wither nor be fruitless. You will be like a tree planted by the rivers of water."
>
> *Steps to Christ*, p. 69

Our mind has to be trained to detach from negative thoughts and think on things that will draw us closer to Jesus. We have the blueprint of the things to think on in the Bible.

"Finally, brethren, whatever things are true, whatever things are noble, whatever things are just, whatever things are pure, whatever things are lovely, whatever things are of good report, if there is any virtue and if there is anything praiseworthy—meditate on these things" (Phil. 4:8).

We must keep God's Word in our mind and heart and walk in them to have hope.

> Blessed are the undefiled in the way, Who walk in the law of the LORD! Blessed are those who keep His testimonies, Who seek Him with the whole heart! They also do no iniquity; They walk in His ways. You have commanded us To keep Your precepts diligently. Oh, that my ways were directed To keep Your statutes! Then I would not be ashamed, When I look into all Your commandments. I will praise You with uprightness of heart, When I learn Your righteous judgments. I will keep Your statutes; Oh, do not forsake me utterly! How can a young man cleanse his way By taking heed according to Your Word. With my whole heart I have sought You; Oh, let me not wander from Your commandments! Your word have I hidden in my heart, That I might not sin against You. (Ps. 119:1–11)

Now let's look at the second commandment on the next round of God's ladder.

THE SECOND COMMANDMENT

This commandment is about worship. God prohibits the worship of idols. We are not to bow before carved statues. Nothing should interfere with our worship of God,

> You shall not make for yourself a carved image—any likeness of anything that is in heaven above, or that is in the earth beneath, or that is in the water under the earth; you shall not bow down to them nor serve them. For I, the LORD your God, am a jealous God, visiting the iniquity of the fathers upon the children to the third and fourth generations of those who hate Me, but showing mercy to thousands, to those who love Me And keep My commandments. (Exod. 20:4–6)

> "I will worship You only; I will disregard all earthly gods"
> (Carscallen version).

God's Ten Commandments

Worshipping only God is the number one requirement of everyone. This commandment tells us that He is a jealous God. Some take that to mean that He is selfish and wants to be exclusive. But what it really shows is that He wants us to return His love so that we might be happy. It is simply unacceptable for us to love anything more than God. As much as God wants us to love our families, He assures us: "... Assuredly, I say to you, there is no one who has left house or brothers or sisters or father or mother or wife or children or lands, for My sake and the gospel's, who shall not receive a hundredfold now in this time—houses and brothers and sisters and mothers and children and lands, with persecutions—and in the age to come, eternal life" (Mark 10:29, 30).

Job is a good example of one who was loyal to God under all circumstances, and God blessed Him for it. Job had lost his home, his children, and all his possessions. He was also stricken with painful sores, but despite everything, he refused to follow the advice of his wife or his friends.

> 'And suddenly a great wind came from across the wilderness and struck the four corners of the house, and it fell on the young people, and they are dead; and I alone have escaped to tell you!' Then Job arose, tore his robe, and shaved his head; and he fell to the ground and worshiped. And he said: 'Naked I came from my mother's womb, And naked shall I return there. The LORD gave, and the LORD has taken away; Blessed be the name of the LORD.' In all this Job did not sin nor charge God with wrong. (Job 1:19–22)

Finally, Job had a talk with God and was humbled. God also rebuked the three friends of Job for adding to Job's suffering by their false assumptions and critical attitudes. Job's material possessions and family were restored, and he received even greater blessings than he had before.

If we put our trust in God, we will also be rewarded. He was not rewarded because he was sinless, but because he had a healthy relationship with God. He was not guilty of the sins his friends accused of him. Remember, righteousness is not the same as sinlessness. "For all have sinned and fall short of the glory of God, being justified freely by His grace through the redemption that is in Christ Jesus" (Rom. 3:23).

> "Job was deprived of his worldly possessions, and so afflicted in body that he was abhorred by his relatives, and friends; yet he maintained his integrity."
>
> *The Acts of the Apostles*, p. 575
>
> "Sickness, suffering, and death are work of an antagonistic power. Satan is the destroyer; God Is the restorer."
>
> *The Ministry of Healing*, p. 113

No one but Jesus Christ has ever been sinless—free from all wrong thoughts and actions. It is the same today. Even Job needed to make some changes in his attitude toward God. Nevertheless, Job was righteous. "… There is none like him on the earth, a blameless and upright man, one who fears god and shuns evil" (Job 1:8).

He carefully obeyed God to the best of his ability in all aspects of his life. And that is all God expects of us. The next rung on God's ladder is about reverence.

THE THIRD COMMANDMENT

The third commandment is about reverence. God instructs us to respect His holy name and not to use His name in vain. The penalty is too great to ignore.

> "You shall not take the name of the LORD Your God in vain, for the LORD will not hold him guiltless who takes His name in vain" (Exod. 20:7, 8).

> "I will reverence Your name and speak of You lovingly" (Carscallen Version).

There are many instances recorded before Mt. Sinai of the sin of disrespecting the name of the Lord. When Moses gave God's instruction to Pharaoh, He scoffed at the authority of His name. The Lord eventually destroyed him because he would not obey. "And Pharaoh said, 'Who is the LORD, that I should obey His voice to let Israel go?' I do not know the LORD, nor will I let Israel go'" (Exod. 5:2).

God's name is special because it carries His personal identity. Using it frivolously or in a curse is so common today that we may fail to realize how serious it is. The way we use God's name conveys how we really feel about Him. We should respect His name and use it appropriately, speaking it in praise or worship rather than in curse or jest. We should not take lightly the abuse of or dishonoring of His Name. I am very thankful that my parents did not allow us children to use God's name in any way that would demean Him. Only the men in that era spoke in a disrespectful way, and they did not do so in the presence of women and children. Unfortunately, that has changed, but God's command for respect and reverence has not.

"Finite man may learn a lesson that should never be forgotten,—to approach God with reverence. We may come boldly into His presence, presenting the Name of Jesus, our righteousness and substitute, but never with the boldness of presumption, as though he were on a level with ourselves. We have heard some address the great and all-powerful and holy God ... as they would not address an equal, or even an inferior. We have seen some behave themselves in the presence of God as they would not dare to do in the presence of an earthly friend. These show that they have not a proper view of God's character and the greatness of His power.... He will not be mocked. God is greatly to be reverenced; wherever His presence is clearly realized, sinful man will bow in the most humble attitude, and from the depths of the soul cry out, 'How dreadful is this place!'"

"The Call of Moses," *The Signs of the Times*, February 26, 1880

God's Ten Commandments

"… He has commanded His covenant forever: Holy and awesome is His name. The fear of the LORD is the beginning of wisdom; A good understanding have all those who do His commandments …" (Ps. 111:9, 10).

"The great principles of education are unchanged. 'They stand fast for ever and ever' (Psalm 111:8); for they are the principles of the character of God. To aid the student in comprehending these principles, and in entering into that relation with Christ which will make them a controlling power in the life, should be the teacher's first effort and his constant aim. The teacher who accepts this aim is in truth a co-worker with Christ, a laborer together with God."

Education, p. 30

If Christ were on earth today, he would find that many clergy use the title Reverend. I am certain that He would repeat this commandment to them. Only Jesus is holy and human, and He is the only one who will always remain that way.

"Therefore let him who thinks he stands take heed lest he fall. No temptation has overtaken you except such as is common to man; but God is faithful, who will not allow you to be tempted beyond what you are able, but with the temptation will also make the way of escape, that you may be able to bear it" (1 Cor. 10:12, 13).

Now that we know that God will provide us a way of escape from sin, let us move up to the next commandment on the fourth rung of His ladder.

THE FOURTH COMMANDMENT

God instructs His people to "remember the Sabbath" and keep it set apart for holy purposes to draw nearer to Him. It is about sanctification and relationship. The commandment is very clear.

> Remember the Sabbath day, to keep it holy. Six days you shall labor and do all your work, but the seventh day is the Sabbath of the LORD your God. In it you shall do no work: you, nor your son, nor your daughter, nor your male servant, nor your female servant, nor your cattle, nor your stranger who is within your gates. For in six days the LORD made the heavens and the earth, the sea, and all that is in them, and rested the seventh day. Therefore the LORD blessed the Sabbath day and hallowed it. (Exod. 20:8–11)

"I will remember You as Creator and keep the Sabbath day holy" (Carscallen Version).

God tells His people to "remember" the Sabbath and keep it set apart for holy purposes to draw nearer to Him. God initiated the seventh day. It's clear He expected continued observance. Obviously, He had given this instruction before or He would not have said "remember." He says, "keep it holy" not "make it holy." The "therefore" tells us He blessed the Sabbath because it was holy and that we should follow His example. Before the Israelites arrived at Mt. Sinai, the Lord ordered preparation for the Sabbath. They were to gather a double portion of manna on the sixth day, so they could rest on the holy seventh day. Some did not heed the instructions, and God was displeased. It helps us to know that His commandments were in operation before they arrived at Mt. Sinai.

It makes no sense to believe modern-day theologians who teach that it took eons of time for each day of Creation to evolve. After working six days, He gives us a day, one twenty-four hour period of night and daylight, to rest.

> Now it happened that some of the people went out on the seventh day to gather, but they found none. And the LORD said to Moses, 'How long do you refuse to keep My commandments and My laws? See! For the LORD has given you the Sabbath; therefore He gives you on the sixth day bread for two days. Let every man remain in his place; let no man go out of his place on the seventh day.' So the people rested on the seventh day. (Exod. 16:27–30)

> "Every week during their long sojourn in the wilderness the Israelites witnessed a threefold miracle, designed to impress their minds with the sacredness of the Sabbath: a double quantity of manna fell on the sixth day, none on the seventh, and the portion needed for the Sabbath was preserved sweet and pure, when if any were kept over at any other time it became unfit for use."
> *Patriarchs and Prophets*, p. 296

Keeping the seventh day holy was a new concept for me. I grew up going to church on Sunday. However, my husband's parents were Seventh-day Adventists when he was young. He had never mentioned it to me before we were married. With nine children and hard financial times, his father decided he had to work on the Sabbath to earn a living. His father contracted cancer and died when he was only forty-nine. My husband was only seventeen years old, but he took up the primary responsibility of providing for his mother and the younger children. The other boys worked when they could to help, but jobs were not always available. On his deathbed, his father told him when he got out of the hospital they were going back to church. But, of course, he didn't get out, so there were no changes in the family. It did influence my husband though, because when we began keeping the Sabbath, he never missed going to church with me and the children unless he was sick.

When we were married, he went to church with me on Sunday, but he became less and less interested. He had plenty of work at home to keep him busy, so I often went alone with the four children. Sometimes I felt like I lost more religion than I gained while trying to keep four children quiet in church all by myself!

My husband had an uncle who had been a missionary in Africa and South America. He had little contact with the family for about fifty years, but when he retired and came back to the states, he came to visit us. He and my husband went to church on Sabbath, which started my quest to know what day I should go to church. In my dilemma my husband pointed to the calendar and showed me that Saturday, the day before Sunday, is the seventh day. That settled it; we started going to church on the Sabbath with our children. No one gave us Bible studies to find out if we understood the other beliefs, and we were baptized in a beautiful river near our home; I cherish that day. Many years later three of our grandchildren were baptized in the same location.

On our yearly visits from Idaho to my parent's home in South Carolina, we tried to share our new found faith with them. My father totally rejected it, especially when it came to the laws about diet.

He said, "If there will only be people in heaven who do not eat pork, you are going to be very lonely up there!" I had never said that, but food was one of his idols, and he had Jewish friends from whom he learned their traditions about food! Thankfully, God has helped me to modify my eating habits.

After my father died, my mother accepted the truth; however, her attitude was "What will people think?" once they realized she had changed churches. She rested both days, however, and when she visited us, she was happy to go to church with us on Sabbath. I expect to see her in heaven. When I was growing up, she never required us to work on Sunday, except

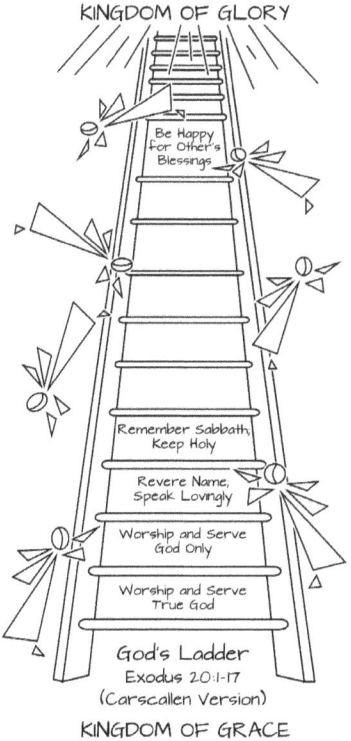

to help with preparing an over-abundance of food for Sunday dinner. We had to get up early, so the food was ready to eat when we got home from church. After dinner, we usually went to visit my paternal grandmother; both of my mother's parents were dead. Sometimes we children went for a long walk on the railroad track while our parents slept. We enjoyed seeing who could walk the rail the longest without falling off. Other times, we would walk about a mile to the highway and wave at every passing car.

We were not allowed to go fishing or crabbing, which was almost the only thing we did for fun. We had an uncle who worked on a plantation on the river not too far from where we lived.

We could fish, crab, or swim behind his house. Some of the older children were bold enough to dive from the high river bank, but it was dangerous if the tide was too low. I remember once we were there and my sister, Mable, dove off the bank and hit a bed of oysters. She came out of the water with blood oozing from her head. It was not a serious cut, but my older sister, Elise, could not stand the sight of blood and promptly fell over backward when she saw her, so Mama had two children to care for at the same time. It's a good thing Elise fainted backward, for if she had gone forward, she would have landed in the water and probably hit the oysters too.

Nowadays, I find myself always searching to learn more. God loved us so much He made the Sabbath for our rest. "And He said to them, 'The Sabbath was made for man, and not man for the Sabbath. Therefore the Son of Man is also Lord of the Sabbath'" (Mark 2:27, 28). *Patriarchs and Prophets* contains a powerful quote about the fourth commandment. "The fourth commandment is the only one of all the ten in which are found both the name and the title of the Lawgiver. It is the only one that shows by whose authority the law is given. Thus it contains the seal of God, affixed to His law as evidence of its authenticity and binding force" (p. 307).

The Sabbath was meant to commemorate God's creation of the heavens and the earth. "For in six days the LORD made the heavens and the earth, the sea ... " (Exod. 20:11).

Again in Deuteronomy, the commandments were given as a safeguard from idolatry. "These words the LORD spoke to all your assembly, in the mountain from the midst of the fire, the cloud, and the thick darkness, with a loud voice; and He added no more. And He wrote them on two tablets of stone and gave them to me" (Deut. 5:22).

"And I gave them My statutes and showed them My judgments, 'which, if a man does, he shall live by them.' Moreover I also gave them My Sabbaths, to be a sign between them and Me, that they might know that I am the LORD who sanctifies them" (Ezek. 20:11, 12).

> "Before entering the Promised Land, the Israelites were admonished by Moses to 'keep the Sabbath day to sanctify it.' Deuteronomy 5:12. The Lord designed that by a faithful observance of the Sabbath command, Israel should continually be reminded of their accountability to Him as their Creator and their Redeemer. While they should keep the Sabbath in the proper spirit, idolatry could not exist; but should the claims of this precept of the Decalogue be set aside as no longer binding, the Creator would be forgotten and men would worship other gods."
>
> *Prophets and Kings*, pp. 181, 182

The seventh day Sabbath points us to Jesus, our Creator and Redeemer.

> If you turn away your foot from the Sabbath, From doing your pleasure on My holy day, And call the Sabbath a delight, The holy day of the LORD honorable, And shall honor Him, not doing your own ways, Nor finding your own pleasure, Nor speaking your own words, Then you shall delight yourself in the LORD: And I will cause you to ride on the high hills of the earth, And feed you with the heritage of Jacob your father. The mouth of the LORD has spoken. (Isa. 58: 13, 14)

Worshipping God on the Sabbath is a delight as He has promised. When we "trample on the Sabbath," we insult God. The joy of the Sabbath is the presence of God. He is present and makes it holy. Therefore, if we engage in activities on the Sabbath, which are not harmful and would be acceptable on any other day, we are not honoring God. Jesus reserved seven miracles for the Sabbath. Healing and helping others are consistent with Sabbath keeping. We can spend time doing works of mercy and benevolence. The Sabbath begins at sunset on the sixth day, Friday; the Bible says so. Each day of Creation was from evening until evening, a twenty-four hour period.

It makes no sense if we believe the theory that it took long periods of time. Should we rest for many years and then work for many years? Our lifetime is not that long! Jesus lived for thirty-three years; He is our example. To believe any form of evolution makes God a liar. Believing in evolution undermines the fact that Jesus is the Son of God.

"... from evening to evening, you shall celebrate your sabbath" (Lev. 23:32). We can break the Sabbath, but we cannot change it. In AD 321 the Roman Emperor Constantine officially declared Sunday the new day of rest for the Empire. Constantine had two great interests: the power of the sun and Christianity. He struck some coins with the image of the cross and others with the image of the sun. He wanted Christians to incorporate the worship of the sun into their religious practices. He was a pagan emperor, and many are still being deceived today as a result of his hunger for power.

A common term for Sunday is to call it the Lord's day. However, Jesus did not worship on Sunday or give any indication that He rejected the Sabbath. Each Sabbath, He went into the synagogue to pray. "So He came to Nazareth, where He had been brought up. And as His custom was, He went into the synagogue on the Sabbath day, and stood up to read" (Luke 4:16).

> "Jesus, while He dwelt on earth, dignified life in all its details by keeping before men the glory of God, and by subordinating everything to the will of His Father ... all are provided for in the promise of His grace."
>
> *Thoughts from the Mount of Blessings*, p. 99

The text that Jesus read from was in Isaiah, and it disclosed what His work was to be. If we are to be like Jesus, we will pattern our work after His, but only by His grace will we be successful. "The Spirit of the LORD is upon Me, Because He has anointed Me To preach the gospel to the poor; He has sent Me to heal the brokenhearted, To proclaim liberty to the captives And recovery of sight to the blind, To set at liberty those who are oppressed; To proclaim the acceptable year of the LORD" (Luke 4:18, 19).

We have just looked at the first four commandments that test our love to God. The next six test our love for humanity.

"... You shall love the Lord your God with all your heart, with all your soul, and with all your mind. This is the first and great commandment. And the second is like it: 'You shall love your neighbor as yourself.' On these two commandments hang all the Law and the Prophets'" (Matt. 22:37–40).

Sometimes it may seem to those around us as though we love them, but unless it comes from the love of God in our hearts, it is only a form of godliness. It may be that we just do not understand. "But you do not have His Word abiding in you, because whom He sent, Him you do not believe. You search the Scriptures, for in them you think you have eternal life; and these are they which testify of Me" (John 5:39).

> "How often, in our own day, is the love of pleasure disguised by a 'form of godliness'! A religion that permits men, while observing the rites of worship, to devote themselves to selfish or sensual gratification, is as pleasing to the multitudes now as in the days of Israel. And there are still pliant Aarons, who, while holding positions of authority in the church, will yield to the desires of the unconsecrated, and thus encourage them in sin."
>
> *Patriarchs and Prophets*, p. 317

I was a slow learner, but I finally got the message. His Word will live within me as long as I will allow. He will direct me if I stay in His Word. It is my choice. God forces no one.

Now let's look at the last six commandments that comprise the second category: love for humanity.

THE FIFTH COMMANDMENT

This commandment is about respect for parental authority. Parents have a tremendous responsibility to teach their children, and the best way to teach is by example. Parents need to be a role model for their children.

"Honor your father and your mother, that your days may be long upon the land which the LORD your God is giving you" (Exod. 20:12).

"I will honor my parents by my obedience in the Lord" (Carscallen version).

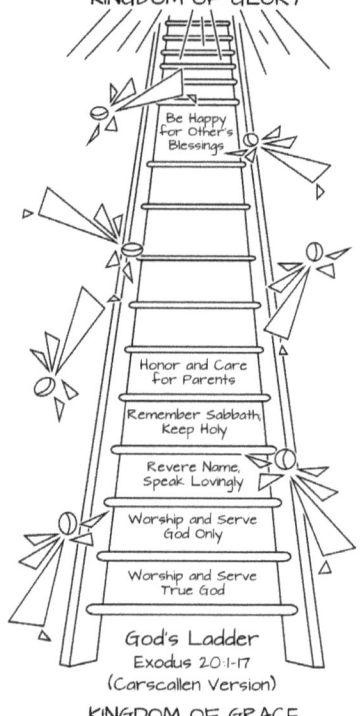

God instructs us to show love for our parents by honoring them, but sometimes parents make it difficult to do so. Jacob, upon whom our pattern of ladders is based, should have learned from his experience with his brother, Esau, but just as his mother had influenced him to deceive his father, he caused jealousy among his children.

"Now Israel loved Joseph more than all his children, because he was the son of his old age. Also he made him a tunic of many colors. But when his brothers saw that their father loved him more than all his brothers, they hated him and could not speak peaceably to him" (Gen. 37:3, 4).

In spite of all the mistreatment by his brothers, Joseph had a forgiving heart.

> When Joseph's brothers saw that their father was dead, they said, 'Perhaps Joseph will hate us, and may actually repay us for all the evil which we did to him.' So they sent messengers to Joseph, saying, 'Before your father died he commanded, saying 'Thus you shall say to Joseph: 'I beg you, please forgive the trespass of your brothers and their sin; for they did evil to you.' Now, please, forgive the trespass of the servants of the God of your father.' And Joseph wept when they spoke to him. Then his brothers also went and fell down before his face, and they said, 'Behold we are your servants.' Joseph said to them, 'Do not be afraid, for am I in the place of God? But as for you, you meant evil against me; but God meant it for good, in order to bring it about as it is this day, to save many people alive. Now therefore, do not be afraid; I will provide for you and your little ones.' And he comforted them and spoke kindly to them. (Gen. 50:15–21)

Joseph had provided for his father since they came to Egypt seeking food. Now, he was willing to care for his father's descendants. This story also confirms this commandment was known before Mt. Sinai. These two Bible passages give the account of Joseph and his brothers. It brings to light the sin of disrespecting our parents through dishonesty. In the first account, the brothers lied to their father about the death of Joseph. In the later account, the brothers ask forgiveness for their trespasses against their father. They knew they had violated the fifth commandment. Also, consider the record of Ham dishonoring Noah by exposing the nakedness of his sleeping father. Ham suffered under a lifelong curse for his sin.

> And Ham, the father of Canaan, saw the nakedness of his father, and told his two brothers outside. But Shem and Japheth took a garment, laid it on both of their shoulders, and went backward and covered the nakedness of their father. Their faces were turned away, and they did not see their father's nakedness. So Noah awoke from his wine, and knew what his younger son had done to him. Then he said: 'Cursed be Canaan; A servant of servants He shall be to his brethren.' And he said: 'Blessed be the LORD, The God of Shem, And may Canaan be his servant. May God enlarge Japheth, And may he dwell in the tents of Shem; And may Canaan be his servant. (Gen. 9:22–27)

I have been honored by my children many times, but there have also been times I felt dishonored. I'm sure that is the situation in most families.

Many years ago one of my daughters took off work and drove a lot of miles to attend the retirement party the school was having for me. It was such a pleasant surprise.

Now I live on my son's property, next door to his house and am honored many times when he and my daughter-in-law do special things for me. All the children came and helped when they put a roof over the trailer in which I live. I am blessed to have loving children; I couldn't begin to name all the ways in which they have honored me.

The penalty for disobedience or disrespect for parents was severe. What would God do today? He told us ahead of time what children would be like in the last days before he returns.

> But know this, that in the last days perilous times will come: For men will be lovers of themselves, lovers of money, boasters, proud, blasphemers, disobedient to parents, unthankful, unholy, unloving, unforgiving, slanders, without self-control, brutal, despisers of good, traitors, headstrong, haughty, lovers of pleasure rather than lovers of God, having a form of godliness but denying its power. And from such people turn away! (2 Tim. 3:1–5)

When I read newspaper accounts of how children have stolen from, or mistreated their parents in any way, it reminds me of this scripture. God gave plenty of instructions to avoid this behavior.

> Hear, O Israel: The LORD our God, the LORD is one! You shall love the LORD your God with all your heart, with all your soul, and with all your strength. And these words which I command you today shall be in your heart. You shall teach them diligently to your children, and shall talk of them when you sit in your house, when you walk by the way, when you lie down, and when you rise up. You shall bind them as a sign on your hand, and they shall be as frontlets between your eyes. You shall write them on the doorposts of your house, and on your gates. (Deut. 6:4–9)

> "As a preparation for teaching His precepts, God commands that they be hidden in the hearts of the parents.... In order to interest our children in the Bible, we ourselves must be interested in it. To awaken in them a love for its study, we must love it. Our instruction to them will have only the weight of influence given it by our own example and spirit."
>
> *Education*, p. 187

This is true whether we are trying to help our own family or others learn to follow after Jesus. His love must first be in our own hearts. All the children loved Jesus because He first loved them. He is the prime example for parents. Unfortunately, I did not know Jesus when my children were young. "Then little children were brought to Him that He might put His hands on them and pray, but the disciples rebuked them. But Jesus said, 'Let the little children come to Me, and do not forbid them; for of such is the kingdom of heaven.' And He laid His hands on them and departed from there" (Matt. 19:13–15).

Paul was a strict law-keeper, and he tried to force Christians to keep the law as he saw it. But God changed all that. I can identify with him.

> As he journeyed he came near Damascus, and suddenly a light shone around him from heaven. Then he fell to the ground, and heard a voice saying to him, 'Saul, Saul, why are you persecuting Me?' And he said, 'Who are You, Lord?' Then the Lord said, 'I am Jesus, whom you are persecuting. It is hard for you to kick against the goads.' So he, trembling and astonished, said, 'Lord, what do You want me to do?' Then the Lord said to him, 'Arise and go into the city, and you will be told what you must do.' (Acts 9:3–6)

> "Paul had prided himself upon his Pharisaical strictness; but after the revelation of Christ to him on the road to Damascus the mission of the Saviour and his own work in the conversion of the Gentiles were plain to his mind, and he fully comprehended the difference between a living faith and a dead formalism. Paul still claimed to be one of the children of Abraham, and kept the Ten Commandments in letter and in spirit as he had ever done before his conversion to Christianity."
>
> *The Story of Redemption*, p. 306

Most of my time with my children was when I was a "Paul." He had to be stricken blind before he saw the Light (Jesus). Thankfully, God has brought about change in my life, and I ask Him to re-create me every day. I believe each of our children has his or her own "Damascus road experience" before they are truly converted. Parents cannot do it for them. Paul's was miraculous. Just as we need to love God and humanity, we must have the law and the gospel.

I believe children can be wrongly influenced if the parents are law-oriented and without a good measure of the gospel in their hearts. Fortunately, Paul had no children, but there will be martyrs in heaven who will be surprised to see him. Imagine the look on Steven's face when he meets Paul among the saved!

Then we see others in the Bible who are servants of God but fail to discipline their children.

Samuel's mother was faithful and had dedicated him to the work of the temple before he was born. Samuel was faithful, but his son, Abijah, was corrupt.

Samson is another example of one who had a godly mother, but when it involved a pagan woman, he demanded his parents to get her for him (see Judges 14:2). He did return to God and used his strength to destroy many pagans even though it ended his own life.

> "No man can rightly present the law of God without the gospel, or the gospel without the law. The law is the gospel embodied, and the gospel is the law unfolded. The law is the root, the gospel is the fragrance blossom and fruit which it bears."
>
> *Christ's Object Lessons*, p. 128

These examples show us that each person has to make his or her own choice independent of the parent's choice for them. However, they need to be taught. Today there are child psychologists and others advising parents on how to rear their children. Some are deceptive.

The Bible is the only true resource; the instructions are all in it. "Train up a child in the way he should go, And when he is old he will not depart from it" (Prov. 22:6).

That is a promise we can depend on. The Bible tells us how to live from the cradle to the grave. The principles to teach children are all there. Jesus is the pattern. They need to be taught to follow Him. They make the choice. And, if they make the right choice, they will always honor and care for their parents.

But God is merciful. For parents who realize they did not follow God's instructions for whatever reason, neglect, busyness, ignorance, etc., He has given many promises. One of my favorite quotations that gives parents assurance is "The love of God still yearns over the one who has chosen to separate himself from Him, and He sets in operation influences to bring him back to the Father's house" (*Christ's Object Lessons*, p. 202).

> "Angels are rearranging environments, changing circumstances, weaving about disinterested souls a network of influence which will some day lead to a surrender. God never forces Himself upon a single life, but there is one way to connect a man to heaven in spite of himself, and that way is through prayer."
>
> *The Story of the Seer of Patmos*, p. 147

Another promise that comes to my mind is "Behold, I will send you Elijah the prophet Before the coming of the great and dreadful day of the LORD. And he will turn The hearts of the fathers to the children, And the hearts of the children to their fathers, Lest I come and strike the earth with a curse" (Mal. 4:5, 6).

> "... When the storm of persecution really breaks upon us, the true sheep will hear the true Shepherd's voice. Self-denying efforts will be put forth to save the lost, and many who have strayed from the fold will come back to follow the great Shepherd."
>
> *Testimonies for the Church*, vol. 6, p. 401

I have shared the following texts with many parents who are concerned about the salvation of their children. They need not worry; we serve a loving God who keeps His promises. "… For I will contend with him who contends with you, And I will save your children" (Isa. 49:25). "There is hope in your future, says the LORD, That your children shall come back to their own border" (Jer. 31:17).

Now let's move up to the sixth rung, so we can take a look at the next commandment.

THE SIXTH COMMANDMENT

The sixth commandment is about respect for human life. God instructs us to demonstrate love, not hatred, toward others by helping to preserve their life.

> "You shall not murder" (Exod. 20:13).

> "I will respect the life of all God's children regardless of their beliefs or behaviors"
> (Carscallen version).

The Bible records Cain's guilt of murdering his brother, Abel. God punished Cain for breaking this commandment. This law was obviously in force at that time. In fact, it was in effect in heaven before the fall of Lucifer.

> And war broke out in heaven: Michael and his angels fought with the dragon; and the dragon and his angels fought, but they did not prevail, nor was a place found for them in heaven any longer. So the great dragon was cast out, that serpent of old, called the Devil and Satan, who deceives the whole world; he was cast to the earth, and his angels were cast out with him. (Rev. 12:7–9)

I wondered, *if Lucifer was causing so much trouble, why did God not just get rid of him completely?* There are examples in the Bible where gross sin resulted in death for the sinner. But God is a God of wisdom as well as love. The following quotation answers my question:

> Had [Satan] been immediately blotted from existence, [the inhabitants of heaven and of other worlds] would have served God from fear rather than love…. Satan's rebellion was to be a lesson to the universe through all coming ages, a perpetual testimony to the nature and terrible results of sin…. When it was announced that with all his sympathizers he must be expelled from the abodes of bliss, then the rebel leader boldly avowed his contempt for the Creator's law.
> (*The Great Controversy*, p. 499)

I'm not sure just when God expelled Satan from heaven, but I do know about his activities on earth. Satan is the "father of lies" (see John 8:44). He deceived Eve and caused the first death, the death of their son.

> Now the serpent was more cunning than any beast of the field which the LORD God had made. And he said to the woman, "Has God indeed said, 'You shall not eat of every tree of the garden'?

God's Ten Commandments

And the woman said to the serpent, 'We may eat the fruit of the trees of the garden; but of the fruit of the tree which is in the midst of the garden, God has said, 'You shall not eat it, nor shall you touch it, lest you die.' Then the serpent said to the woman, 'You will not surely die.' (Gen. 3:1–4)

> "The only one who promised Adam life in disobedience was the great deceiver. And the declaration of the serpent to Eve in Eden—'Ye shall not surely die'—was the first sermon ever preached upon the immortality of the soul. Yet this declaration, resting solely upon the authority of Satan, is echoed from the pulpits of Christendom and is received by the majority of mankind as readily as it was received by our first parents."
>
> *The Great Controversy*, p. 533

Now Adam knew Eve his wife, and she conceived and bore Cain, and said, 'I have acquired a man from the LORD.' Then she bore again, this time his brother Abel. Now Abel was a keeper of sheep, but Cain was a tiller of the ground. And in the process of time it came to pass that Cain brought an offering of the fruit of the ground to the LORD. Abel also brought of the firstborn of his flock and of their fat. And the LORD respected Abel and his offering, but He did not respect Cain and his offering. And Cain was very angry, and his countenance fell. So the LORD said to Cain, 'Why are you angry? And why has your countenance fallen? If you do well, will you not be accepted? And if you do not do well, sin lies at the door. And its desire is for you, but you should rule over it.' Now Cain talked with Abel his brother; and it came to pass, when they were in the field, that Cain rose up against Abel his brother and killed him. (Gen. 4:1–8)

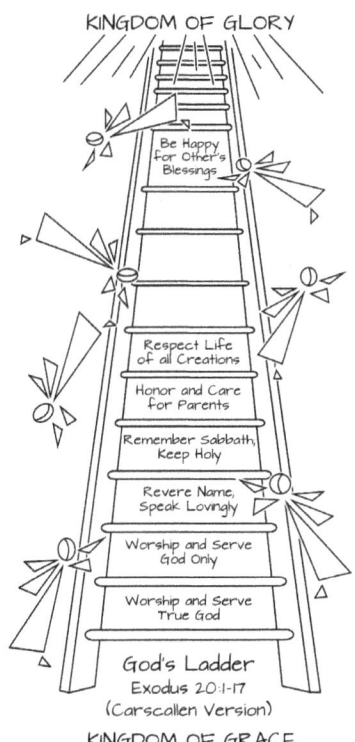

Adam and Eve both knew the command of God, but they yielded to Satan's temptation. Ever since that time, it has been more and more difficult for humankind to resist his temptations. But God has promised that if we submit to Him, even though we sin and even murder, He will forgive us.

"Therefore submit to God. Resist the devil and he will flee from you. Draw near to God and He will draw near to you. Cleanse your hands, you sinners; and purify your hearts, you double-minded. Lament and mourn and weep! Let your laughter be turned to mourning and your joy to gloom. Humble yourselves in the sight of the Lord, and He will lift you up" (James 4:7).

> "But man was not abandoned to the result of the evil he had chosen. In the sentence pronounced upon Satan was given an intimation of redemption.... This sentence, spoken in the hearing of our first parents, was to them a promise. Before they heard of the thorn and the thistle, of the toil and sorrow that must be their portion, or of the dust to which they must return, they listened to words that could not fail of giving them hope. All that had been lost by yielding to Satan could be regained through Christ."
>
> *Education,* p. 27

The promise given to Adam and Eve was that God would send His son to redeem them from the penalty of death. Satan was still there, so he spoke to him in the hearing of Adam and Eve. "So the LORD God said to the serpent: 'Because you have done this, You are cursed more than all cattle, And more than every beast of the field; On your belly you shall go, And you shall eat dust All the days of your life. And I will put enmity Between you and the woman, And between your seed and her Seed; He shall bruise your head, And you shall bruise His heel" (Gen. 3:14, 15).

In speaking to the Jews about Abraham and who exactly the children of Abraham are, Jesus said, "You are of your father the devil, and the desires of your father you want to do. He was a murderer from the beginning, and does not stand in the truth, because there is no truth in him. When he speaks a lie, he speaks from his own resources, for he is a liar and the father of it" (John 8:44).

God made provisions for people who have killed someone accidentally. He thinks of everything necessary for our salvation.

> The cities of refuge of refuge were so distributed as to be within a half day's journey of every part of the land. The roads leading to them were always to be kept in good repair; all along the way signposts were to be erected bearing the word 'Refuge' in plain , bold characters, that the fleeing one might not be delayed for a moment.... The cities of refuge appointed for God's ancient people were a symbol of the refuge provided in Christ. The same merciful Saviour who appointed those temporal cities of refuge has by the shedding of His own blood provided for the transgressors of God's law a sure retreat, into which they may flee for safety from the second death. No power can take out of His hands the souls that go to Him for pardon. (*Patriarchs and Prophets*, pp. 515, 516)

The heart has no room for hatred. "Do not marvel, my brethren, if the world hates you. We know that we have passed from death to life, because we love the brethren. He who does not love his brother abides in death. Whoever hates his brother is a murderer, and you know that no murderer has eternal life abiding in him" (1 John 3:13–15).

"You have heard that it was said to those of old, 'You shall not murder, and whoever murders will be in danger of the judgment'" (Matt. 5:21).

The Jews persisted until they finished their plan to have Christ crucified. He took all the sin of the world upon Himself in order to ensure that, along with Adam and Eve, we might have eternal life. The plan of redemption was set in motion, but the command is still "You shall not murder."

> "The completeness of Christian character is attained when the impulse to help and bless others springs constantly from within. It is the atmosphere of this love surrounding the soul of the believer that makes him a savor of life unto life and enables God to bless his work."
>
> *The Acts of the Apostles,* p. 551

Our next step is the seventh commandment. It is just as clear as this one is. We have no need to murder; God will take care of that.

Let's go on up to the next rung on God's ladder: adultery.

THE SEVENTH COMMANDMENT

The seventh commandment is about purity in relationships. When God created a male and female, He made a plan for them to be faithful to each other.

"You shall not commit adultery" (Exod. 20:14).

"I will keep myself sexually pure" (Carscallen version).

When we speak of adultery, we usually refer to unfaithfulness to marriage vows. " ... whoever divorces his wife for any reason except sexual immorality causes her to commit adultery" (Matt. 5:32).

However, sexual immorality involves more than the husband-wife relationship. The Bible also speaks of fornication, incest, homosexuality, and relations with beasts.

Spiritual adultery was rampant when the nation of Israel went after and worshipped false gods. God asks us to demonstrate our love by being loyal to Him and obeying His commandments. If we are obedient, we will not commit adultery.

The Bible identifies adultery as sinful in the accounts of Pharaoh taking Abraham's wife into his house and the account of Sodom and Gomorrah. The best example to prove God's commandment on adultery was known before Mt. Sinai is the account of Joseph, who refused to have an affair with Potiphar's wife. Joseph said, "How then can I do this great wickedness, and sin against God?" (Gen. 39:9).

Let's look at what the Bible says about these events.

> Now there was a famine in the land, and Abram went down to Egypt to dwell there, for the famine was severe in the land. And it came to pass, when he was close to entering Egypt, that he said to Sarai his wife, 'Indeed I know that you are a woman of beautiful countenance. Therefore it will

happen, when the Egyptians see you, that they will say, 'This is his wife'; and they will kill me, but they will let you live. Please say you are my sister, that it may be well with me for your sake, and that I may live because of you.' So it was, when Abram came into Egypt, that the Egyptians saw the woman, that she was very beautiful. The princes of Pharaoh also saw her and commended her to Pharaoh. And the woman was taken to Pharaoh's house. He treated Abram well for her sake. He had sheep, oxen, male donkeys, male and female servants, female donkeys, and camels. But the LORD plagued Pharaoh and his house with great plagues because of Sarai, Abram's wife. And Pharaoh called Abram and said, 'What is this you have done to me? Why did you not tell me that she was your wife? Why did you say, 'She is my sister'? I might have taken her as my wife. Now therefore, here is your wife; take her and go your way.' So Pharaoh commanded his men concerning him; and they sent him away, with his wife and all that he had. (Gen. 12:10–20)

> "During his stay in Egypt, Abraham gave evidence that he was not free from human weakness and imperfection. In concealing the fact that Sarah was his wife, he betrayed a distrust of the divine care, a lack of that lofty faith and courage so often and nobly exemplified in his life…. Through Abraham's lack of faith, Sarah was placed in great peril…. But the Lord, in His great mercy, protected Sarah by sending judgments upon the royal household. By this means the monarch learned the truth in the matter, and, indignant at the deception practiced upon him, he reproved Abraham and restored to him his wife…."
>
> *Patriarchs and Prophets*, p. 130

So Abraham lost faith in God's protection, even after all God has promised him and thus far had blessed him. This example shows how lying compounds the effects of sin. When he lied, Abraham's problems multiplied. He knew about the sin of adultery, and instead of protecting his wife, he allowed Satan to tempt him into sin. But, he proved himself worthy in dealing with Sodom and Gomorrah. Adultery involves more than illicit sex with another man's wife.

And the LORD said, 'Because of the outcry against Sodom and Gomorrah is great, and because their sin is very grave, I will go down now and see whether they have done altogether according to the outcry against it that has come to Me; and if not, I will know.' Then the men turned away from there and went toward Sodom, but Abraham still stood before the LORD. And Abraham came near and said, 'Would You also destroy the righteous with the wicked?' (Gen. 18:20–23)

Because his nephew, Lot, had chosen to live in Sodom when they parted, Abraham pleaded with God. He considered Lot righteous, and in God's mercy, only Lot and his two daughters were saved. His wife regretfully looked back and was turned into a "pillar of salt" (see Gen. 19:26). His daughters later committed incest with their father and produced problem children.

Perhaps the story of Joseph relates to the most regular description of adultery. I remembered his story of being deceived by his brothers and sold into slavery, but despite his troubles, he remained loyal to God.

> And it came to pass after these things that his master's wife cast longing eyes on Joseph, and she said, 'Lie with me.' But he refused and said to his master's wife, 'Look, my master does not know what is with me in the house, and he has committed all that he has to my hand. There is no greater in this house than I, nor has he kept back anything from me but you, because you are his wife. How then can I do this great wickedness and sin against God?' So it was, as she spoke to Joseph day by day, that he did not heed her, to lie with her or to be with her. (Gen. 39:7–10)

Joseph was later sent to prison because of the false accusations of Potiphar's wife, but he never yielded His faith in God. He was later rewarded.

"How was Joseph enabled to make such a record of firmness of character, uprightness, and wisdom?—In his early years he had consulted duty rather than inclination; and the integrity, the simple trust, the noble nature, of the youth bore fruit in the deeds of the man. A pure and simple life had favored the vigorous development of both physical and intellectual powers.... 'The fear of the Lord, that is wisdom; and to depart from evil is understanding' (Job 28:28).... But character is not inherited. It cannot be bought. Moral excellence and fine mental qualities are not the result of accident. The most precious gifts are of no value unless they are improved. The formation of a noble character is the work of a lifetime and must be the result of diligent and persevering effort. God gives opportunities; success depends upon the use made of them."

Patriarchs and Prophets, pp. 222, 223

David, instead of resisting the temptation, committed adultery, and as a result the child of the adulterous relationship died. He even had the husband killed to try to cover up his sin. It was the sin of self-exaltation that prepared the way for David's fall. However, David was later called a man after God's own heart (see Acts 13:22).

We must keep focused on Christ and His example to be free from breaking this commandment.

The eighth commandment is next, and God expects obedience to all of His commandments.

THE EIGHTH COMMANDMENT

The eighth commandment is about honesty and respect for the property of others. God has told us not to steal.

> "You shall not steal" (Exod. 20:15).

> "I will respect the property of others" (Carscallen version).

The Bible speaks specifically about stealing from God.

> 'For I am the LORD, I do not change; Therefore you are not consumed, O sons of Jacob. Yet from

the days of your fathers You have gone away from My ordinances And have not kept them. Return to Me, and I will return to you,' Says the LORD of hosts. But you said, 'In what way shall we return?' 'Will a man rob God? Yet you have robbed Me! But you say, 'In what way have we robbed You?' In tithes and offerings. You are cursed with a curse for you have robbed Me, Even this whole nation. Bring all the tithes into the storehouse, That there may be food in My house, And try Me now in this,' Says the LORD of hosts, 'If I will not open for you the windows of heaven And pour out for you such blessing That there will not be room enough to receive it. And I will rebuke the devourer for your sakes, So that he will not destroy the fruit of your ground, Nor shall the vine fail to bear fruit for you in the field,' Says the LORD of hosts; 'And all nations will call you blessed, For you will be a delightful land,' says the LORD of hosts. (Mal. 3:6–12)

God is very patient and longsuffering with the sins of His people. He bestows such abundant rewards on us; why would we not want to return to Him what He asks of us? But He is not pleased if we give out of duty instead of love. "But this I say: He who sows sparingly will also reap sparingly, and he who sows bountifully will also reap bountifully. So let each one give as he purposes in his heart, not grudgingly or of necessity; for God loves a cheerful giver" (2 Cor. 9:6, 7).

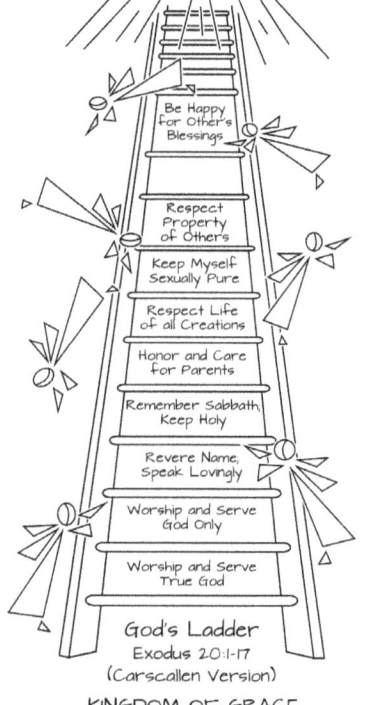

> "The sower multiplies his seed by casting it away. So it is when those who are faithful in distributing God's gifts. By imparting they increase their blessings. God has promised them a sufficiency that they may continue to give."
>
> *Christ's Object Lessons*, p. 86

Many are tempted to use their means in self-indulgence, appetite, personal adornment, expensive cars, or worldly pleasures, but "He whose heart is aglow with the love of Christ will regard it as not only a duty, but a pleasure, to aid in the advancement of the highest, holiest work committed to man—the work of presenting to the world the riches of goodness, mercy, and truth" (*The Acts of the Apostles*, pp. 338, 339).

In the Old Testament, Jeremiah records the question asked by God.

'Will you steal ... and walk after other gods whom you do not know, and then come and stand before Me in this house which is called by My name, and say, 'We are delivered to do all these abominations?' ... I will cast you out of My sight, As I have cast out all your brethren—the whole tribe of Ephraim. Therefore do not pray for this people, nor lift up a cry or prayer for them, nor make intercession to Me; for I will not hear you.' (Jer. 7:9, 10, 15, 16)

> "It is not because He is unwilling to forgive that He turns from the transgressor; it is because the sinner refuses to make use of the abundant provisions of grace, that God is unable to deliver from sin."
>
> *Prophets and Kings*, p. 323

Before Joseph moved his father and brothers to Egypt, he had been giving his brothers food to take back to their father. They did not know that the man who was in charge of approving the amounts of the food provided was their brother, Joseph, whom they had thrown in a pit and left to die. He did not die, but he was sold into slavery. Beyond that, they had had no contact with him. When the brothers went for food, they did not recognize Joseph, but Joseph recognized them. Jacob would not allow Benjamin, the youngest, to go with them. But after the second trip, Joseph demanded that they bring him.

When Benjamin's sack was filled, Joseph had the servant put his silver cup in the bag, to give him a reason to accuse them of theft. They knew that stealing was a sin, and at that time, it was punishable by death. His ploy was to test his brothers to see if there had been a change in their character. They stood the test. They had changed, and the family was united in the best location of Egypt (see Gen. 42).

Jesus told the disciples: "Do not lay up for yourselves treasures on earth, where moth and rust destroy and where thieves break in and steal; but lay up for yourselves treasures in heaven, where neither moth nor rust destroys and where thieves do not break in and steal. For where your treasure is, there your heart will be also" (Matt. 6:19–21).

In spite of Christ's warning, we have an example of lying, stealing, hypocrisy, and covetousness all in one sinful act. And there were severe consequences.

> But a certain man named Ananias, with Sapphira his wife, sold a possession. And he kept back part of the proceeds, his wife also being aware of it, and brought a certain part and laid it at the apostles' feet. But Peter said, 'Ananias, why has Satan filled your heart to lie to the Holy Spirit and keep back part of the price of the land for yourself? While it remained, was it not your own? And after it was sold, was it not in your own control? Why have you conceived this thing in your heart? You have not lied to men but to God.' Then Ananias, hearing these words, fell down and breathed his last. So great fear came upon all those who heard these things. And the young men arose and wrapped him up, carried him out, and buried him. Now it was about three hours later when his wife came in, not knowing what had happened. And Peter answered her, 'Tell me whether you sold the land for so much?' She said, 'Yes, for so much.' Then Peter said to her, 'How is it that you have agreed together to test the Spirit of the Lord? Look, the feet of those who have buried your husband are at the door, and they will carry you out.' Then immediately she fell down at his feet and breathed her last. And the young men came in and found her dead, and carrying her out, buried her by her husband. (Acts 5:1–10)

> "We are to engage in no business, follow no pursuit, seek no pleasure, that would hinder the outworking of His righteousness in our character and life. Whatever we do is to be done heartily, as unto the Lord.... If we follow His example, His assurance to us is that all things needful in this life 'shall be added.' Poverty or wealth, sickness or health, simplicity or wisdom—all are provided for in the promise of His grace."
>
> *Thoughts from the Mount of Blessing,* p. 99

As I said before, God takes care of everything–His Grace is sufficient!

The next rung we shall ascend to is number nine on God's ladder.

THE NINTH COMMANDMENT

This ladder is about honesty. The Lord instructs us not to lie or deceive others. If our past has been one of lying or gossiping, sometimes this can be difficult to overcome.

"You shall not bear false witness against your neighbor" (Exod. 20:16).

"I will only speak the truth and do so in a loving manner." (Carscallen version).

Jacob's sons, who had mistreated their brother, Joseph, were having difficulty convincing him that they were honest men.

> Joseph saw his brothers and recognized them, but he acted as a stranger to them and spoke roughly to them. Then he said to them, 'Where do you come from?' And they said, 'From the land of Canaan to buy food.' So Joseph recognized his brothers, but they did not recognize him. Then Joseph remembered the dreams which he had dreamed about them, and said to them, 'You are spies! You have come to see the nakedness of the land!' And they said to him, 'No, my lord, but your servants have come to buy food. We are all one man's sons; we are honest men; your servants are not spies.' But he said to them, 'No, but you have come to see the nakedness of the land.' And the said, 'Your servants are twelve brothers, the sons of one man in the land of Canaan; and in fact, the youngest is with our father today, and one is no more.' But Joseph said to them, "It is as I spoke to you, saying, 'You are spies!' In this manner you shall be tested: By the life of Pharaoh, you shall not leave this place unless your youngest brother comes here. Send one of you, and let him bring your brother; and you shall be kept in prison, that your words may be tested to see whether there is any truth in you; or else, by the life of Pharaoh, surely you are spies!' So he put them all in prison three days. Then Joseph said to them the third day, 'Do this and live, for I fear God: If you are honest men, let one of your brothers be confined to your prison house; but you, go and carry grain for the famine of your houses. And bring your youngest brother to me; so your words will be verified, and you shall not die.' And they did so. (Gen. 42:7–20)

> "The three days in the Egyptian prison were days of bitter sorrow as the brothers reflected upon their past sins."
>
> *Patriarchs and Prophets*, p. 225

We have seen the results under the fifth commandment. They were reunited. Often people will believe a lie before they will believe the truth. It was that way with those who denied Jesus.

"Because I tell the truth, you do not believe me. Which of you convicts Me of sin? And if I tell the truth, why do you not believe Me? He who is of God hears God's words; therefore you do not hear, because you are not of God" (John 8:45–47).

The first recorded lie after Creation is recorded in Genesis 3:4, when Satan contradicted God's word and told Eve, "You will not surely die." We discussed this at length under the eighth commandment.

The eighth and ninth commandments are closely related. The eighth speaks to stealing material possessions, and the ninth is more about character defamation.

The story of Jacob and Esau, as told in Genesis, demonstrates that lying and deceit was known to be evil. We have covered at length the story of Jacob and Esau. Jacob suffered many years as a result of his "false witnessing," but because of our merciful God, he was given that beautiful dream of the angels ascending and descending a ladder to and from heaven. And, ultimately, he was forgiven when he wrestled with God.

"Bearing false witness" is better known as "gossiping." And I have been guilty of breaking that commandment far more than I like to admit. It was usually to my children about the negative things I knew other children or their parents were doing that were not in accord with God's word. I did it to show them it was wrong and to discourage

> "Closely allied to gossip is the covert insinuation, the sly innuendo, by which the unclean in heart seek to insinuate the evil they dare not openly express. Every approach to these practices the youth should be taught to shun as they would shun the leprosy."
>
> *Education*, p. 236

them from doing the same thing. I was wrong, and I finally learned what the Bible says to do in situations like that. I should have been speaking to the person instead of speaking about them. God has given us clear counsel in the Bible.

God not only tells us what not to do, but also what we should do.

Moreover if your brother sins against you, go and tell him his fault between you and him alone. If he hears you, you have gained your brother. But if he will not hear, take with you one or two more, that 'by the mouth of two or three witnesses every word may be established.' And if he refuses to hear them, tell it to the church. But if he even refuses to hear the church, let him be to you like a heathen and a tax collector. (Matt. 18:15-17)

> "But it is to the wrongdoer himself that we are to present the wrong. We are not to make it a matter of comment and criticism among ourselves; nor even after it is told to the church, are we at liberty to repeat it to others. A knowledge of the faults of Christians will be only a cause of stumbling to the unbelieving world; and by dwelling upon these things, we ourselves can receive only harm; for it is by beholding that we become changed."
>
> *The Desire of Ages*, p. 441

It was not that anyone was sinning against me that I spoke to a church issue; I thought they were sinning against God. And now I know that He will handle it. Often, "silence is golden." Sometimes God says: "Be still, and know that I am God ..." (Ps. 46:10).

Speaking the truth is hard if we are called to admonish a brother or sister. If it has to be done, it must only be done in love, and it might result in the salvation of that soul. Before doing anything, one must spend a lot of time in prayer asking God for guidance. "A word fitly spoken is like apples of gold in settings of silver" (Prov. 25:11).

I still fall into the old habit sometimes; however, if there is some way we can help the person, we have a responsibility to do it without telling others. I remember some of the words to an old song by Johnny Mercer that said "You've got to accentuate the positive, eliminate the negative, latch on to the affirmative, and don't mess with Mr. In-Between!" They had it right! I think of that sometimes, but now I have more light on this commandment. We do have some responsibility to others who might not know they are sinning.

> "For evils that we might have checked, we are just as responsible as if we were guilty of the acts ourselves ... While we seek to correct the errors of a brother, the Spirit of Christ will lead us to shield him, as far as possible, from the criticism of even his own brethren, and how much more from the censure of the unbelieving world. We ourselves are erring, and need Christ's pity and forgiveness, and just as we wish Him to deal with us, He bids us deal with one another."
>
> *The Desire of Ages*, p. 441

If I were sinning and did not realize what I was doing was sinful, I would hope someone cared enough about me to help me change. However, there is always the risk that the sinner might be offended. Always remember the Golden Rule: "Therefore, whatever you want men to do to you, do also to them, for this is the Law and the Prophets" (Matt. 7:12).

Let's move on to the top rung now.

The Tenth Commandment

The tenth commandment warns us about coveting anything that belongs to another. The greatest blessing we can have is being content with what we have; it is then that we have peace. We do not have peace for ourselves if we are not happy that God has blessed others also.

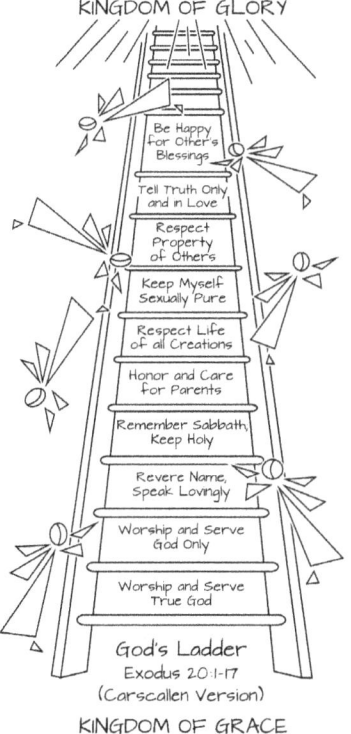

> "You shall not covet your neighbor's house; you shall not covet your neighbor's wife, nor his male servant, nor his female servant, nor his ox, nor his donkey, nor anything that is your neighbor's" (Exod. 20:17).

> "I will be happy for the blessings of others and be thankful for my own" (Carscallen version).

Paul tells us that those who covet another person's belongings will not have a place in God's kingdom. "For this you know that no ... covetous man, who is an idolater, has any inheritance in the kingdom of Christ and God" (Eph. 5:5).

Covetousness was Satan's problem. He wanted Christ's position; he wanted to be equal to God. And because of his jealousy, he was evicted from heaven. Because of sin, we are born as selfish infants and must at some point die to self and have the new birth experience if we are to enter heaven. When we overcome this temptation to covet, we are ready for the kingdom of glory. But we, like Paul, must keep the law, even though we know we can't keep it in our own strength. It is the law of love that converts us. "The law of the Lord is perfect converting the soul ... " (Ps. 19:7).

Paul understood that the wisdom and justice of the law was based on the principle of love. But he knew this for himself so well that he was in anguish.

> For we know that the law is spiritual, but I am carnal, sold under sin. For what I am doing, I do not understand. For what I will to do, that I do not practice; but what I hate, that I do. If, then, I do what I will not to do, I agree with the law that it is good. But now, it is no longer I who do it, but sin that dwells in me. For I know that in me (that is, in my flesh) nothing good dwells; for to will is present with me, but how to perform what is good I do not find. For the good that I will to do, I do not do; but the evil I will not to do, that I practice. Now if I do what I will not to do, it is no longer I who do it, but sin that dwells in me. I find then a law, that evil is present with me, the one who wills to do good. For I delight in the law of God according to the inward man. (Rom. 7:14–22)

It is only the gospel of Jesus Christ that can free us, and Paul realized that.

> Let brotherly love continue. Do not forget to entertain strangers, for by so doing some have unwittingly entertained angels.... Let your conduct be without covetousness; be content with such

things as you have. For He Himself has said, 'I will never leave you nor forsake you.' So we may boldly say: 'The LORD is my helper; I will not fear. What can man do to me ...?' Jesus Christ is the same yesterday, today, and forever. (Heb. 13:1–8)

> "The law reveals to man his sins, but it provides no remedy. While it promises life to the obedient, it declares that death is the portion of the transgressor. The gospel of Christ alone can free him from the condemnation or the defilement of sin."
>
> *The Great Controversy,* pp. 467, 468

Paul knew that without Jesus he could do nothing. I now realize that as well. I have had a glimpse of Him and want to know more and more. I believe that when the gospel and the law are understood together, covetousness will cease. "Now godliness with contentment is great gain" (1 Tim. 6:6).

> "The truth is to be planted in the heart. It is to control the mind and regulate the affections. The whole character must be stamped with the divine utterances. Every jot and tittle of the word of God is to be brought into the daily practice. He who becomes a partaker of the divine nature will be in harmony with God's great standard of righteousness, His holy law. This is the rule by which God measures the actions of men. This will be the test of character in the judgment."
>
> *Christ's Object Lessons,* p. 314

Our church has been praying for revival for a long time. It was emphasized that there is one thing that will help bring about that revival, which is a restoration of God's commandments in our lives. Peter told us on his ladder that after we receive the Holy Spirit, we needed more knowledge. He continued on to name the character traits we must develop if we are to reach the top round of love. But knowledge of the content of the Ten Commandments is a must if we are going to keep them in our hearts to observe. As I've said before, if we love Jesus, we will keep the Ten Commandments.

"It is only as the law of God is restored to its rightful position that there can be a revival of primitive faith and godliness among His professed people" (*The Great Controversy,* p. 478). That primitive godliness is the character of God as we see it in Jesus. The law not only paints a picture of His character; it is His character.

"... I will put My laws in their mind and write them on their hearts; and I will be their God, and they shall be My people" (Heb. 8:10).

> "The law of God, from its very nature, is unchangeable. It is a revelation of the will and the character of its Author. God is love, and His law is love. Its two great principles are love to God and love to man.... The character of God is righteousness and truth; such is the nature of His law.... Such a law, being an expression of the mind and will of God, must be as enduring as its Author."
>
> *The Great Controversy,* p. 467

> "And if we consent, He will so identify Himself with our thoughts and aims, so blend our hearts and minds into conformity to His will, that when obeying Him we shall be but carrying out our own impulses.... When we know God as it is our privilege to know Him, our life will be a life of continual obedience. Through an appreciation of the character of Christ, through communion with God, sin will become hateful to us."
>
> *The Desire of Ages,* p. 668

Rather than worry or be anxious about our condition, we need to turn our eyes away from self, and look to Jesus. Overcoming covetousness is putting on humility.

God has led me from my ignorance into the light of His love and His law. I am dependent on Him to keep me on the ladder to heaven, so I might enjoy eternal life with Jesus, my family, and friends. I believe His promises and each of the Ten Commandments is a promise. All together they are like a chain held together by His love. If one link in a chain breaks, it is all broken. It is the same with the Ten Commandments. But if we stumble on God's ladder, the angels are there to catch us. God and the law are the same traits of character. Pastor Doug Batchelor enumerated the following Bible references in a sermon I listened to on television.

God is JUST – Rom. 3:26	His law is JUST – Rom. 7:12
God is TRUE – John 3:33	His law is TRUE – Neh. 9:13
God is PURE – 1 John 3:3	His law is PURE – Ps. 19:7, 8
God is LIGHT – 1 John 1:5	His law is LIGHT – Prov. 6:23
God is FAITHFUL – 1 Cor. 1:9	His law is FAITHFUL – Ps. 119:86
God is GOOD – Nah. 1:7	His law is GOOD – Rom. 7:12, 16
God is SPIRITUAL – John 4:24	His law is SPIRITUAL – Rom. 7:14
God is HOLY – Isaiah 6:3, 1 Peter 1:15	His law is HOLY – Exod. 20:8, Rom. 7:12
God is TRUTH – John 14:6	His law is TRUTH – Ps. 119:142, 151
God is LIFE – John 14:6	His law is LIFE – Matt. 19:17
God is RIGHTEOUSNESS – Jer. 23:6	His law is RIGHTEOUSNESS – Ps. 119:172
God is PERFECT – Matt. 5:48	His law is PERFECT – James 1:25
God is ETERNAL – Deut. 33:27	His law is ETERNAL – Ps. 111:7, 8
God is PEACE – Isa. 9:6	His law is PEACE – Ps. 119:165
God is UNCHANGING – Mal. 3:6	His law is UNCHANGING – Ps. 111:7, 8
God is SWEET – Ps. 34:8	His law is SWEET – Ps. 119:103
God is WISE – Rom. 16:26, 27	His law is WISE – Ps. 19:7
God is OUR MEDITATION – Ps. 63:6	His law is OUR MEDITATION – Ps. 1:2
God is JUDGE – Ps. 50:6	His law is JUDGE – James 2:12
God is ENLIGHTENMENT – Eph. 1:17, 18	His law is ENLIGHTENMENT – Ps. 19:8

God is CLEAN – Ps. 19:9	His law is CLEAN – Ezek. 22:26
God is BLESSED – Ps. 28:6	His law is BLESSED – Exod. 20:11
God is KNOWLEDGE – Isa. 11:2	His law is KNOWLEDGE – Ps. 119:66
God is HOPE – Ps. 130:7	His law is HOPE – Ps. 119:74
God is LIFE – Ps. 36:9	His law is LIFE – Prov. 3:1, 2
God is UNDERSTANDING – Ps. 147:5	His law is UNDERSTANDING – Ps. 119:99
God is HAPPINESS – Ps. 146:5	His law is HAPPINESS – Prov. 29:18
God is JOY – Ps. 16:11	His law is JOY – Ps. 119:162
God is WONDERFUL – Isa. 9:6	His law is WONDERFUL – Ps. 119:18
God is LIBERTY – Isa. 61:1	His law is LIBERTY – James 1:25, Ps. 119:45
God is COMFORT – Ps. 23:4	His law is COMFORT – Ps. 119:50
God is OUR SONG – Rev. 15:3	His law is OUR SONG – Ps. 119:54
God is MERCIFUL – Exod. 34:6, 7	His law is MERCIFUL – Ps. 119:58

Having reached the apex of God's ladder, I am happy when I see how God is blessing others. I no longer covet that which belongs to another, and I have peace in my mind and heart because I am thankful for what I have. "Great peace have those who love Your Law, And nothing causes them to stumble" (Ps. 119:165).

"I delight to do Your will, O my God, And Your law is within my heart" (Ps. 40:8). I do truly get pleasure when I know I am worshipping and serving God. It is my heart's desire now and forevermore. God's law is unchanging, and we can depend on His fulfillment of it. Now I know that His law is one law consisting of ten principles of love. Living these principles can only be done by relying on the power of the Holy Spirit. He will keep me knowledgeable of sin that I might flee from it. It is important to remember that the character of God and the Law of God are the same.

Let us now go to His Son, Jesus' ladder to help understand what life is like after committing to keep His commandments. Jesus definitely puts the commandments in the positive and He gives us no doubt about what we should do, but the best part is that He also tells us what our reward will be if we keep them.

Chapter Four
JESUS' LADDER

When I introduced the title for this book, I told you about how simple God has made salvation for us and how Jesus taught me how to reach the top rung of love through the study of Peter's ladder. Then He gave the commandments, which we obey through the power of the Holy Spirit. Now He tells the disciples what kinds of people can have the blessing of joy in their lives.

> Blessed are the poor in spirit, For theirs is the kingdom of heaven. Blessed are those who mourn, For they shall be comforted. Blessed are the meek, For they shall inherit the earth. Blessed are those who hunger and thirst for righteousness, For they shall be filled. Blessed are the merciful, For they shall obtain mercy. Blessed are the pure in heart, For they shall see God. Blessed are the peacemakers, For they shall be called sons of God. Blessed are those who are persecuted for righteousness' sake, For theirs is the kingdom of heaven. Blessed are you when they revile and persecute you, and say all kinds of evil against you falsely for My sake. Rejoice and be exceedingly glad, for great is your reward in heaven, for so they persecuted the prophets who were before you. (Matt. 5:3–12)

Jesus took the disciples up on the mountainside, and after He had ordained the twelve, He bestowed blessings upon them. He wanted them to have joy; He wants the same for us. We wanted our children to experience joy also. I can relate to those people who climbed up the hill. After we became Christians, when our children were young, we often packed a lunch and climbed to the top of the hill across the road from our house on Sabbath afternoons. It was a fun climb because there were a lot of wild flowers and animals to see. Too often when we stayed home there were intrusions of our Sabbath observance by farmers who wanted lumber or sawdust from the sawmill my husband operated with his three brothers. They did not operate the mill on Sabbath; but I've wondered since if we missed many opportunities to share our faith by avoiding those encounters. Yet, I know it was a blessing for my husband to be free from work and have the time to spend with me and the children. He knew the names of most of the wild flowers and all the trees, so it was an opportunity to help them complete some of the requirements for their Pathfinder honors.

Now I live overlooking a lake. I can imagine many scenes on the Sea of Galilee. Beyond the lake are wooded hills. I sit and visualize Jesus and the disciples as they sat on the hillside and learned at his feet. He knew just what the disciples needed to learn and gave encouragement to all those who joined them.

> "Jesus, while He dwelt on earth, dignified life in all its details by keeping before men the glory of God, and by subordinating everything to the will of His Father.... All are provided for in the promise of His grace."
>
> *Thoughts from the Mount of Blessing*, p. 99

Jesus' ladder presents the steps of salvation, in ten blessings. But, what is a blessing? What does the word blessed mean? Bible translators use different words to describe blessed. In my search, I discovered several: happy, fortunate, spiritually prosperous, to be envied, and full of deep joy. I like "full of deep joy," but I like Webster's definition "enjoying the bliss of heaven," even better.

God emphasizes our need to exercise our faith and accept His blessings, which only comes through the righteousness of Christ. I repeat this again because it took me a long time to learn "of myself I can do nothing." Christ is the ladder. He is our salvation. He is our righteousness.

Jesus taught us to pray and said that He would answer our prayers if we met the conditions He gave us for these ten blessings. John includes a description of the conditions for answered prayer. We must pray for these blessings if we are to receive them.

"And whatever you ask in My name, that I will do, that the Father may be glorified in the Son" (John 14:13).

"If you ask anything in My name, I will do it" (John 14:14).

"If you abide in Me, and My words abide in you, you will ask what you desire, and it shall be done for you" (John 15:7).

"You did not choose Me, but I chose you and appointed you that you should go and bear fruit, and that your fruit should remain, that whatever you ask the Father in My name He may give you. These things I command you, that you love one another" (John 15:16, 17).

These verses contain five conditions for answered prayer, all contingent on the love we reached on Peter's ladder and obedience on God's ladder. These five conditions are:

- that we ask in Jesus' name
- that we abide in Jesus
- that Jesus' words abide in us
- that we go and bear fruit and that fruit remain in us
- that we glorify the Father God and His Son, Jesus

Let us begin our journey up Jesus' ladder now.

Poor in Spirit

Because we already love Jesus and keep God's commandments, we can now mount Jesus' ladder of blessings and be filled with joy when we reach the top. "Blessed are the poor in spirit For theirs is the kingdom of heaven" (Matt. 5:3).

The poor in Spirit are those who recognize their sinfulness and realize they need to be redeemed. The word "happy" is often used instead of "blessed."

"Christ's first words to the people on the mount were words of blessing. Happy are they, He said, who recognize their spiritual poverty, and feel their need of redemption...The proud heart strives to earn salvation; but both our title to heaven and our fitness for it are found in the righteousness of Christ" (*The Desire of Ages*, pp. 299, 300).

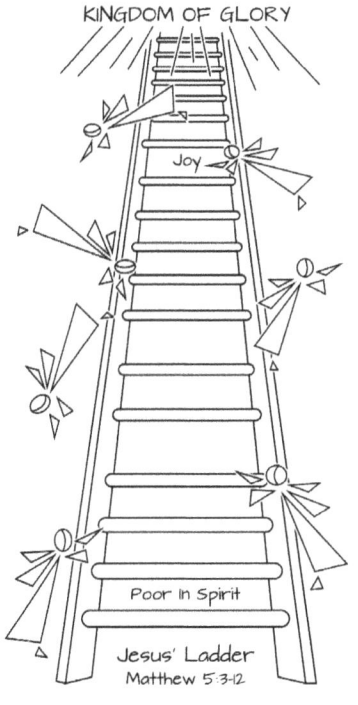

It is the proud heart that "strives to earn salvation," so pride must be overcome. I learned on Peter's ladder that no matter how hard I try, I cannot earn salvation; it is a gift. We discussed that on both Peter's ladder and God's ladder. We will understand even more when we get to John's ladder of revelation.

But did I become proud because I had learned so much already? If so, pride must go. Pride is one of the sins of the world, and I only want to do God's will. "For all that is in the world—the lust of the flesh, the lust of the eyes, and the pride of life—is not of the Father but is of the world" (1 John 2:16). "Pride goes before destruction, And a haughty spirit before a fall. Better to be of a humble spirit with the lowly ..." (Prov. 16:18, 19).

My mother was a very proud woman. She was good at pretending that things were always better than they were, and I'm afraid I followed in her footsteps. When I started to school and told her I needed something to share for "show-and-tell," she warned me to never tell what went on at home. I didn't know that things went on at home that should be kept secret. We were taught that children should "be seen and not heard," and I must have lived quietly in my own world. So, when it was my turn, she always provided some object that I could show and tell the class about. I have prayed that God would take away my pride and "make me humble," and I believe He is in the process of answering that prayer.

"He who feels whole, who thinks that he is reasonably good, and is contented with his condition, does not seek to become a partaker of the grace and righteousness of Christ. Pride feels no need, and so it closes the heart against Christ and the infinite blessings He came to give. There is no room for Jesus in the heart of such a person. Those who are rich and honorable in their own eyes do not ask in faith, and receive the blessing of God. They feel they are full, therefore they go away empty. Those who know that they cannot possibly save themselves, or of themselves do any righteous action, are the ones who appreciate the help that Christ can bestow. They are the poor in spirit, whom He declares to be blessed."

Thoughts from the Mount of Blessings, p. 7

We must recognize our "spiritual poverty" and know that we are not worthy of God's love, but if we come to Jesus just as we are, He will meet us, just as the father did in the story of the prodigal son after he wasted his inheritance.

> I will arise and go to my father, and will say to him, 'Father, I have sinned against heaven and before you, and I am no longer worthy to be called your son. Make me like one of your hired servants.' And he arose and came to his father. But when he was still a great way off, his father saw him and had compassion, and ran and fell on his neck and kissed him. And the son said to him, 'Father, I have sinned against heaven and in your sight, and am no longer worthy to be called your son.' But the father said to his servants, 'Bring out the best robe and put it on him, and put a ring on his hand and sandals on his feet. And bring the fatted calf here and kill it, and let us eat and be merry; for this my son was dead and is alive again; he was lost and is found.' And they began to be merry. (Luke 15:18–24)

Our Father God longs to embrace us just as He did this son who was lost.

What a picture here of the sinner's state! Although surrounded with the blessings of His love, there is nothing that the sinner, bent on self-indulgence and sinful pleasure, desires so much as separation from God.... Whatever the appearance may be, every life centered in self is squandered. Whoever attempts to live apart from God is wasting his substance.... The love of God still yearns over the one who has chosen to separate from Him, and He sets in operation influences to bring him back to the Father's house.... In his restless youth the prodigal looked upon his father as stern and severe.... So those who are deceived by Satan look upon God as hard and exacting.... His law they regard as a restriction upon men's happiness, a burdensome yoke from which they are glad to escape. But he whose eyes have been opened by the love of Christ will behold God as full of compassion.... And heaven and earth shall unite in the Father's song of rejoicing: 'For this my son was dead, and is alive again; he was lost, and is found.

Christ's Object Lessons, pp. 200–207

His arms are always outstretched to receive those who are lost. He says, "Come to Me, all you who labor and are heavy laden, and I will give you rest. Take My yoke upon you and learn from Me, for I am gentle and lowly in heart, and you will find rest for your souls. For My yoke is easy and My burden is light" (Matt. 11:28–30).

Now that we understand what "spiritual poverty" is, let us, in humility, take a step up to the next rung on Jesus' Ladder.

THOSE WHO MOURN

In my human way of thinking, it seemed strange that we must mourn before we will be comforted. But when I discovered my need for humility, I understood; mourning is a blessing. "Blessed are those who mourn, for they shall be comforted" (Matt. 5:4).

The mourning Jesus speaks of here is true sorrow for sin. When I realized it was my sins Jesus died for, it brought true repentance to my heart. I confessed my sins of pride and selfishness, and I know it was the result of the knowledge of the Holy Spirit I received on Peter's ladder that prompted me. We cannot even repent on our own; Jesus gives repentance. We are not worthy of it, but Jesus is.

> "Ignorance is no excuse for error or sin, when there is every opportunity to know the will of God. A man is traveling and comes to a place where there are several roads and a guideboard indicating where each one leads. If he disregards the guideboard, and takes whichever road seems to him to be right, he may be ever so sincere, but will in all probability find himself on the wrong road."
>
> *The Great Controversy*, pp. 597, 598

I told you that I was thankful for Acts 17:30, where it says that "God winked at their ignorance," but now that I have more knowledge, I can no longer claim that promise.

I know that God's will is in His Word, so I must search diligently. He reveals to us our guilt so that we might come to Him and give our burdens to Him. He weeps for us just as He did when He walked on earth. "Now as He drew near, He saw the city and wept over it, saying, 'If you had known, even you, especially in this your day, the things that make for your peace! But now they are hidden from your eyes'" (Luke 19:41, 42).

As He looked out over Jerusalem, He wept. Like Christ, we must weep for sins of the world as well as for those who refuse to come to Him in contrition for their sins. He permits trials that we might become partakers of His holiness. Trials are for removing the imperfections of our character. We can only perfect our character through the power of the Holy Spirit. Others might tarnish our reputation, but only we can permit sin to spoil our character.

Unfortunately, I was like Jacob. It took a lot of wrestling with what I thought was the enemy before I realized that my trials were for my benefit, not for punishment.

> "The trials of life are God's workmen, to remove the impurities and roughness from our character. Their hewing, squaring, and chiseling, their burnishing and polishing, is a painful process; it is hard to be pressed down to the grinding wheel. But the stone is brought forth prepared to fill its place in the heavenly temple. Upon no useless material does the Master bestow such careful, thorough work. Only His precious stones are polished after the similitude of a palace."
>
> *Thoughts from the Mount of Blessings*, p. 10

"Blessed be the God and Father of our Lord Jesus Christ, the Father of mercies and God of all comfort, who comforts us in all our tribulation, that we may be able to comfort those who are in any trouble, with the comfort with which we ourselves are comforted by God" (2 Cor. 1:3, 4).

> "Real sorrow for sin is the result of the working of the Holy Spirit. The Spirit reveals the ingratitude of the heart that has slighted and grieved the Savior, and brings us in contrition to the foot of the cross. By every sin Jesus is wounded afresh; and as we look upon Him whom we have pierced, we mourn for the sins that have brought anguish upon Him. Such mourning will lead to the renunciation of sin."
>
> *The Desire of Ages*, p. 300

There were only a few times that I saw my husband cry, but he wept uncontrollably after he came up from the water of baptism. He remembered how his father had died just after he had told him his decision to get back into the church and lead their family. My husband's tears were of true repentance and joy that he would now be a model for his sons. I might never have truly known Jesus if I had not had sorrow in my life. It is a painful process, but all must experience it to remove the flaws from our character and to better understand what Jesus did for us.

I should have known that God loved me because I could sing the song "Jesus Loves Me," but I had no idea what the words meant. Now I know what sin is, and I fully understand that God does not want me to disobey His commandments. He longs for us to look to him in simple faith, keep our mind on Him, and meditate on his loving kindness. He lifts us above the sorrow and trials to the joy that only He can give.

" ... I will turn their mourning to joy, will comfort them, and make them rejoice rather than sorrow" (Jer. 31:13).

" ... To comfort all who mourn, to console those who mourn in Zion, to give them beauty for ashes, the oil of joy for mourning, the garment of praise for the spirit of heaviness; that they may be called trees of righteousness, the planting of the LORD, that He may be glorified" (Isa. 61:2, 3).

And God always fulfills His promise: "For they indeed for a few days chastened us as seemed best to them, but He for our profit, that we may be partakers of His holiness. Now no chastening seems to be joyful for the present, but painful; nevertheless, afterwards it yields the peaceable fruit of righteousness to those who have been trained by it" (Heb. 12:10).

"It yields the peaceable fruit of righteousness"—that is the goal of this ladder.

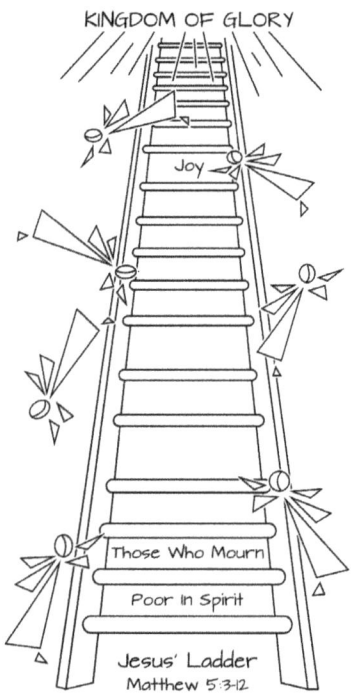

KINGDOM OF GLORY
Joy
Those Who Mourn
Poor In Spirit
Jesus' Ladder
Matthew 5:3-12
KINGDOM OF GRACE

Not long after we were baptized, there was a child dedication at church. After those who had planned ahead were brought forward, the pastor asked, "Are there any other parents who would like to dedicate a child? I looked at my husband, and he looked at me and nodded. We stood and marched our four children to the platform. We didn't realize the pastor needed time to talk to us, prepare certificates, etc. I have wondered since if our older children might have been embarrassed because they were almost old enough to make their own decision. (I relate this only to verify how fully we had surrendered our lives and the lives of our children over to the Lord.) Thankfully, all of them were baptized of their own freewill and in their own timing. Now they are responsible for what they do with the blessing.

As we mourn for our sins that have brought anguish upon Jesus, and express our sorrow for them, we become meek. That is the next step on the ladder.

THE MEEK

Meekness is one of the foundational requirements in seeking Christ's righteousness. The meek have recognized that they are lacking in the Spirit and have expressed sorrow for their sins. Their sins are forgiven. I realized that God saw me as no better and no worse than any other of His children, and I came to understand that His love and death on the cross covered all my sins. I thank God for his forgiveness of my ignorance, pride, and selfishness as I mourned to overcome them.

"Blessed are the meek for they shall inherit the earth" (Matt. 5:5). God has given us the promise that if we are meek, we shall be given a place on the earth after He has cleansed it from all sin and made new. But to receive the promise, I must meet the conditions. I know that I can only do this through the new birth experience.

> "It is the love of self that brings unrest. When we are born from above, the same mind will be in us that was in Jesus, the mind that led Him to humble Himself that we might be saved. Then we shall desire to sit at the feet of Jesus, and learn of Him.... The value of our work is in proportion to the impartation of the Holy Spirit."
>
> *The Desire of Ages,* pp. 330, 331

We are not saved by our works; however, God expects us to do the work of learning more and more about Jesus, and the more time we spend in the Word, in humility seeking knowledge, the more we will become like Him. He gives the grace we need.

"'God resists the proud, But gives grace to the humble.' Therefore submit to God. Resist the devil and he will flee from you. Draw near to God and He will draw near to you. Cleanse your hands, you sinners; and purify your hearts, you double-minded. Lament and mourn and weep! Let your laughter be turned to mourning and your joy to gloom. Humble yourselves in the sight of he Lord, And He will lift you up" (James 4:6–10).

Jesus revealed the meekness we should all desire. "Let this mind be in you which was also in Christ Jesus, who being in the form of God, did not consider it robbery to be equal with God, but made Himself of no reputation, taking the form of a bondservant, and coming in the likeness of men. And being found in appearance as a man, He humbled Himself and became obedient to the point of death, even the death of the cross" (Phil. 2:5–8).

> "The difficulties we have to encounter may be very much lessened by the meekness which hides itself in Christ. If we possess the humility of our Master, we shall rise above the slights, the rebuffs, the annoyances, to which we are daily exposed, and they will cease to cast a gloom over the spirit.... Lowliness of heart is the strength that gives victory to the followers of Christ; it is their connection with the courts above."
>
> *The Desire of Ages*, p. 301

"Though the Lord is on high, Yet He regards the lowly; But the proud He knows from afar" (Ps. 138:6).

Again, I am thankful that Jesus took away the pride that had kept me distant from Him, and instead had me draw toward Him in a full surrender. Without Him, I could not have made it through.

> "Those who reveal the meek and lowly spirit of Christ are tenderly regarded by God. They may be looked upon with scorn by the world, but they are of great value in His sight. Not only the wise, the great, the beneficent, will gain a passport to the heavenly courts ... the humble in heart, whose highest ambition is to do God's will,—these will gain an abundant entrance. They will be among that number who have washed their robes and made them white in the blood of the Lamb."
>
> *The Desire of Ages*, pp. 301, 302

My highest ambition now is to do the will of God, and I claim the promise that I will be given entrance to heaven. I've learned that in being meek, I will think of myself as being no better and no worse than anyone else. We all have equal opportunity if we keep advancing to the next higher step on the ladder. He promised: "... He will beautify the humble with salvation" (Ps. 149:4).

But there is so much more I need to learn. John said, "If we confess our sins, He is faithful and just to forgive us our sins and to cleanse us from all unrighteousness" (1 John 1:9).

I have confessed my sins and have claimed the promise of cleansing, but each morning as I study my Bible and learn more of the spotless life of Jesus, I see that only through the power of the Holy Spirit can I become like Him. I must experience the new birth every day.

"Take My yoke upon you and learn from Me, for I am gentle and lowly in heart, and you will find rest for your souls. For My yoke is easy and My burden is light" (Matt. 11:29, 30).

I believe my mother planted the seed of the Word in my mind when I was a baby. I don't remember her reading the Bible to me; however, my older siblings have told me that before we lost the farm, it was different. After supper each evening, she would gather all the children around the table, along with those employed to work on the farm and read the Bible to us. After my birth, she was sick much of the time. I do remember her quoting lots of scripture after I was older, but I didn't understand the meaning.

We had an elderly couple living across the railroad tracks from us. They were very kind people, and they cared about our family, which had seven children total and had just moved under trying circumstances. During my mother's many stays in the hospital, all the other children were in school, and I was sent to the neighbors' until my brothers and sisters got home from school. It was a large two-story house with rocking chairs and a swing on the porch. I could see our house from the porch, and I would sit and rock myself or swing until I saw the school bus let my siblings out. I was so happy to see them; I would run home as fast as my five-year-old legs would take me.

When they were no longer able to live alone in the big house, they sold it to my father. There were thirty acres with the house, but the land was poor—nothing like the rich black soil he farmed by the river where we lived before the bank foreclosed in 1929. Even when there was a good crop, it seemed like the prices dropped before he got the produce to market. Much of his salary as deputy sheriff went into the farm.

My father learned to play cards with the other county officials, which took its toll on his income as well considering he was always the loser. But we grew a large garden, had our own chickens, cows, and hogs, so we were well-fed, if not healthy-fed! Of course, all this required much work by Mama and the younger children who were still living at home.

Those were hard times for my mother, but we were fortunate that the sheriff needed another deputy, and he gave Papa the job. The pay was not great, but it kept food on the table for our large family. Mama always worried about Papa because it was a dangerous job. Once he had to shoot a man in self-defense, so she had a good reason to be anxious. Yet, even in her anxiety about him, she never gave up her faith in Jesus. Mama was a "people-pleaser," and some people would even characterize me as a "people-pleaser." I wonder if that is the label that should be given to those, like me, who want to be like Jesus by being kind and helpful to others. But it certainly has obtained a negative connotation.

We grew fields of corn, which had to be hoed and harvested by hand. Besides having it to feed the chickens and animals, it was for our own food. This involved a lot of preparation for canning for the winter when the corn was freshly picked. After the ears were dry, we had to shuck and shell the ears to be taken to the grist mill to be ground. After it was ground at the mill, we sifted the finest ground through a screen sieve to have cornmeal to make cornbread and corn dumplings, and then we sifted what was left through a larger sized screen for grits. The husk that was left was fed to the hogs.

One year, Papa planted a field of cotton so my sister, who was still at home with me, and I could harvest it, and Mama would have the cotton for quilt batting. Keeping the weeds out of the rows with hoes wasn't so bad, but when it came time to pick the cotton—what misery! Our fingers were sore and bleeding by the end of the second day, and Mama insisted that Papa hire someone to pick the rest. The cotton gin was not too far away, and we got to see how it operated.

We also grew potatoes and were paid ten cents a barrel to pick up the potatoes behind the plow. We did have a hired man who did the plowing. The modern machinery potato farmers use now was not invented yet, or if it was, it was too expensive for us to own.

My brother, who was working away from home, purchased ten acres joining our property just for the cost of the taxes, and he let Papa use it. It had pecan trees on part of it, and that involved picking the pecans off the ground when they were ripe and fell off. Then on winter evenings we would sit by the fireplace and crack and shell the nuts. Mama got to keep the money for the shelled pecans that were sold to buy our school clothes. She also had money from selling eggs, chickens, butter, and sewing dresses for the neighbors.

Papa got a job for Mama through his connections at the County Court House. The job was to record the birth of the babies born in the neighborhood. Most of the women had their babies at home and did not go in to register them and obtain a birth certificate. After word started to get around, mothers came to our house with their babies to register them. Sometimes Mama would hear of someone who had a baby but did not come, so she would go to their house. She was paid fifty cents for each birth certificate she turned in. She always gave the mother a vanilla crème pie after she registered the baby. She had some superstition that a fruit pie would give the baby colic! Everyone loved her and spoke of her lovingly. I believe God implanted His love in me through her. He gave these words to Jeremiah: "Before I formed you in the womb I knew you; Before you were born I sanctified you; I ordained you a prophet to the nations" (Jer. 1:5).

David wrote "For You formed my inward parts; You covered me in my mother's womb. I will praise you, for I am fearfully and wonderfully made. Marvelous are Your works, And that my soul knows very well" (Ps. 139:13, 14).

Now we are ready to advance to the next step that makes our burden light–His righteousness.

SEEK RIGHTEOUSNESS

This is the step similar to the one we reached as virtue, on Peter's ladder, and that of serving the true God only, on God's ladder. It is when we are willing to submit to His will–willing to make a complete surrender. "Blessed are those who hunger and thirst for righteousness, for they shall be filled" (Matt. 5:6).

I realized that Jesus died on the cross for my sins, and now they are forgiven, so I look to the cross where He shed His blood to remind myself that is what His righteousness cost.

Seeking for Christ's righteousness is not a one-time thing. It must be constant, every day. I realized I had to make a full surrender daily, and in the blessing, He promised power to do it–the power of the Holy Spirit. But I must seek for it. I "hungered and thirsted" for His righteousness as I studied His Word.

" ... You will seek the LORD your God, and you will find Him if you seek Him with all your heart and with all your soul" (Deut. 4:29). " ... And those who seek me diligently will find me" (Prov. 8:17).

I had discovered the real meaning of faith and virtue on Peter's ladder. Now I knew I needed to search the scriptures more diligently, daily even, if I were to preserve the knowledge I had gained. If I am not advancing on Jesus' ladder, I shall be falling behind.

> "If you have a sense of need in your soul, if you hunger and thirst after righteousness, this is an evidence that Christ has wrought upon your heart, in order that He may be sought unto to do for you, through the endowment of the Holy Spirit, those things which it is impossible for you to do for yourself.... To Jesus, who emptied Himself for the salvation of lost humanity, the Holy Spirit was given without measure. So it will be given to every follower of Christ when the whole heart is surrendered for His indwelling.... When we submit ourselves to Christ, the heart is united with His heart, the will is merged with His will, the mind becomes one with His mind, the thoughts are brought into captivity to Him; we live His life. This is what it means to be clothed with the garment of His righteousness. Then as the Lord looks upon us He see, not the fig-leaf garment, not the nakedness and deformity of sin, but His own robe of righteousness, which is perfect obedience to the law of Jehovah.... Righteousness is right doing, and it is by their deeds that all will be judged. Our characters are revealed by what we do. The works show whether the faith is genuine."
> *Thoughts from the Mount of Blessings*, pp. 19, 21; *Christ's Object Lessons*, p. 312

I am reminded of Jacob's ladder when Jesus encounters the woman at the same well that Jacob dug long after he had received his dream of the ladder. At this well, Jesus pointed out how to get on the ladder and stay on.

> So He came to a city of Samaria which is called Sychar, near the plot of ground that Jacob gave to his son Joseph. Now Jacob's well was there. Jesus therefore, being wearied from His journey, sat thus by the well. It was about the sixth hour. A woman of Samaria came to draw water. Jesus said to her, 'Give Me a drink.' For His disciples had gone away into the city to buy food. Then the woman of Samaria said to Him, 'How is it that You, being a Jew, ask a drink from me, a Samaritan woman?' For Jews have no dealings with Samaritans. Jesus answered and said to her, 'If you knew the gift of God, and who it is who says to you, 'Give Me a drink,' you would have asked Him, and He would have given you living water'.... His disciples came, and they marveled that He talked with a woman; yet no one said, 'What do You seek?' or, 'Why are You talking with her?' The woman then left her waterpot, went her way into the city.... (John 4:5–28)

The Samaritan woman, for whom we have no name, was convinced that this man was the Messiah, and accepted His righteousness. Just as she believed Him, I too believed, and began to tell my relatives and friends about Jesus and the commandments we learned in chapter three. However, they were not convinced, and I began to feel resistance until some of our friends withdrew completely. My husband and I were seeking together, and that made it easier. But I was glad I had learned the promise following the positive blessings: that I would be reviled and persecuted. God always warns us before things happen.

> "This [Samaritan] woman represents the working of a practical faith in Christ. Every true disciple is born into the kingdom of God as a missionary. He who drinks of the living water becomes a fountain of life. The receiver becomes a giver. The grace of Christ in the soul is like a spring in the desert, welling up to refresh all, and making those who are ready to perish eager to drink of the water of life."
>
> *The Desire of Ages*, p. 195

God never asks us to do anything without first preparing us for the work. He had a plan of which I knew nothing at the time. It did not come until I had fully surrendered my life to Jesus.

The children were all gone and my husband and I were alone, and we were sometimes lonely for them. I told you already about the song God gave me while driving to work. I frequently prayed as I drove, but usually it was a prayer from the Bible or a prayer song. This one became my own (see page 107). Within six months after I wrote the song and named it "All on the Altar," my husband got a call to Africa where our son was a student missionary.

I had decided to take a year's sabbatical from school and go to South Carolina to spend time near my mother who was not well. I phoned the school district and spoke with the superintendent about a teaching job. When I told him about my credentials in special education, he offered me a job on the phone. We had just enough time to pack up what we would need for the year in our car, and then we drove to South Carolina. My brother owned the building where my mother lived and had an upstairs apartment vacant, so we moved into the same house where she lived.

We were there only a few weeks until our son in Africa asked his dad to come and help him do some building. At first, my husband thought he couldn't leave me alone, but I convinced him I could handle it.

We had a beautiful first granddaughter, Julie, and my husband wanted to spend some time with her before he left, so I suggested that he fly home and spend some time with her family and the other children, and I would join them for Christmas vacation. However, he had only been gone a few days when I began wondering why I didn't go with him.

I called the church headquarters and asked them if it would possible for me to go to Africa with him. They replied that they expected the wife to go along. I just had time to turn in my resignation without a penalty and prepare to go to Idaho to be with the family for Christmas, as we had originally planned. My husband flew back to South Carolina, and the day my Christmas vacation began, we left for our five day drive back to Idaho. We had a wonderful Christmas with the children, and in January, we left for Zambia, Africa.

We spent six months at Yuka Mission Hospital. My husband supervised the building of an addition to the hospital. This freed our son, Carey, to go to the villages nearby and test for leprosy, so those afflicted could get treatment from the doctor at the hospital. The hospital did not have a kitchen. Food was cooked outdoors in a large kettle on an open fire. All the patients were mixed together in one ward—malaria, TB, leprosy, and all the other prevalent diseases were there together. My husband also helped build houses that were needed for the hospital workers to live in, and the framework for a church was also finished before we left. I spent my time teaching the doctor and the pastor's children and worked with the women lepers.

I found boxes of sample blocks of men's suits and other clothing that someone had sent to the hospital for the patients. Even though some of the women only had stubs for fingers, due to injuring them, I was amazed at how quickly they mastered the art of sewing with needles and thread. Many made beautiful quilts for themselves. I learned that it was not the disease of leprosy that caused the fingers to fall off, but because leprosy deadens the nerves, it was usually the burns they received while cooking on open fires that caused the damage.

We enjoyed worshipping with the Africans outdoors under a large tree that provided shade. The board benches for seats were not comfortable, but with the enthusiasm of the people singing and praying, the discomfort was quickly forgotten. In places like this, one knows that God is near. You can see things happen that can only be described as miracles, so it was a blessed time for us. Many of our experiences with the people there strengthened our faith. I shall never forget one event in particular.

Each Sabbath afternoon, my husband and I went to a small village about a mile from where we lived at the hospital. Along the way many children joined us, singing as we walked. We could not speak their language, but we had an interpreter, a song book in their language, and a picture roll, so I was prepared to tell Bible stories.

One Sabbath, a messenger came to tell us that the interpreter could not come; his father was ill, and he had gone to his village to care for him. We understood because the natives were very loyal to their parents. However, it caused a dilemma because I had no one to interpret for me. We decided to go nevertheless because we knew they would be gathered and waiting. At least we could sing some songs with them and show the pictures depicting Bible stories.

We sang many songs; their harmony needed no accompaniment, for it sounded like angels must be singing with them. However, when I got up and started telling the story and pointing to the pictures, they looked at each other in bewilderment—no understanding. Then one of the men came and stood beside me and interpreted. At least I assume he was sharing the story I told because I could see their eyes light up and joy on their faces. I tried to communicate with the man after we finished, but he could not understand and reply in English. I called it "the gift of tongues," which that man had when it was needed. He understood my language and communicated it in their native tongue. Truly when God calls, He makes the provisions, if we are willing. Ultimately, we would not have had that experience if our son had not been willing. I will always remember the day he decided to be a student missionary.

The phone rang one Sabbath, and it was Carey, who was a student at Walla Walla College at the time. Without a lot of preliminary conversation, he asked, "How would you feel about my going to Zambia next year?" Zambia—I had never heard of Zambia, but I had heard of the African adventures of his Great Uncle Arthur, who spent many years in the jungles. He went on to explain that he had been invited to Yuka Mission Hospital to be a student missionary.

Of course I was delighted that he had chosen to serve the Lord in that area, so I immediately gave my approval and his father had no objections either. When he came home for the summer, we began to make plans. His dad would furnish the trees and help him make poles to sell to earn money for his trip. In addition to money, he had to get a passport, all the required immunization shots, shop for suitable clothing and boots for protection from snake bites, and get a visa. He needed to do all that while working at his regular summer job to earn money for his college tuition when he returned. Amazingly, he was able to get all of the money he needed.

I had always had a fear of snakes, so we found the thickest high top boots available, which alleviated my fears. I knew that if God wanted him there, He would protect him if he did his part, which was to wear those thick leather boots at all times. He got the shots—there were no reactions. His passport came in the mail. He had applied for a visa, but it had yet to come.

Reservations were already made, but with one week before his departure date, the visa had still not arrived, and I was getting concerned. Everything else was in order, so I called the General Conference, and they said the visa had been sent, but it did not come that day or the next. I was just sure that it had gone astray some place, so I went in and spoke with the postmaster. Perhaps it was registered and required a signature or something, or perhaps it had gone to the wrong Potlatch—that's where we lived then. We didn't use zip codes back then.

I explained the situation to the postmaster, and he was very helpful. He called Spokane, which was the last sorting station before Potlatch. They checked, but it was not there. He gave me the phone numbers for all the other Potlatch post offices in the United States, so I went home and called each one of them. No one had the missing visa.

The day came for Carey to fly out of Spokane, but he still did not have his visa. We had faith that somehow it would come in time. That morning, Carey had his suitcase packed except for a few final items lying beside it to put in, and we waited for the mailman to come. Another disappointment—no visa, and you do not get into Zambia without a visa. So that was final for Carey, he thought; he went to work with his dad about twenty-five miles from where we lived.

But I just couldn't let it go. If God had called him to work there, and he was willing to go, why was this happening? I thought on one last ditch effort. I thought if this comes tomorrow, we will really feel bad. I called the postmaster in Spokane and said, "I know this is a far-out request, but if you have a visa come today for Carey Carscallen at Potlatch, Idaho, would you please call me?" He probably thought I was nuts! Our daughter was living in Moscow where my husband and Carey were working, so I gave him her number to call. Then I called her, and told her to rush over to the building site and tell them rush home if he called.

Talk about last minute answers to prayer. It happened! The postmaster called my daughter; she rushed over to where they were working, and they rushed home. Carey showered and changed his clothes while I put the final things in his suitcase, and off we went to Spokane. We had two hours to get him on that plane. But first we had to go to the auxiliary post office and get the visa.

Ordinarily, we planned two hours just to get to the airport; this time a few speed limits were broken. We found the post office without any problem, picked up the visa, and got to the airport just fifteen minutes before the scheduled departure time. However, the plane was an hour late so we had time to sit down, relax, and say our final goodbyes.

Now if Carey had not had faith enough to believe it would come and had not had everything packed or if I had not persisted in attempting to find the lost visa, would he ever have gone as a missionary? And, today as dean of architecture, would he be taking students on mission trips to Bolivia to work on an orphanage and schools for children who are on drugs or abandoned by their parents who generally are on drugs? Only God knows, but we know it was He who made it all possible.

> "Education, culture, the exercise of the will, human effort, all have their proper sphere, but here they are powerless.... There must be a power working from within, a new life from above, before men can be changed from sin to holiness. That power is Christ. His grace alone can quicken the lifeless faculties of the soul, and attract it to God, to holiness."
>
> *Steps to Christ*, p. 18

After our experience in Africa, I knew that Jesus' righteousness was working through us as God protected us from malaria, leprosy, snake bites, and many other dangers that lurked about us every day while we served the Lord.

Our daughters like adventure also. Nelle chose to go to Mexico with a group and study Spanish. Jane elected to do a European tour to study world history. What a fun way they chose to get college credits for subjects that would have required much more time and effort.

The words to the song I had written come to mind often to renew my vow to God and submit all to him; it is only then that I shall receive the promise. He said, "... Seek Me and live ..." (Amos 5:4).

Our experience in Africa was like living in a different world. It was like living life to the fullest in the presence of God. But we must continually seek to know and serve as Jesus did, wherever He places us. " ... 'If anyone thirsts, let him come to Me and drink. He who believes in Me, as the Scripture has said, out of his heart will flow rivers of living water" (John 7:37, 38). We also received the promise David spoke of: "O, taste and see that the Lord is good ..." (Ps. 34:8).

The next round on Jesus' ladder relates to the merciful. I can never thank God enough for His mercy.

THE MERCIFUL

Who are the merciful? They are those who have realized their need for the Holy Spirit, mourned for their sinful condition, become humble, and sought after God's righteousness in meekness. In God's mercy, He has forgiven them of their sins. "Blessed are the merciful, For they shall obtain mercy" (Matt. 5:7).

When we receive God's mercy and forgiveness, it is then that we are willing to be merciful and forgiving to others. As all the other character traits, it can only be done by the power of the Holy Spirit. We can get to the place where we can say like Jesus did as He hung on the cross, "... Father forgive them, for they know not what they do..." (Luke 23:34).

God's mercy is referred to numerous times in scripture. I shall quote only a few which impressed me. "The earth, O LORD, is full of Your mercy; Teach me Your statutes" (Ps. 119:64).

I believe we must know His statutes, the Ten Commandments. We have just reviewed them as Ten Promises on God's ladder. He tells us to whom He shows mercy, and that His mercy endures forever: "but showing mercy to thousands, to those who love Me and keep My commandments" (Exod. 20:6).

We are seeking joy on this ladder, and we shall have it when we reach the top round. "For I desire mercy and not sacrifice, And the knowledge of God more than burnt offerings" (Hosea 6:6). "Let us therefore come boldly to the throne of grace, that we may obtain mercy, and find grace to help in time of need" (Heb. 4:16). "For judgment is without mercy to the one who has shown no mercy. Mercy triumphs over judgment" (James 2:13).

I realized that I must show mercy and compassion to others if I am to be given mercy when my name comes up for judgment. It is the mercy we have through the Holy Spirit that saves us. We have none of our own. "For He says to Moses, 'I will have mercy on whomever I will have mercy, and I will have compassion on whomever I will have compassion. So then it is not of him who wills, nor of him who runs, but of God who shows mercy" (Rom. 9:15, 16).

> "God has given us His holy precepts, because He loves mankind. To shield us from the results of transgression, He reveals the principles of righteousness.... God desires us to be happy, and He gave us the precepts of the law that in obeying them we might have joy."
> *The Desire of Ages*, p. 308

We must realize that this verse describes us: "But I am like a green olive tree in the house of God; I trust in the mercy of God forever and ever" (Ps. 52:8).

He forgave us freely; none have earned God's forgiveness. "But when the kindness and the love of God our Savior toward man appeared, not by works of righteousness which we have done, but according to His mercy He saved us, through the washing of regeneration and renewing of the Holy Spirit" (Titus 3:4, 5).

Paul tells us that God freely forgives us if, in our ignorance, we fail to show mercy; however, he shows the mercy given to him in his life, so we will no longer be ignorant. "Although I was formerly a blasphemer, a persecutor, and an insolent man; but I obtained mercy because I did it ignorantly in unbelief" (1 Tim. 1:13).

I mourn once more when I think of all the unmerciful things I did before I learned of the power available to me through the Holy Spirit. And then the text comes to mind: "Truly, these times of ignorance God overlooked, but now commands all men everywhere to repent, because He has appointed a day on which He will judge the world in righteousness ..." (Acts 17:30, 31).

But as I said before, I am no longer in "my times of ignorance," so I must depend on the Holy Spirit to perform the things I have learned. I am so thankful that I learned of His love, mercy, and compassion to sinners like me before Satan tried his utmost to discourage me. Within a three year period, our house burned and we lost most of our possessions, I retired from work, and my husband died. Thankfully, I had learned to trust in Jesus prior to Satan's attacks.

God is truly merciful!

The next round we ascend to is being pure in heart.

All On the Altar

PURE IN HEART

Those who are pure in heart are free from pride and self-seeking tendencies. They have recognized that they lacked the power of the Holy Spirit, have mourned for their lack and become meek. Seeing their sorrow for their sins, God has empowered them with His Spirit as they sought His righteousness. They practice in their own life the principle of self-sacrificing love, the pure love that we learned about when we got to the top of Peter's ladder and that we saw in the character of God on His ladder.

"Blessed are the pure in heart, For they shall see God" (Matt. 5:8).

There is no more pretending to be something one is not, no more pride or hypocrisy when we reach this round on the ladder. Being pure in heart is equivalent to the round of godliness on Peter's ladder. We are nearing the heavenly kingdom, and we must not fall now. However, in His mercy, which we just discussed, He will pick us up and put us back on the ladder at just the place we need to be to feel secure.

> "No matter how high the profession, he whose heart is not filled with love for God and his fellow men is not a true disciple of Christ.... In his zeal he might even meet a martyr's death, yet if not actuated by love, he would be regarded by God as a deluded enthusiast or an ambitious hypocrite."
>
> *The Acts of the Apostles*, pp. 318, 319

While I thought my outward behavior was acceptable, I began to see that I did not have a pure heart. A passage in an old book I discovered helped me in my understanding of love.

> "You will give yourselves to [sic] many things, give yourself first to Love. Hold things in their proportion. *Hold things in their proportion.* Let at least the first great object of our lives be to achieve the character defended in these words, the character—and it is the character of Christ—which is built around Love.... I was not told when I was a boy that 'God so loved the world that He gave His only begotten Son, that whosoever believeth in Him should have everlasting life.' What I was told, I remember, was, that God so loved the world that, if I trusted in Him, I was to have a thing called peace, or I was to have rest, or I was to have joy, or I was to have safety. But I had to find out for myself that whosoever trusteth in Him—that is, whosoever loveth Him, for trust is only the avenue to Love—hath everlasting life.'" (*The Greatest Thing in the World*, pp. 25, 26)

This reminded me of a false concept I was taught of God's love when I was a child. My mother told me that if I was "good," God would love me and that God did not love those who did bad things, or in her words "children who were ugly or naughty." Unfortunately, I told my children the same thing before I learned the truth. She did not describe what the bad things were, and I was always afraid that I would do something "ugly." I lived in fear that I would do something wrong. Somehow, God put it in my heart as a child to do what was right–but I didn't really know what was right. It was a great relief after I began to study my Bible to learn that God loves everyone. He loves the obedient and the disobedient; however, even though His love is unconditional, there are conditions to salvation.

Once, when my sister and I had some disagreement, I hit her. I felt so bad that I cried. I also remember being in the third grade when the teacher left the room and told us to be quiet–no talking while she was gone or we would have to stay in at recess. I did not talk, but others did, and she heard from outside, and kept her promise to keep us in at recess. When she did let us out, I went to the restroom and cried. I had a "tender heart." It was true emotion. I was so hurt by being punished for something I had not done that I could not hold the tears back any longer. Someone must have told the teacher because she came in and consoled me. Crying was something I had willed not to do when I was very young. I had seen my father use his belt on my older brothers, and tell them if they cried, they would "get some more." But this time I lost my control. I'm still not sure why it hurt so bad when I was accused of something I did not do, but I think it was shame that I felt, not guilt. But it seems my heart was easily broken. Yet there are times when it is appropriate to have a broken heart, despite the pain it brings. After I became converted and learned that Jesus died from a broken heart, I turned my hurts over to Him. He always comes to my rescue and helps me through the rough times.

> "Let your heart break for the longing it has for God, for the living God. The life of Christ has shown what humanity can do by being partaker of the divine nature. All that Christ received from God we too may have. Then ask and receive. With the persevering faith of Jacob, with the unyielding persistence of Elijah, claim for yourself all that God has promised."
>
> *Christ's Object Lessons*, p. 149

God has promised to make us "pure in heart" if we keep our focus on His Word, so I shall continue to claim His promise. I have learned that even a pure heart is a gift of God. There were people I wanted to love, so I began to pray, "Father, I know you love this person. Please help me to learn to love him, too." And He did. I began to assimilate the words Paul wrote.

> Though I speak with the tongues of men and of angels, but have not love, I have become sounding brass or a clanging cymbal. And though I have the gift of prophecy, and understand all mysteries and all knowledge, and though I have all faith, so that I could remove mountains, but have not love, I am nothing. And though I bestow all my goods to feed the poor, and though I give my body to be burned, but have not love, it profits me nothing. Love suffers long and is kind; love does not envy; love does not parade itself, is not puffed up, does not behave rudely, does not seek its own, is not provoked, thinks no evil; does not rejoice in iniquity, but rejoices in the truth; bears all things, believes all things, hopes all things, endures all things. Love never fails. But whether there are prophecies, they will fail; whether there are tongues, they will cease; whether there is knowledge, it will vanish away.

For we know in part and we prophesy in part. But when that which is perfect has come, then that which is in part will be done away. When I was a child, I spoke as a child, I understood as a child, I thought as a child; but when I became a man, I put away childish things. For now we see in a mirror, dimly, but then face to face. Now I know in part, but then I shall know just as I also am known. And now abide faith, hope, love, these three; but the greatest of these is love. (1 Cor. 13:1–13)

This round on Jesus' ladder equates with "godliness" on Peter's ladder. I'm thankful for Peter's example of one who has denied Christ but later repented for his denial with a sorely broken heart. I am even more thankful that we serve a God of love who delights in the forgiveness of His children.

> "The truth is to be planted in the heart. It is to control the mind and regulate the affections. The whole character must be stamped with the divine utterances. Every jot and tittle of the word of God is to be brought into the daily practice."
>
> *Christ's Object Lessons*, p. 314

We cannot show true kindness to our brothers and sisters in the church if we have not attained to being merciful and pure in heart. I truly want to receive the promise given to the pure in heart: "they shall see God" (see Matt. 5:8). If we are not pure in heart, we cannot become peacemakers.

Let's move up to the next rung on Jesus' ladder and see how He describes peacemakers.

THE PEACEMAKERS

If we have remained on the "pure in heart" round of Jesus' ladder and see God in the form of Jesus, we are prepared to take one step further and learn to be a peacemaker.

"Blessed are the peacemakers, For they shall be called sons of God" (Matt. 5:9).

Jesus gave us this most precious promise, to be called a child of God. But God has called all of us to be His children; whether we respond to His call is our choice.

Often we think of a peacemaker as one who arbitrates differences between men, but the peacemakers spoken of here are in a different category. They have peace within themselves and peace with others. We are to show the love of Christ to all with whom we come in contact in our daily life.

> "We ourselves owe everything to God's free grace. Grace in the covenant ordained our adoption. Grace in the Saviour effected our redemption, our regeneration, and our exaltation to heirship with Christ. Let this grace be revealed to others."
>
> *Christ's Object Lessons*, p. 250

"... just as He chose us in Him before the foundation of the world, that we should be holy and without blame before Him in love, having predestined us to adoption as sons by Jesus Christ to Himself, according to the good pleasure of His will, to the praise of the glory of His grace, by which He made us accepted in the Beloved" (Eph. 1:4–6).

> "Christ's followers are sent to the world with the message of peace. Whoever, by the quiet, unconscious influence of a holy life, shall reveal the love of Christ; whoever, by word or deed, shall lead another to renounce sin and yield his heart to God, is a peacemaker.... The spirit of peace is evidence of their connection with heaven. The sweet savor of Christ surrounds them. The fragrance of the life, the loveliness of the character, reveal to the world the fact that they are children of God. Men take knowledge of them that they have been with Jesus. 'Everyone that loveth is born of God.' 'If any man have not the Spirit of Christ, he is none of His;' but 'as many as are led by the Spirit of God, they are the sons of God.' 1 John 4:7; Romans 8:9, 14"
>
> *Thoughts from the Mount of Blessing*, p. 28

God gave us His peace when we reached the top rung on His ladder, and David said: "Great peace have they who love Your law, And nothing causes them to stumble" (Ps. 119:165).

It is a peace which we cannot pretend to have; it must be the grace of Christ in our heart directing us to whomever we might share our faith with, either by our words or our actions.

> "Men cannot manufacture peace. Human plans for the purification and uplifting of individuals or of society will fail of producing peace, because they do not reach the heart. The only power that can create or perpetuate true peace is the grace of Christ. When this is implanted in the heart, it will cast out the evil passions that cause strife and dissension."
>
> *The Desire of Ages*, p. 305

> "Christ has promised the gift of the Holy Spirit to His church, and the promise belongs to us as much as to the first disciples. But like every other promise, it is given on conditions. There are many who believe and profess to claim the Lord's promise; they talk about Christ and about the Holy Spirit, yet receive no benefit. They do not surrender the soul to be guided and controlled by the divine agencies. We cannot use the Holy Spirit. The Spirit is to use us. Through the Spirit God works in His people 'to will and to do of His good pleasure.' (Philippians 2:13). But many will not submit to this. They want to manage themselves. This is why they do not receive the heavenly gift. Only to those who wait humbly upon God, who watch for His guidance and grace, is the Spirit given. The power of God awaits their demand and reception. This promised blessing, claimed by faith, brings all other blessings in its train. It is given according to the riches of the grace of Christ, and He is ready to supply every soul according to the capacity to receive."
>
> *The Desire of Ages*, p. 672

In the Old Testament, God gave the promise of peace to the children of Israel through the priest. "And the LORD spoke to Moses, saying: 'Speak to Aaron and his sons, saying, 'This is the way you shall bless the children of Israel. Say to them: 'The LORD bless you and keep you; The LORD make His face shine upon you, And be gracious to you; The LORD lift up His countenance upon you, And give you peace'" (Num. 6:22–26).

Before Jesus returned to His Father, He left the promise of the Holy Spirit and peace for His followers. "But the Helper, the Holy Spirit, whom the Father will send in My name, He will teach you all things, and bring to your remembrance all things that I said to you. Peace I leave with you, My peace I give to you; not as the world gives do I give to you. Let not your heart be troubled, neither let it be afraid" (John 14:26, 27).

The next step on Jesus' ladder sometimes makes it difficult to maintain the idea that Micah claims the peacemakers will be the remnant of Jacob, now spiritual Israel. Soon the waiting will be over. "Then the remnant of Jacob Shall be in the midst of many peoples, Like dew from the LORD, Like showers on the grass, That tarry for no man Nor wait for the sons of men" (Mic. 5:7).

> "Those who take Christ at His word, and surrender their souls to His keeping, their lives to His ordering, will find peace and quietude. Nothing of the world can make them sad when Jesus makes them glad by His presence. In perfect acquiescence there is perfect rest.... Our lives may seem a tangle; but as we commit ourselves to the wise Master Worker, He will bring out the pattern of life and character that will be to His own glory."
>
> *The Desire of Ages*, p. 331

Reaching this round on Jesus' ladder puts us where we need to be to His own glory (see John 7:18). If we reach this point, we will be ready to meet Jesus.

However, the next step makes it hard for some to maintain that peace and have the joy only God gives. Let's go up and see if we have what it takes to remain on Jesus' ladder.

THE PERSECUTED

On God's Ten Commandment ladder, He told us not to murder. Sometimes it seems like death would be a blessing rather than go through some of the persecution seen in history as well as today. But we have to remember that God is always there for us; He will see us through anything–even persecution.

"Blessed are those who are persecuted for righteousness' sake, For theirs is the kingdom of heaven" (Matt. 5:10).

In this world where sin reigns, we cannot be like Jesus without being persecuted. Unfortunately, if

> "When we see Jesus, a Man of Sorrows and acquainted with grief, working to save the lost, slighted, scorned, derided, driven from city to city till His mission was accomplished: when we behold Him in Gethsemane, sweating great drops of blood, and on the cross dying in agony—when we see this, self will no longer clamor to be recognized."
>
> *The Desire of Ages*, p. 439

Jesus' Ladder 113

we have attained to God's love as Peter showed us, become at peace with ourselves and others as God's ladder taught, and now have reached this rung on Jesus' ladder, persecution is a given.

Isaiah foretold the suffering of Jesus: "Surely He has borne our griefs And carried our sorrows; Yet we esteemed Him stricken, smitten by God, and afflicted. But He was wounded for our transgressions, He was bruised for our iniquities; The chastisement for our peace was upon Him, And by His stripes we are healed. All we like sheep have gone astray; We have turned, every one, to his own way; And the LORD has laid on Him the iniquity of us all" (Isa. 53:4–6).

> "In all ages Satan has persecuted the people of God. He has tortured them and put them to death, but in dying they became conquerors...Through trials and persecution, the glory—character—of God is revealed in His chosen ones. The church of God, hated and persecuted by the world, are educated and disciplined in the school of Christ. They walk in narrow paths on earth; they are purified in the furnace of affliction. They follow Christ through sore conflicts; they endure self-denial and experience bitter disappointments; but their painful experience teaches them the guilt and woe of sin, and they look upon it with abhorrence. Being partakers of Christ's sufferings, they are destined to be partakers of His glory."
>
> *Thoughts from the Mount of Blessings*, pp. 30–31

Jesus' death on the cross made it all possible. But even worse than physical persecution is being reviled by the words of someone whom you love dearly. To be denounced abusively when one is not guilty. This was Christ's experience, and I believe most of us have been hurt by words from someone we love as well. Jesus has already suffered for us, so we can go to Him for consolation.

From the time sin entered the world man has been reviled and persecuted. Cain spoke abusively to his brother, Abel, and then killed him. The saying "Sticks and stones may break my bones, but words can never harm me" is generally not true. However, it can be, if we have put on the character of God as revealed in the Ten Commandments.

"Blessed are you when they revile and persecute you, and say all kinds of evil against you falsely for My sake. Rejoice and be exceedingly glad, for great is your reward in heaven, for so they persecuted the prophets who were before you" (Matt. 5:11–12).

There are many who were not prophets who have dealt with this, who have been reviled and persecuted because of their faith, both in the Biblical record and in more recent times.

Noah preached repentance before the flood, and he was mocked as a fanatic and an alarmist. Moses was continually derided by the children of Israel as he led them to the Promised Land. John the Baptist preached repentance, and he was beheaded. Stephen was stoned to death because of his loyalty to God. Today, in some countries there are church members who are in prison for witnessing their faith to others. John tells us why. Could I be as faithful to God's Word?

"I, John ... was on the island that is called Patmos for the word of God and for the testimony of Jesus Christ" (Rev. 1:9).

When faith seemed to waver with other Christians, John would remind them: "That which was from the beginning, which we have heard, which we have seen with our eyes, which we have looked upon, and our hands have handled, concerning the Word of life ... that which we have seen and heard we declare to you, that you also may have fellowship with us; and truly our fellowship is with the Father and with His Son Jesus Christ" (1 John 1:1–3).

> "As a witness for Christ, John entered into no controversy, no wearisome contention. He declared what he knew, what he had seen and heard. He had been intimately associated with Christ, had listened to His teachings, had witnessed His mighty miracles. Few could see the beauties of Christ's character as John them. For him the darkness had passed away; on him the true light was shining. His testimony in regard to the Savior's life and death was clear and forcible."
>
> *The Acts of the Apostles*, p. 555

My purpose for writing this book is to declare what I have learned from Bible writers and other Christian authors. I believe, and now I desire to witness, and though it may mean I will have to deal with reviling from others, and ultimately, persecution, I pray that the power of the Holy Spirit will keep me faithful.

> "But when tribulation comes upon us, how many of us are like Jacob! We think it the hand of an enemy; and in the darkness we wrestle blindly until our strength is spent, and we find no comfort or deliverance.... We also need to learn that trials mean benefit, and not to despise the chastening of the Lord nor faint when we are rebuked of Him."
>
> *Thoughts from the Mount of Blessings*, pp. 11, 12

> "Christ is acquainted with all that is misunderstood and misrepresented by men. His children can afford to wait in calm patience and trust, no matter how much maligned and despised; for nothing is secret that shall not be made manifest, and those who honor God shall be honored by Him in the presence of men and angels."
>
> *Thoughts from the Mount of Blessing*, p. 32

Peter records this to remind us. "Knowing this first: that scoffers will come in the last days, walking according to their own lusts, and saying, 'Where is the promise of His coming? For since the fathers fell asleep, all things continue as they were from the beginning of creation'" (2 Peter 3:3, 4).

The last rung on Jesus' Ladder is to rejoice. How can we rejoice in spite of persecution?

Let's move up and follow Jesus' instructions.

Rejoice

As we rejoice in our blessings, we are happy; we have joy in our hearts. That joy can only come as we give ourselves totally to Jesus for service to others.

"Rejoice and be exceedingly glad, for great is your reward in heaven, for so they persecuted the prophets who were before you" (Matt. 5:12).

What a reward God has waiting for us in heaven! It is so wonderful that Paul describes this way. "Eye has not seen, nor ear heard, Nor have entered into the heart of man The things which God has prepared for those who love Him" (1 Cor. 2:9).

Those who put their trust in Him rejoice. "But let all those rejoice who put their trust in You; Let them ever shout for joy, because You defend them; Let those also who love Your name Be joyful in You. For You, O LORD, will bless the righteous; With favor You will surround him as with a shield" (Ps. 5:11, 12).

Many verses speak to rejoicing in the New Testament.

- "Your father Abraham rejoiced to see My day, And he saw it and was glad" (John 8:56).

- "You have heard Me say to you, 'I am going away and coming back to you.' If you loved Me, you would rejoice ..." (John 14:28).

- "Therefore you now have sorrow; but I will see you again and your heart will rejoice, and your joy no one will take from you" (John 16:22).

- "Now when they came up out of the water, the Spirit of the Lord caught Philip away, so that the eunuch saw him no more; and he went on his way rejoicing" (Acts 8:39).

- " ... does not rejoice in iniquity, but rejoices in the truth" (1 Cor. 13:6).

- "Rejoice with those who rejoice, and weep with those who weep" (Rom. 12:15).

- "Then the seventy returned with joy, saying, 'Lord, even the demons are subject to us in Your name.' And He said to them, 'I saw Satan fall like lightning from heaven. Behold, I give you the authority to trample on serpents and scorpions, and over all the power of the enemy, and nothing shall by any means hurt you. Nevertheless do not rejoice in this, that the spirits are subject to you, but rather rejoice because your names are written in heaven'" (Luke 10:17–20).

- "Rejoice in the Lord always. Again I say, rejoice!" (Phil. 4:4).

If we obey the words of Jesus, we will rejoice. Sometimes it may seem hard, but we will be successful if we follow His method.

> "Under a storm of stinging, faultfinding words, keep the mind stayed upon the word of God. Let mind and heart be stored with God's promises. If you are ill-treated or wrongfully accused, instead of returning an angry answer, repeat to yourself the precious promises: "Be not overcome of evil, but overcome evil with good. (Romans 12:21)"
>
> *The Ministry of Healing,* p. 486

Some may think the Sermon on the Mount is too idealistic, but the more I come to know Jesus, the more I realize that these blessings lie at the heart of His message.

I wonder what the result would be if we promoted having the Beatitudes posted on the walls of our public buildings as some have the Ten Commandments? Perhaps it would make more sense to people who want to see God's law upheld, for it is simple and practical, and there could be no misunderstanding. Both the commandments and the Beatitudes are the words of God Himself. Think about it.

We shall go to Paul's ladder now to consider the fruit we are expected to bear.

Chapter Five
Paul's Ladder: The Fruit of the Spirit

We have been propelled by the Holy Spirit to the top of Peter's ladder, which is Love. And from this step we are ready to enter the kingdom of glory. God is love, and we ascended His ladder of peace and contentment, in place of covetousness, which also placed us ready to enter His glory. Then we received the joy of the Lord as Jesus Himself guided us up to the top of His ladder of blessings, again to the gate of God's kingdom. This love, peace, and joy have penetrated our hearts and minds. Each step was a character trait which Christ's followers must possess to be ready to meet Jesus at His return. Paul was there to learn from Peter. He knew God's law, and he saw Jesus' ladder, but he still ascended his ladder the hard way.

If we have put on the virtues of Christ Jesus, then as we ascend Paul's ladder, we are ready to put those virtues into action for the benefit of others. In order to do this we must exercise the self-control we put on after we had gained the knowledge of the Holy Spirit on Peter's ladder. I prefer to call it "Spirit-control." Are you ready to share your fruit with others as Paul did after he was converted? "But the fruit of the Spirit is love, joy, peace, longsuffering, kindness, goodness, faithfulness, gentleness, self-control. Against such there is no law" (Gal. 5:22, 23).

The first three of the fruits are love, joy, and peace. These are directed to God. The next three, patience, kindness, goodness, are directed toward others. The last three faithfulness, gentleness, and self-control, are directed toward self. All are gifts from God. All reveal one's character. Note that "fruit of the Spirit" is singular—we must bear all of the fruit to be a complete person.

Looking at the ladder from the bottom, going up, we have already discussed love, joy, and peace on Peter and Jesus' ladders and accepted them as gifts of the Holy Spirit. These result in patience, kindness, and goodness toward others. Then faithfulness, gentleness, and self-control are certain to follow. Remember, they are all gifts of the Holy Spirit. Paul accepted them. It was the power of the Holy Spirit that took him to the top of the ladder. That same power will take us to the top.

Paul warned that we might be drawn from the simplicity that is in Christ. He wrote "But I fear, lest somehow, as the serpent deceived Eve by his craftiness, so your minds may be corrupted from the simplicity that is in Christ" (2 Cor. 11:3).

Again, I ask myself, *if salvation is so simple, why do we make it hard for ourselves?*

However, there is hope for us if we stay on the ladder by the power of the Holy Spirit, and let His power do the work for us. Paul counseled and prayed. His conversion on the road to Damascus had changed him. He had seen Jesus, and he preached about Christ until his dying day. In spite of the deceptive light and power of Satan, the fruit of God's Spirit will be manifest through us if we wear the armor of God, as Paul explains:

> Put on the whole armor of God, that you may be able to stand against the wiles of the devil. For we do not wrestle against flesh and blood, but against principalities, against powers, against the rulers of the darkness of this age, against spiritual hosts of wickedness in the heavenly places. Therefore take up the whole armor of God, that you may be able to withstand in the evil day, and having done all, to stand. Stand therefore, having girded your waist with truth, having put on the breastplate of righteousness, and having shod your feet with the preparation of the gospel of peace; above all, taking the shield of faith with which you will be able to quench all the fiery darts of the wicked one. And take the helmet of salvation, and the sword of the Spirit, which is the word of God; praying always with all prayer and supplication in the Spirit, being watchful to this end with all perseverance and supplication for all the saints—and for me, that utterance may be given to me, that I may open my mouth boldly to make known the mystery of the gospel, for which I am an ambassador in chains; that in it I may speak boldly, as I ought to speak. (Eph. 6:11–20)

It's about putting on the character of God and letting His Spirit guide us. When we are filled with His Spirit, we will be compelled to pray, speak, and do.

> "As men seek to come into harmony with God, they will find that the offense of the cross has not ceased. Principalities and powers and wicked spirits in high places are arrayed against all who yield obedience to the law of heaven. Therefore, so far from causing grief, persecution should bring joy to the disciples of Christ, for it is an evidence that they are following in the steps of their Master."
>
> *Thoughts from the Mount of Blessings,* pp. 29, 30

Paul's writings were hard for me to understand as I read them; however, Peter had warned me, and so I diligently studied to learn more about the armor of God. "And consider that the longsuffering of our Lord is salvation—as also our beloved brother Paul, according to the wisdom given to him, has written to you, as also in all his epistles, speaking in them of these things, in which are some things hard to understand, which untaught and unstable people twist to their own destruction, as they do also the rest of the Scriptures" (2 Peter 3:15–16).

I realized that I had to carefully study Paul's writings, lest I be deceived. Perhaps I would have to struggle as Jacob did as he wrestled with the angel and won the victory.

> "Not until he fell crippled and helpless upon the breast of the covenant angel did Jacob know the victory of conquering faith and receive the title of a prince with God."
>
> *Thoughts from the Mount of Blessing,* p. 62

Paul's Ladder: The Fruit of the Spirit

I was encouraged by counsel I received from other inspired writings, such as this: "If you will go to work as Christ designs that His disciples shall, and win souls for Him, you will feel the need of a deeper experience and a greater knowledge in divine things, and will hunger and thirst after righteousness. You will plead with God, and your faith will be strengthened, and your soul will drink deeper drafts at the well of salvation. Encountering opposition and trials will drive you to the Bible and prayer" (*Steps to Christ*, p. 80). And that is what happened! I began to devour the words of scripture which I read. After seeing God's promises on Jacob's ladder, discovering what true love is on Peter's ladder, understanding what peace is on God's ladder, and finding joy on Jesus' ladder, along with all the other character traits enumerated on each of those ladders, I needed to know how to put them into action in my daily life. So instead of mounting Paul's ladder and reviewing all the virtuous characteristics we attained to already, let's find out what we should do with the character traits we have put on, realizing that all must result from self-control—our choosing the control of the Holy Spirit.

> "As you receive the Spirit of Christ—the Spirit of unselfish love and labor for others—you will grow and bring forth fruit. The graces of the Spirit will ripen in your character. Your faith will increase, your convictions deepen, your love be made perfect. More and more you will reflect the likeness of Christ in all that is pure, noble, and lovely."
>
> *Christ's Object Lessons*, p. 68

Just as we receive love, joy, peace, and all the other graces as gifts from God, so is self-control a gift. All are externally originated and given to believers to the measure that they are willing to receive them. None are internally generated. It is just the same with self-control. Yet, some think that they control themselves. This is an exhibition of self-exaltation, as they demonstrate to us that they can be good on their own.

God-given "self-esteem" requires abandonment of any notion of self-importance or self-success. It means that we realize our true worth and ultimate identity as God's children, redeemed by His love. Thus, self-control is equal to self-denial, or being crucified with Christ.

"I have been crucified with Christ; it is no longer I who live, but Christ lives in me; and the life which I now live in the flesh I live by faith in the Son of God, who loved me and gave Himself for me" (Gal. 2:20).

> "Whenever man accomplishes anything, whether in spiritual or in temporal lines, he should bear in mind that he does it through co-operation with his Maker. There is great necessity for us to realize our dependence on God."
>
> *Christ's Object Lessons*, p. 82

"Then Jesus said to His disciples, 'If anyone desires to come after Me, let him deny himself, and take up his cross, and follow Me'" (Matt. 16:2).

It must be a daily surrender. "It is the work of God in laying the glory of man in the dust, and doing for man that which it is not in his power to do for himself. When men see their own nothingness, they are prepared to be clothed with the righteousness of Christ" (*The Faith I Live By*, p. 111).

Our feelings and emotions are not dependable to act upon. We must know God's will. "The heart is deceitful above all things, and desperately wicked; Who can know it? I, the LORD, search the heart, I test the mind, Even to give every man according to his ways, According to the fruit of his doings" (Jer. 17:9, 10).

> "Beset with temptations without number, we must resist firmly or be conquered.... Paul's sanctification was the result of a constant conflict with self. He said: 'I die daily.' 1 Corinthians 15:31. His will and his desires every day conflicted with duty and the will of God. Instead of following inclination, he did God's will, however crucifying to his own nature. God leads His people on step by step."
>
> *Testimonies for the Church*, vol. 8, pp. 312, 313

My feelings had been so repressed when I was a young child that I hardly knew what feelings were. I lived in constant fear that I would do something wrong, but I had no idea what that wrong was. I learned a lot about feelings when I was teaching special needs children and began to examine my own. I finally realized I did not control my feelings; I only turned them inward. Years later, I learned that the root of my problem was bitterness. God speaks to that: "Pursue peace with all people, and holiness, without which no one can see the Lord: looking carefully lest anyone fall short of the grace of God; lest any root of bitterness springing up cause trouble, and by this many become defiled" (Heb. 12:14, 15).

In an article by Jim Wilson titled "How to be Free From Bitterness," I learned that bitterness accumulates. The roots go down deeper each time it manifests itself. Bitterness makes you sick if it is kept suppressed for long periods of time. I learned that guilt is what I felt when I sinned against someone else, and bitterness is what I felt when someone sinned against me or even if I thought they sinned against me. I learned that there are three solutions to bitterness:

1. Keep the bitterness in, and make yourself sick.

2. Let it out on others and spread the sickness around.

3. Make God's solution your own.

God's solution is to dig up the root. Get rid of it. But this takes the grace of God.

> Who is wise and understanding among you? Let him show by good conduct that his works are done in the meekness of wisdom. But if you have bitter envy and self-seeking in your hearts, do not boast and lie against the truth. This wisdom does not descend from above, but is earthly, sensual, demonic. For where envy and self-seeking exist, confusion and every evil thing are there. But the wisdom that is from above is first pure, then peaceable, gentle, willing to yield, full of mercy and good fruits, without partiality and without hypocrisy. Now the fruit of righteousness is sown in peace by those who make peace." (James 3:13–18)

Turning them over to Jesus and asking Him to be in control has been a long time coming. But I am thankful to have done so because now I get hurt much less when I am reviled by the words of others. I have learned to respond by saying, "Father, forgive them, for they know not what they do" (see Luke 23:34).

> "No man can of himself understand his errors.... In one way only can a true knowledge of self be obtained. We must behold Christ.... When we contemplate His purity and excellence, we shall see our own weakness and poverty and defects as they really are. We shall see ourselves lost and hopeless ... We shall see that if we are ever saved, it will not be through our own goodness, but through God's infinite grace."
>
> *Christ's Object Lessons*, p. 159

God gave me peace on His ladder, and Jesus' ladder taught me that I can retain that peace and have joy in spite of persecution. Once I was able to experience that "wonderful peace, coming down from the Father above" that Warren Cornell wrote about in the hymn "Wonderful Peace," I was able to give the glory to God. Now I can say with the angels at the birth of Jesus: "Glory to God in the highest, And on earth peace, goodwill, toward men" (Luke 2:14).

With the "peace of God, which surpasses all understanding" in my heart, there is no longer any need to fear (see Phil. 4:7). I can be happy because I know how much God loves me. "While the Christian's life will be characterized by humility, it should not be marked with sadness and self-depreciation. It is the privilege of everyone so to live that God will approve and bless him. It is not the will of our heavenly Father that we should be ever under condemnation and darkness" (*The Great Controversy*, p. 477).

"So Jesus said to them again, 'Peace to you; As the Father has sent Me, I also send you'" (John 20:21).

It is only after we have received Jesus' peace that we can be sent where God wants us to go. We only have to be willing, or willing to be made willing. "And He said to them, 'Go into all the world and preach the gospel to every creature'" (Mark 16:15).

> "Service to God includes personal ministry. By personal effort we are to co-operate with Him for the saving of the world.... All who are ordained unto the life of Christ are ordained to work for the salvation of their fellow men. Their hearts will throb in unison with the heart of Christ. The same longing for souls that He has felt will be manifest in them. Not all can fill the same place in the work, but there is a place and a work for all."
>
> *Christ's Object Lessons*, pp. 300, 301

As soon as my husband and I were baptized and joined the church, we were given positions of responsibility, which we gladly fulfilled. The children were young, so I taught in the children's division. Later, I served as Sabbath school superintendent, church clerk, treasurer, deaconess, and elder, as well as on conference and union committees. Unfortunately, I have always tried to be a "people pleaser," as well as wanting to "please God," and it was hard for me to say "no" when I was asked to serve.

God also made it possible for me to go to college and get a degree, which would enable me to help financially when the children were ready for college. I had compassion for people and decided to major in social work, so I could help people in need. But God had other plans for me. I still lacked one year of getting my degree at the University of Idaho. I started taking classes there when I began driving the children to Moscow, so they could attend church school. We still had two children in academy and two in college. My husband had retired with a disability, so he decided to enroll in classes that would enable him to operate a printing press. He had exceptional mechanical skills.

At that time we decided to move to College Pace, Washington, near Walla Walla, Washington where we could all go to school and cut out much of our expenses. I did not realize that Walla Walla College did not have a degree in social work until after we had moved. When I showed up to register, I was informed of this. What a disappointment! I was so looking forward to having instructions from Christian teachers, who would teach from the biblical perspective, but that dream was gone. I wanted to get any other degree it would take at least two years because I did not have the required Bible classes. However, there was a caring pastor counselor there, who advised me to go over to nearby Whitman College. I could major in sociology there.

When I presented my transcripts to admissions at Whitman, they enrolled me in classes that would result in a double major of sociology and elementary education, which had been my ambition throughout my elementary and high school days. God knew what I needed.

After I graduated I applied for a social work position. The interview was scheduled to be on the Sabbath. I asked for a change in time but was denied. I knew I could protest because, by law, they would have to accommodate my religious beliefs. I decided that there might be more pitfalls along the way and decided to apply for a teaching position. There was an opening at Rogers, which was the elementary church school in College Place. I applied there and was offered the position to teach second grade, which was my first choice. However, I had to decline.

My husband was ready to move back home to Potlatch because the printing presses were becoming obsolete because of new technology, and his teacher informed him that the church would never offer him a job because of his age. Again, God had other plans. I phoned the superintendent of the Potlatch school district to find out if they had any teaching positions open.

After he spoke with the principal of the elementary school, he called back and offered me a job teaching second grade! But that was not to be either. God had other plans. Two weeks before school started, the second grade teacher, who was supposed to retire, changed her mind and asked to remain teaching. The principal called and asked if I would take the job of teaching remedial reading, so I accepted. I had never even taught reading and had no special training to teach remedial reading. However, I remembered the Bible passage my mother had often quoted: "Not that I speak in regard to need, for I have learned in whatever state I am, to be content: I know how to be abased, and I know how to abound. Everywhere and in all things I have learned both to be full and to be hungry, both to abound and to suffer need. I can do all things through Christ who strengthens me" (Phil. 4:11–13).

After I started teaching in public school, I thought a good thing to do would be to sell the children's story books since I knew so many children who really needed reading skills, and I could encourage the parents to help by reading to them. I made contact with the conference and expressed my desire to sell books in the summer.

They seemed pleased and invited me to the retreat for their book salesmen. I attended, listened carefully to the instructions given, and went home with the counsel to wait until I was called and then a worker would go out with me the first week. They never called, and I reasoned again that this was not God's plan for me, so I did not pursue it further. However, I knew these children had other problems besides poor reading skills, and I took evening and summer classes to learn about special education, and eventually, I earned a master's degree. Then, I was qualified to start a special education program for the school district.

I enjoyed learning new things, so I continued taking classes in the evenings and during the summers after our children were away and added school psychologist and counselor to my credentials. There was never a dull moment at work. We had a small school district, and I wore many hats and enjoyed my job.

God gave us each different gifts and abilities, as Paul said:

> There are diversities of gifts, but the same Spirit. There are differences of ministries, but the same Lord. And there are diversities of activities, but it is the same God who works all in all. But the manifestation of the Spirit is given to each one for the profit of all: for to one is given the word of wisdom through the Spirit, to another the word of knowledge through the same Spirit, to another faith by the same Spirit, to another gifts of healings by the same Spirit, to another the working of miracles, to another prophecy, to another discerning of spirits, to another different kinds of tongues, to another the interpretation of tongues. But one and the same Spirit works all these things, distributing to each one individually as He wills. (1 Cor. 12:4–11)

These are spiritual gifts, but we are also given physical gifts or abilities. Learning to ride a bicycle was one of the hardest physical things I had to learn. I had wanted a bicycle for years, and I had even prayed that God would send me one. It didn't happen. As a child I never had a bicycle of my own, but my brothers had an old boy's bicycle. The seat was so high that my feet could barely reach the pedals. When they were not around, I would try to ride it. I would just get one leg over the bar and to the pedal on the opposite side when I would fall over. I did finally master it, but not until after receiving many hurts and bruises. That has been the story of my life–trying to do things on my own without a teacher.

I knew nothing about child-rearing when I had my children. That was my primary reason for beginning to take classes at the university. I'm so thankful that Jesus has always intervened and rescued me, even though most of the knowledge I needed came later in life.

Although I worked for the public school district, I was willing to do testing for students in the church school when the teachers asked for my help. Seeing the need in our small school, I reasoned that our church school teachers might profit by having a special education consultant for the conference, so I proposed that they add an itinerant teacher. Since all of my own children were in academy and college by this time, and my husband was retired, I thought it would be an interesting challenge as well as a service to the teachers and children. However, the response I got was "We have no need for special education in our church schools." I accepted the rejection and continued in my position in public school. I retired after twenty years of service.

I did not realize it at the time but now I know how much I was greatly influenced by the humanistic teaching, which resulted from my education in secular public institutions. Again, the verse my mother often spoke came to my mind. "And we know that all things work together for good to those who love God, to those who are the called according to His purpose" (Rom. 8:28).

The administrators respected my religious beliefs by not requiring any Friday night duties such as supervision at ball games and joining the teachers' union; however, there were times when I felt resentment from some of the teachers.

> "The last rays of merciful light, the last message of mercy to be given to the world, is a revelation of His character of love. The children of God are to manifest His glory. In their own life and character they are to reveal what the grace of God has done for them. The light of the Sun of Righteousness is to shine forth in good works—in words of truth and deeds of holiness."
> *Christ's Object Lessons*, pp. 415, 416

I realize now that my actions at that time where only a "form of godliness," but God did not leave me there. Now I know that our "good works" are nothing if we do it for selfish reasons. Our works do not save us. It is the righteousness of Christ in us shining forth that manifests the glory of God.

We are told that this is done through the church, and we make up the church.

> The church, being endowed with the righteousness of Christ, is His depository, in which the wealth of His mercy, His love, His grace, is to appear in full and final display.... The gift of His Holy Spirit, rich, full, and abundant, is to be to His church as an encompassing wall of fire, which the powers of hell shall not prevail against. In their untainted purity and spotless perfection, Christ looks upon His people as the reward of all His suffering, His humiliation, and His love, and the supplement of His glory–Christ, the great center from which radiates all glory (*Testimonies to Ministers and Gospel Workers*, pp. 18, 19).

The thought that we can be the "supplement of His glory" is a thrilling one to me.

We can only be this supplement if we get our direction from God's Word and show forth the fruit of His Spirit–His character traits.

Jesus warns us of false prophets, and in Matthew, He tells us one of the ways to distinguish the true from the false. He says:

> Beware of false prophets, who come to you in sheep's clothing, but inwardly they are ravenous wolves. You will know them by their fruits. Do men gather grapes from thornbushes or figs from thistles? Even so, every good tree bears good fruit, but a bad tree bears bad fruit. A good tree cannot bear bad fruit, nor can a bad tree bear good fruit. Every tree that does not bear good fruit is cut down and thrown into the fire. Therefore by their fruits you will know them. (Matt. 7:15–20)

Have you ever known someone who is always busy helping others, but they always have a happy and peaceful look on their face? I believe that is the gift of God as Isaiah describes it. "The work of righteousness will be peace, And the effect of righteousness, quietness and assurance forever" (Isa. 32:17).

It has been such a joy to me to learn these things, to have the peace that is above understanding, and to know that it is God directing my life day by day for as long as I choose to stay surrendered to Him. I will not forget my song of commitment.

> "Men and women enjoying the religion of Jesus Christ will not be uneasy, restless, discontented, changeable; the peace of Christ in the heart will give solidity to character. You must not let anything rob your soul of peace, of restfulness, of the assurance that you are accepted just now. Appropriate every promise; all are yours on condition of your complying with the Lord's prescribed terms. Entire surrender of your ways, which seem so very wise, and taking Christ's ways, is the secret of perfect rest in His love."
>
> *My Life Today*, p. 176

Throughout the book of Psalms, I have found many instances where the author laments the fact that wicked people seem to get ahead in life. What should we do when we find ourselves becoming envious of those who appear to have it all, even though they acquired their wealth or success through questionable means? We found the answer on God's ladder. We must have the ability to be thankful for the blessings of others. God will take care of His people. "Mark the blameless man, and observe the upright; For the future of that man is peace" (Ps. 37:37).

The Greek word for patience is *hupomone*, which means "fortitude, steadfast endurance." We received this patience on Peter's ladder. Some translations use the word "longsuffering," which Webster's defines as "patiently enduring lasting offense or hardship" (Merriam-Webster, http://www.merriam-webster.com/dictionary/longsuffering, [accessed May 10, 2013]). Paul had learned patience. "Now may the Lord direct your hearts into the love of God and into the patience of Christ" (2 Thess. 3:5).

> "The heart that is in harmony with God is a partaker of the peace of heaven, and will diffuse its blessed influence all around. The spirit of peace will rest like dew upon hearts weary and troubled with worldly strife."
>
> *Reflecting Christ*, p. 278

He also had learned that he had no goodness in himself. "As it is written: 'There is none righteous, no, not one; There is none who understands; There is none who seeks after God'" (Rom. 3:10, 11).

Paul expresses the need to turn to righteousness so well. "And so all Israel will be saved as it is written: 'The Deliverer will come out of Zion, And He will turn away ungodliness from Jacob; For this is My covenant with them, When I take away their sins'" (Rom. 11:26, 27).

When my husband died, someone said to me "He was a very gentle man." I had never identified his character traits, except love—above all else, I knew he loved me. But I wondered what she meant by her remark. I had a faint idea; he didn't have a mean bone in his body! I thought about how you handle things gently if you don't want them to break. So I referred to Webster's Dictionary. The definition of gentle is "considerate or kindly; not harsh, severe, or violent." And gentleness is defined as "the quality or state of being gentle; especially: mildness of manners or disposition" (Merriam-Webster, http://www.merriam-webster.com/dictionary/gentleness, [accessed May 10, 2013]). Yes, he was very gentle. I was the harsh, severe member of the family when it came to requiring obedience from our children. How I regret some of that ... but I believe they have forgiven me, and I know God has. As Peter instructed in the Bible, I have added "knowledge to virtue" throughout my years, and the power of the Holy Spirit is growing me in grace, but I have a ways to go yet.

Peter showed that by adding virtue-grace-power, we would gain more knowledge, and to that knowledge we would add all the other character traits leading to love and self-control.

Peter placed self-control after knowledge on his ladder and followed with patience and perseverance. Did you ever see a patient person who did not have self control? Now, on Paul's ladder we can benefit from the knowledge to which Peter referred. It is the gift of the Holy Spirit that draws us to accept the gift of faith, and it is the power of the Holy Spirit that takes us to the top.

Finally at the top, I understood that it is Christ's gentleness, faithfulness, goodness, kindness, patience, peace, love, and joy, which would demonstrate the self-control that I needed.

I now knew that I had only fooled myself by doing all "the right things" without recognizing that if I did do anything right, it was the Holy Spirit working within me. Previously, I only had a "form of godliness."

I had self-control! I was in control, but I finally got the message that what I needed was God-control. We cannot do this work ourselves, but we can choose to let the Holy Spirit be in control. Christ alone can renew the heart and give us the strength to always use integrity, firmness, and perseverance in doing His work.

We have confessed our deficit of the Holy Spirit, mourned because of our sinfulness, demonstrated our meekness by our humility, sought His righteousness, been merciful and pure in heart, and become a peacemaker. Now, in spite of the trials that have come as a result of staying on the ladder with Jesus, Paul, just as Peter and Jesus have done, shows us the character traits our behavior must be initiated by–the power of the Holy Spirit.

Paul learned these lessons well. From starting as a Jew who persecuted or killed every follower of Christ, to ending up as a follower who put forth the same zeal to gain more followers as he had in trying to exterminate those who worshipped the true God. The Holy Spirit was truly the one responsible for his transformation.

> "Strength of character consists of two things—power of will and power of self-control.... The real greatness and nobility of the man is measured by the power of the feelings that he subdues, not by the power of the feelings that subdue him. The strongest man is he, who, while sensitive to abuse, will yet restrain passion and forgive his enemies. Such men are true heroes."
>
> *Testimonies Treasures*, vol. 1, p. 602

Peter's, God's, Jesus', and Paul's ladders follow the model of the ladder Jacob dreamed about, which reached from earth to heaven. The Holy Spirit, through Paul, has shown us the fruit representing Christ's character. And Jesus has said, "You will know them by their fruits" (Matt. 7:16). James' desire has become mine: to "show you my faith by my works" (see James 2:18), which must be the work of the Holy Spirit.

"Therefore be patient, brethren, until the coming of the Lord. See how the farmer waits for the precious fruit of the earth, waiting patiently for it until it receives the early and latter rain. You also be patient. Establish your hearts, for the coming of the Lord is at hand" (James 5:7, 8).

> "The highest evidence of nobility in a Christian is self-control. He who can stand unmoved amid a storm of abuse is one of God's heroes.... The largest share of life's annoyances, its heartaches, its irritations, is due to uncontrollable temper. In one moment, by hasty, passionate, careless words, may be wrought evil that a whole lifetime's repentance cannot undo.... Overwork sometimes causes a loss of self-control. But the Lord never compels hurried, complicated movements. Many gather to themselves burdens that the merciful heavenly Father did not place on them. Duties He never designed them to perform chase one another wildly. God desires us to realize that we do not glorify His name when we take so many burdens that we are overtaxed and, becoming heart-weary and brain-weary, chafe and fret and scold. We are to bear only the responsibilities that the Lord gives us, trusting in Him, and thus keeping our hearts pure and sweet and sympathetic."
>
> *Reflecting Christ*, p. 292

One of my biggest regrets before I came to know Jesus is taking on so many educational ventures and church responsibilities when my children were young. I did a lot of chafing, fretting and scolding when they were not warranted. Now I know that "In his own strength man cannot rule his spirit. But through Christ he may gain self-control" (*Reflecting Christ*, p. 293).

"For it is God who works in you both to will and to do for His good pleasure" (Phil. 2:13).

Who is in control of my life? Paul admonishes us to examine ourselves and find out. "But let each one examine his own work, and then he will have rejoicing in himself alone, and not in another. For each one shall bear his own load" (Gal. 6:4, 5).

An article entitled "Pray for the Latter Rain" published in the Review and Herald on March 2, 1897 says, "Unless we are daily advancing in the exemplification of the active Christian virtues, we shall not recognize the manifestations of the Holy Spirit in the latter rain."

> "Christ says: 'I have chosen you, and ordained you, that you should go and bring forth fruit, and that your fruit should remain.' As Christ's ambassador, I would entreat of all who read these lines to take heed while it is called today. 'If ye will hear his voice, harden not your hearts.' Without waiting a moment, inquire, What am I to Christ? and what is Christ to me? What is my work? What is the character of the fruit I bear?"
>
> "Ordained to Bring Forth Fruit,"
> *Review and Herald*, February 12, 1895

How can one know whether he or she is daily advancing in the exemplification of the "active Christian virtues?"

> "The individual members of the church should be jealous for their own souls, critically watching their own actions, lest they should move from selfish motives and be a cause of stumbling to their weak brethren."
>
> *Testimonies for the Church*, vol. 4, p. 489

> "Self-knowledge leads to humility and to trust in God, but it does not take the place of efforts for self-improvement. He who realizes his own deficiencies will spare no pains to reach the highest possible standard of physical, mental, and moral excellence."
>
> *Counsels to Parents, Teachers, and Students*, p. 67

We are further counseled to ask ourselves some hard questions.

> We are to reflect His glory. Have we done this in the past? Have we revealed the character of our Lord by precept and example? Have we not joined in the work of the enemy of souls and misrepresented our heavenly Father? Have we not been passing judgment on our brethren, criticizing their words and actions? Then the love of God has not been enthroned in our souls. Let us make a decided change. (*Faith and Works*, p. 61)

God will reveal our character defects if we ask Him. Often it is through life's trials.

> It is in mercy that the Lord reveals to men their hidden defects. He would have them critically examine the complicated emotions and motives of their own hearts, and detect that which is wrong, and modify their dispositions and refine their manners. God would have His servants become acquainted with their own hearts. In order to bring to them a true knowledge of their condition, He permits the fire of affliction to assail them, so that they may be purified. The trials of life are God's workmen to remove the impurities, infirmities, and roughness from our characters, and fit them for the society of pure, heavenly angels in glory.... The fire will not consume us, but only remove the dross, and we shall come forth seven times purified, bearing the impress of the Divine. (*My Life Today*, p. 92)

Jesus prayed for unity in the church.

> I do not pray for these alone, but also for those who will believe in Me through their word; that they all may be one, as You, Father, are in Me, and I in You; that they also may be one in Us, that the world may believe that You sent Me. And the glory which You gave Me I have given them, that they may be one just as We are one: I in them, and You in Me; that they may be made perfect in one, and that the world may know that You have sent Me, and have loved them as You have loved Me. (John 17:20–23)

Ellen White wrote "If the professed followers of Christ would accept God's standard, it would bring them into unity; but so long as human wisdom is exalted above the Holy Word, there will be divisions and dissension" (*Patriarchs and Prophets*, p. 124).

What is "God's standard?" About the time I read this quotation, I was searching for an area to study for my doctoral dissertation, and I decided that this was it! So I met with my committee and presented my proposal: "Values of Seventh-day Adventist Families in Northwestern United States." They denied my proposal because they said, "You cannot measure values." However, they were impressed at what I wanted to do and suggested that I change the title to "Standards of Family Life Among Seventh-day Adventists in Northwestern United States." That better identified the purpose of my study which was "to identify the standards Seventh-day Adventists in the Upper-Columbia Conference felt to be important to successful family living, and to determine the extent to which they perceived they were achieving those standards." The Upper-Columbia Conference was my laboratory.

Group-dynamic process sessions were held to obtain data which was used to construct a questionnaire. The questionnaire was administered to 1474 people from eighteen churches that were randomly selected as well as residence students at Upper Columbia Academy and Walla Walla College. They responded by rating ten items in five areas: family communication, use of time, worship habits, health practices, and other-orientation.

A comparison of scores between importance and achievement implied that believing something is important does not necessarily mean that one is also achieving that goal. On the other hand, these results may be influenced by poor self-concepts among sample members or unrealistic self-evaluations.

I will only mention two things that impressed me. First, that family worship scored lowest in achievement, and secondly, use of time scored lowest in importance. We all have the same amount of time each day, and how we use it determines what we achieve. Perhaps we should think about using more of our time in family worship or for our own worship if we are alone.

Psychologists have discovered that the emotional center of the brain is influenced by many factors, beginning with our inherited temperament. That explains why some people are excitable by nature, while others are passive or indifferent. After that, life's experiences, education, beliefs, and most significantly, the mind, influences how we feel. But we can be assured that there is hope for change in the mental faculties through Christ.

> "When the sunlight of God's love illuminates the darkened chambers of the soul, then restless weariness and dissatisfaction will cease, and satisfying joys will give vigor to the mind and health and energy to the body."
>
> *The Ministry of Healing*, p. 247

I must remember there are two sources of power and light seeking to draw us—the deceptive light and power of Satan, and the true light that gives us the love, joy, and peace that Paul chose. I have chosen as Paul did.

We must have the Spirit of God, and not the spirit of Satan, the deceiver. If my pride and self-centeredness is gone then I will produce the fruit that grows by love and comes by faith.

> "When men and women are truly converted, they will conscientiously regard the laws of life that God has established in their being, thus seeking to avoid physical, mental, and moral feebleness. Obedience to these laws must be made a matter of personal duty. We ourselves must suffer the ills of violated law. We must answer to God for our habits and practices. Therefore the question for us is not, 'What will the world say?' but, 'How shall I, claiming to be a Christian, treat the habitation God has given me?'"
>
> "A Habitation for the Spirit," *The Review and Herald*, December 31, 1908

> "Those who rose up with Jesus would send up their faith to Him in the holiest, and pray, 'My Father, give us Thy Spirit.' Then Jesus would breathe upon them the Holy Ghost. In that breath was light, power, and much love, joy and peace. I turned to look at the company who were still bowed before the throne; they did not know that Jesus had left it. Satan appeared to be by the throne, trying to carry on the work of God. I saw them look up to the throne, and pray, 'Father, give us Thy Spirit.' Satan would then breathe upon them an unholy influence; in it there was light and much power, but no sweet love, joy, and peace. Satan's object was to keep them deceived and to draw back and deceive God's children."
>
> *Early Writings*, pp. 55, 56

"But someone will say, 'You have faith, and I have works.' Show me your faith without your works, and I will show you my faith by my works" (James 2:18). "Who is he who overcomes the world, but he who believes that Jesus is the Son of God" (1 John 5:5). "... In the world you will have tribulation; but be of good cheer, I have overcome the world" (John 16:33).

> "Whatever may be our inherited or cultivated tendencies to wrong, we can overcome through the power that He is ready to impart."
>
> *God's Amazing Grace*, p. 254

> "God will accept only those who are determined to aim high. He places every human agent under obligation to do his best. Moral perfection is required of all. Never should we lower the standard of righteousness in order to accommodate inherited and cultivated tendencies to wrongdoing. We need to understand that imperfection of character is sin. All righteous attributes of character dwell in God as a perfect, harmonious whole, and every one who receives Christ as a personal Saviour is privileged to possess these attributes."
>
> *My Life Today*, p. 271

Paul tells us what we need to do: "... Be transformed by the renewing of your mind, that you may prove what is good and acceptable and perfect will of God" (Rom. 12:2). He also tells us what he did: "But I discipline my body and bring it into subjection, lest, when I have preached to others, I myself should become disqualified" (1 Cor. 9:27). And he tells us he did it by his faith: "Trust in the Lord with all your heart And lean not on your own understanding; In all your ways acknowledge Him, And He shall direct your paths" (Prov. 3:5, 6).

Our spiritual, physical, and mental healing depends on these three issues. We must "be transformed" by the renewal of our minds. We must "discipline" our bodies. And, we must "Trust in the Lord" with all our hearts and lean not on our own understanding. Sounds simple, doesn't it? But we have learned that "of ourselves we can do nothing." It is the power of the Holy Spirit that God gave us when we accepted His robe of righteousness that will work in us and through us. I believe Jesus' path is straight and easy to follow, but it is in a vertical direction. We must climb the ladder, step-by-step, and not fall off as it becomes narrower.

Ladders are wide at the bottom and get narrower and narrower as the top is reached. That is the way it was with Jacob's ladder. The closer we get to the top, the dross has been refined more and more until we become that polished jewel that shines with the brightness of the image of God. We can only enter the kingdom of glory if we become like Jesus. He said, "Enter by the narrow gate; for wide is the gate and broad is the way that leads to destruction, and there are many who go in by it. Because narrow is the gate and difficult is the way which leads to life, and there are few who find it" (Matt. 7:13).

However, to encourage us, He also said, "Come to Me, all you who labor and are heavy laden, and I will give you rest. Take My yoke upon you and learn from Me, for I am gentle and lowly in heart, and you will find rest for your souls. For My yoke is easy and My burden is light" (Matt. 11:28–30).

> "[Jesus] was never elated by applause, nor dejected by censure or disappointment.... But many who profess to be His followers have an anxious, troubled heart ... They do not make a complete surrender to Him; for they shrink from the consequences that such a surrender may involve.... It is the love of self that brings unrest. When we are born from above, the same mind will be in us that was in Jesus, the mind that led Him to humble Himself that we might be saved."
>
> *The Desire of Ages*, 330, 331

It is not about what we do; it's about what Christ has done for us. How important it is to give all our young people the opportunity of a Christian education.

> True education imparts this wisdom. It teaches the best use not only of one but of all our powers and acquirements.... Character building is the most important work ever entrusted to human beings; and never before was its diligent study so important as now. Never was any previous generation called to meet issues so momentous; never before were young men and young women confronted by perils so great as confront them today. (*Education*, p. 225)

There is also much counsel from scripture and the writings of Ellen White regarding pastors.

> To every young man who enters the ministry, Paul's words to Timothy are spoken 'Take heed unto thyself, and unto the doctrine.' [1 Timothy 4:16.] 'Thyself' needs the first attention. First give yourself to the Lord for purification and sanctification. A godly example will tell more for the truth than the greatest eloquence, unaccompanied by a well-ordered life. Trim the lamp of the soul, and replenish it with the oil of the Spirit. Seek from Christ that grace, that clearness of comprehension, which will enable you to do successful work. Learn from Him what it means to work for those for whom He gave His life. 'Take heed,' first to yourself, and then to the doctrine. Do not let your heart become hardened by sin. Closely examine your manners and habits. Compare them with the word of God, and then cut away from the life every wrong habit and indulgence. (*Gospel Workers 1915*, pp. 104, 105)

Paul counsels us to "cut away from the life every wrong habit and indulgence." This requires effort on our part, but we can only do it with His power dwelling within us. Each must study the Bible, pray, consult with other Christians, etc.

> "If the soul is to be purified and ennobled, and made fit for the heavenly courts, there are two lessons to be learned—self-sacrifice and self-control. Some learn these important lessons more easily than do others, for they are exercised by the simple discipline the Lord gives them in gentleness and love. Others require the slow discipline of suffering, that the cleansing fire may purify their hearts of pride and self-reliance, of earthly passion and self-love, that the true gold of character may appear and that they may become victors through the grace of Christ."
>
> *Faith and Works*, p. 86

"And my God shall supply all your need according to His riches in glory by Christ Jesus" (Phil. 4:19). "I can do all things through Jesus Christ who strengthens me" (Phil. 4:13).

> "The individual members of the church should be jealous for their own souls, critically watching their own actions, lest they should move from selfish motives and be a cause of stumbling to their weak brethren."
>
> *Testimonies for the Church*, vol. 4, p. 489

Paul was very vocal on this matter. "For if we would judge ourselves, we should not be judged" (1 Cor. 11:31). But he does imply that pastors have a responsibility to judge or reprove those in the church. "For what have I do with judging those also who are outside? Do you not judge those who are inside? But those who are outside God judges ..." (1 Cor. 5:12, 13).

As we are transformed, we will be compelled to try to help others.

Paul's Ladder: The Fruit of the Spirit

> "Jesus reproved His disciples. He warned and cautioned them; but John and his brethren did not leave Him; they chose Jesus, notwithstanding the reproofs. The Saviour did not withdraw from them because of their weakness and errors. They continued to the end to share His trials and to learn the lessons of His life. By beholding Christ, they became transformed in character."
>
> *The Desire of Ages*, p. 296

> Brethren, if a man is overtaken in any trespass, you who are spiritual restore such a one in a spirit of gentleness, considering yourself lest you also be tempted. Bear one another's burdens, and so fulfill the law of Christ. For if anyone thinks himself to be something, when he is nothing, he deceives himself. But let each one examine his own work, and then he will have rejoicing in himself alone, and not in another. For each one shall bear his own load. Let him who is taught the word share in all good things with him who teaches. Do not be deceived, God is not mocked; for whatever a man sows, that he will also reap. For he who sows to his flesh will of the flesh reap corruption, but he who sows to the Spirit will of the Spirit reap everlasting life. And let us not grow weary while doing good, for in due season we shall reap if we do not lose heart. Therefore, as we have opportunity, let us do good to all, especially to those who are of the household of faith. (Gal. 6:1–10)

Speaking of Paul: "The inmost thoughts and emotions of his heart were transformed by divine grace; and his nobler faculties were brought into harmony with the eternal purposes of God. Christ and His righteousness became to Saul more than the whole world" (*The Acts of the Apostles*, p. 120).

Each of us is free to choose for ourselves which spirit we allow to lead us.

> Every seed sown produces a harvest of its kind. So it is in human life. We all need to sow the seeds of compassion, sympathy, and love; for we shall reap what we sow. Every characteristic of selfishness, self-love, self-esteem, every act of self-indulgence, will bring forth a like harvest. He who lives for self is sowing to the flesh, and of the flesh he will reap corruption. (*Christ's Object Lessons*, p. 84)

It was the same ladder that Jacob saw in his vision that Paul saw on the road to Damascus. It was shining so bright with the glory of God that it blinded him.

> This man of faith beholds the ladder of Jacob's vision, representing Christ, who has connected earth with heaven, and finite man with the infinite God. His faith is strengthened as he calls to mind how patriarchs and prophets have relied upon the One who is his support and consolation, and for whom he is giving his life .... Like a trumpet peal his voice has rung out through all the ages since, nerving with his own courage thousands of witnesses for Christ and wakening in thousands of sorrow-stricken hearts the echo of his own triumphant joy: '... I have fought a good fight, I have finished my course, I have kept the faith: henceforth there is laid up for me a crown

of righteousness, which the Lord, the righteous Judge, shall give me at that day....' (*The Acts of the Apostles*, pp. 512, 513)

My goal is to "fight a good fight" of faith as Paul did and be ready for God's kingdom. James has told us what true religion is and being able to put that into practice is also through the gift of grace God has given us.

- "Pure and undefiled religion before God and the Father is this: to visit orphans and widows in their trouble, and to keep oneself unspotted from the world" (James 1:27).
- "He shall be like a tree Planted by the rivers of water That brings forth fruit in its season Whose leaf also shall not wither; And whatever he does shall prosper" (Ps. 1:3).
- Paul was like that tree after he was converted. He bore much fruit. "But the fruit of the Spirit is love, joy, peace, longsuffering, kindness, goodness, faithfulness, gentleness, self-control. Against such there is no law" (Gal. 5:22, 23).

Remember that there is just one fruit of the Spirit, and that one fruit includes all of the Christian graces enumerated in verses 22 and 23. In other words, all of these traits are to be present in the life of the Christian, and it cannot be said that he is bearing the fruit of the Spirit if one is missing. On the other hand, there are many different forms in which evil manifests itself, and only one of the evil traits need to be present for a man to be classified as one who produces the works of the flesh.

> Now the works of the flesh are evident, which are: adultery, fornication, uncleanness, lewdness, idolatry, sorcery, hatred, contentions, jealousies, outbursts of wrath, selfish ambitions, dissensions, heresies, envy, murders, drunkenness, revelries, and the like; of which I tell you beforehand, just as I also told you in time past, that those who practice such things will not inherit the kingdom of God. (Gal. 5:19–21)

"True sanctification is nothing more or less than to love God with all the heart, to walk in His commandments and ordinances blameless. Sanctification is not an emotion but a heaven-born principle, that brings all the passion and desires under the control of the Spirit of God; and this work is done through our Lord and Savior. Spurious sanctification does not glorify God but leads those who claim it to exalt and glorify themselves. Whatever comes in our experience, whether of joy or sorrow, that does not reflect Christ and point to Him as its author, bringing glory to Him and sinking self out of sight, is not true Christian experience."

Faith and Works, p. 87

When trials come sometimes fear arises, and we may think of our trials as punishment. That was the concept that Job's friends put to him. But like Job, we can say, "Though He slay me, yet will I trust Him ..." (Job 13:15).

Paul's Ladder: The Fruit of the Spirit

> "The love of God will strengthen the soul, and through the virtue (power) of the merits of the blood of Christ we may stand unscathed amid the fire of temptation and trial; but no other help can avail to save but Christ, our righteousness, who is made unto us wisdom and sanctification and redemption."
>
> *Faith and Works*, p. 86

God is a God of love, and He is allowing Satan to fill his cup of iniquity. Our reaction to the trials we have is our own choice. Like Joshua, I choose Jesus. "And if it seems evil to you to serve the LORD, choose for yourselves this day whom you will serve, whether the gods which your fathers served that were on the other side of the River, or the gods of the Amorites, in whose land you dwell. But as for me and my house, we will serve the LORD" (Josh. 24:15).

Let us look as Paul's ladder one more time. It has the traits that we must emulate in our own lives if we will be ready to meet Jesus when He returns.

I shall continue to study so that I am certain that I know God's will when I need to make a choice.

God had a plan from the beginning. I was hearing so much about evolution, I decided to go back to the very beginning and look at Creation week, so I could see how all this got started in the first place. Those seven days fit exactly on Jacob's ladder as God designed, to meet man's needs before He created them.

Let's take a look at how He prepared the place for humanity to live before He created them and the wonderful gifts He gave to them after they were created.

> "The closer you come to Jesus, the more faulty you will appear in your own eyes; for your vision will be clearer, and your imperfections will be seen in broad and distinct contrast to His perfect nature. This is evidence that Satan's delusions have lost their power; that the vivifying influence of the Spirit of God is arousing you. No deep-seated love for Jesus can dwell in the heart that does not realize its own sinfulness. The soul that is transformed by the grace of Christ will admire His divine character; but if we do not see our own moral deformity, it is unmistakable evidence that we have not had a view of the beauty and excellence of Christ. The less we see to esteem in ourselves, the more we shall see to esteem in the infinite purity and loveliness of our Savior. A view of our sinfulness drives us to Him who can pardon; and when the soul, realizing its helplessness, reaches out after Christ, He will reveal Himself in power. The more our sense of need drives us to Him and to the word of God, the more exalted views we shall have of His character, and the more fully we shall reflect His image."
>
> *Steps to Christ*, pp. 64, 65

Chapter Six
GOD'S CREATION LADDER

Did God create the world? If so, just how did he do it? These questions never occurred to me until after I started searching the Bible for answers to help me with how to "train up my children in the way they should go" (see Prov. 22:6). I had never asked myself, *Who am I? Why am I here? Where am I going?* So, how could I help them? In my search, I found the answers to both God's purpose and my own. Creation is still a subject of much debate. Some say the universe appeared after a sudden explosion. Others say God started the process, and the universe evolved over billions of years. Almost every ancient religion has its own story to explain how the world came to be. Almost every scientist has an opinion on the origin of the universe. But only the Bible shows one Supreme God creating the earth out of his great love and giving all people a special place in it. He gave us a perfect environment to live in where He would visit us. He created it for His chosen people to inhabit, which means He has chosen all of us.

> In the beginning God created the heavens and the earth. The earth was without form, and void; and darkness was on the face of the deep. And the Spirit of God was hovering over the face of the waters. Then God said, 'Let there be light'; and there was light. And God saw the light, that it was good; and God divided the light from the darkness. God called the light Day, and the darkness he called Night. So the evening and the morning were the first day. Then God said, 'Let there be a firmament in the midst of the waters, and let it divide the waters from the waters.' Thus God made the firmament, and divided the waters which were under the firmament from the waters which were above the firmament; and it was so. And God called the firmament Heaven. So the evening and the morning were the second day. Then God said, 'Let the waters under the heavens be gathered together into one place, and let the dry land appear'; and it was so. And God called the dry land Earth, and the gathering together of the waters He called Seas. And God saw that it was good. Then God said, 'Let the earth bring forth grass, the herb that yields seed, and the fruit tree that yields fruit according to its kind, whose seed is in itself, on the earth'; and it was so. And the earth brought forth grass, the herb that yields seed according to its kind, and the tree that yields fruit, whose seed is in itself according to its kind. And God saw that it was good. So the evening and the morning were the third day. Then God said, 'Let there be lights in the firmament of the heavens to divide the day from the night; and let them be for signs and seasons, and for days and years; and let them be for lights in the firmament of the heavens to give light on the earth'; and it was so. Then God made two great lights: the greater light to rule the day, and the lesser light to rule the night. He made the stars also. God set them in the firmament of the heavens to give light on the earth, and to rule over the day and over the night, and to divide the light from the

darkness. And God saw that it was good. So the evening and the morning were the fourth day. Then God said, 'Let the waters abound with an abundance of living creatures, and let birds fly above the earth across the face of the firmament of the heavens.' So God created great sea creatures and every living thing the moves, with which the waters abounded, according to their kind, and every winged bird according to its kind. And God saw that it was good. And God blessed them saying, 'Be fruitful and multiply, and fill the waters in the seas, and let birds multiply on the earth.' So the evening and the morning were the fifth day. Then God said, 'Let the earth bring forth the living creature according to its kind: cattle and creeping thing and beast of the earth, each according to its kind'; and it was so. And God made the beast of the earth according to its kind, cattle according to its kind, and everything that creeps on the earth according to its kind. And God saw that it was good. Then God said, 'Let Us make man in Our image, according to Our likeness; let them have dominion over the fish of the sea, over the birds of the air, and over the cattle, over all the earth and over every creeping

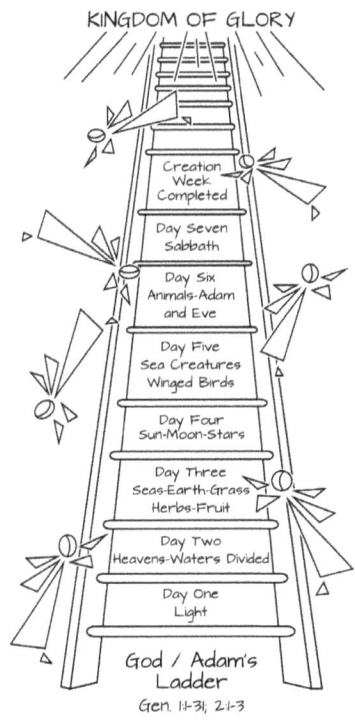

thing that creeps on the earth.' So God created man in His own image; in the image of God He created him; male and female He created them. Then God blessed them, and God said to them, 'Be fruitful and multiply; fill the earth and subdue it; have dominion over the fish of the sea, over the birds of the air, and over every living thing that moves on the earth.' And God said, 'See, I have given you every herb that yields seed which is on the face of all the earth and every tree whose fruit yields seed; to you it shall be for food. Also, to every beast of the earth, to every bird of the air, and to everything that creeps on the earth, in which there is life, I have given every green herb for food'; and it was so. Then God saw everything that He had made, and indeed it was very good. So the evening and the morning were the sixth day. Thus the heavens and the earth, and all the host of them, were finished. And on the seventh day God ended His work which He had done, and He rested on the seventh day from all His work which He had done. Then God blessed the seventh day and sanctified it, because in it He rested from all His work which God had created and made. (Gen. 1:1–2:3)

What an achievement for just seven days! Some question the length of each day, but the Bible is clear. A day consists of one evening and one morning. "… So the evening and the morning were the first day" (Gen. 1:5).

One twenty-four hour period is one literal day. It should not be confused with a prophetic day, which is when a day is represented as one year.

Some evolutionary theories teach randomness, chance, accidents, death, etc. They propose that if a creature happened to evolve something—say, a good pair of eyes—that enabled it to survive, it survived; if not, it died off and the blind species became extinct. Life on the earth was a vicious battle between creatures where only the strongest, or fittest, remained.

On the other hand, the Creation story in the Bible reveals that everything was perfectly planned, precise, and calculated. God created the world in an orderly fashion. He made those things that were necessary to sustain the life of the creation that followed, until He had all that would be necessary for humanity to live in a perfect world. He created men and women as unique beings capable of communicating with Him. No other part of creation can claim that remarkable privilege. He created it just the way He wanted it; He created, a perfect world.

> "Millions of years, it is claimed, were required for the evolution of the earth from chaos; and in order to accommodate the Bible to this supposed revelation of science, the days of creation are assumed to have been vast, indefinite periods, covering thousands or even millions of years. Such a conclusion is wholly uncalled for. The Bible record is in harmony with itself and with the teaching of nature. Of the first day employed in the work of creation is given the record, 'The evening and the morning were the first day.' Genesis 1:5. And the same in substance is said of each of the first six days of creation week. Each of these periods Inspiration declares to have been a day consisting of evening and morning, like every other day since that time. In regard to the work of creation itself the divine testimony is, 'He spake, and it was done; He commanded, and it stood fast.' Psalm 33:9. With Him who could thus call into existence unnumbered worlds, how long a time would be required for the evolution of the earth from chaos? In order to account for His works, must we do violence to His word?"
>
> *Education*, pp. 128, 129

CREATION: DAY ONE

Let's look at each day of creation in ascending order on the ladder as God prepares the place for humanity to live in, to care for the lower creatures, and to keep it the way that He made it.

"Then God said, 'Let there be light'; and there was light. And God saw the light, that it was good; and God divided the light from the darkness. God called the light Day, and the darkness He called Night. So the evening and the morning were the first day" (Gen. 1:3–5).

The first step on the ladder taught me that I must have the light of Jesus in my life. On the first day of the week, God created the most necessary thing for humanity's existence: light. I believe that the light was meant to represent the Lamb, Jesus, who would later be sacrificed for us. He said, "… I am the light of the world. He who follows Me shall not walk in darkness, but have the light of life" (John 8:12).

"And God said," with each day of Creation, makes it evident that God created the world by speaking it into existence. It might be hard to comprehend, but the Bible says God is so powerful than even the utterance of His words has profound creative power. He inspired His servant, David, to write "For He spoke, and it was done; He commanded, and it stood fast" (Ps. 33: 9).

> "God is light; and in the words, 'I am the light of the world,' Christ declared His oneness with God, and His relation to the whole human family. It was He who at the beginning had caused 'the light to shine out of darkness.' 2 Corinthians 4:6. He is the light of sun and moon and star. He was the spiritual light that in symbol and type and prophecy had shone upon Israel. But not to the Jewish nation alone was the light given. As the sunbeams penetrate to the remotest corners of the earth, so does the light of the Sun of Righteousness shine upon every soul."
>
> *The Desire of Ages*, p. 464

He also made clear how long it took. "For in six days the LORD made the heavens and the earth, the sea, and all that is in them, and rested the seventh day..." (Exod. 20:11).

> "When consideration is given to man's opportunities for research; how brief his life; how limited his sphere of action; how restricted his vision; how frequent and how great the errors in his conclusions, especially as concerns the events thought to antedate Bible history; how often the supposed deductions of science are revised or cast aside; with what readiness the assumed period of the earth's development is from time to time increased or diminished by millions of years; and how the theories advanced by different scientists conflict with one another,—considering all this, shall we, for the privilege of tracing our descent from germs and mollusks and apes, consent to cast away that statement of Holy Writ, so grand in its simplicity, 'God created man in His own image, in the image of God created He him'? Genesis 1:27. Shall we reject that genealogical record,—prouder than any treasured in the courts of kings,—'which was the son of Adam, which was the son of God'? Luke 3:38. Rightly understood, both the revelations of science and the experiences of life are in harmony with the testimony of Scripture to the constant working of God in nature."
>
> *Education*, p. 130

Currently, science seems to be supporting the Bible record that God's speaking could have brought about the "matter and forces" by the vibrations of His vocal cords.

In the program *The Elegant Universe* on PBS, NOVA reports that the newest research indicates that all life in the universe came from sound.

"According to string theory, absolutely everything in the universe–all of the particles that make up matter and forces–is comprised of tiny vibrating fundamental strings" (*The Elegant Universe*, NOVA).

Interestingly, this is close to what the Bible has always said. God is not only powerful, but orderly. When I put the days of Creation on Jacob's ladder, I could see how they were created in the order needed to provide for the needs of the man and woman created on the sixth day. His method is illustrated in Mark. "... The kingdom of God is as if a man should scatter seed on the ground, and should sleep by night and rise by day, and the seed should sprout and grow, he himself does not know how. For the earth yields crops by itself: first the blade, then the head, after that the full grain in the head" (Mark 4:26–28).

We should aim to keep growing with Jesus in our hearts, just as the grain grows. Unfortunately, I had spent my life on self. Even though I did not realize it at the time, I was a "people-pleaser" and a demanding parent to glorify myself.. I needed to die to self.

> "The life spent on self is like the grain that is eaten. It disappears, but there is no increase. A man may gather all he can for self; he may live and think and plan for self; but his life passes away, and he has nothing. The law of self-serving is the law of self-destruction."
>
> *The Desire of Ages*, p. 624

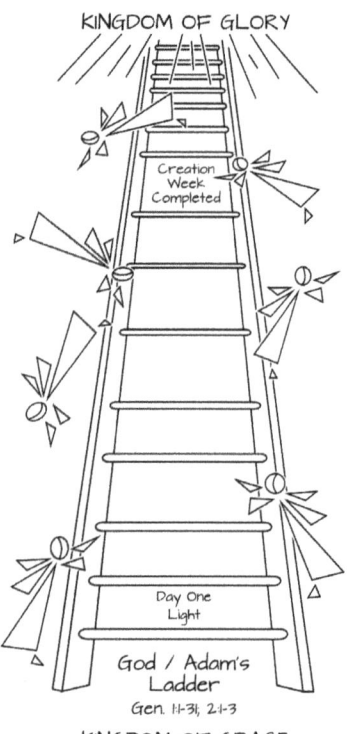

I began to spend more time studying my Bible, and eventually, I began to understand. "By the word of the LORD the heavens were made, And all the host of them by the breath of His mouth" (Ps. 33:6). "By faith we understand that the worlds were framed by the word of God, so that the things which are seen were not made of things which are visible" (Heb. 11:3).

"The LORD is my light and my salvation; Whom shall I fear? The LORD is the strength of my life; Of whom shall I be afraid?" (Ps. 27:1). This light given to the world on the first day of creation will remain a light to all who believe until we enter the New Jerusalem, where there will be no need for additional light. "The city had no need of the sun or the moon to shine in it, for the glory of God illuminated it. The Lamb is its light" (Rev. 21:23).

Long before God sent His Son to earth to be the light, Job spoke of light shining. It had to be the light of the first day of Creation; the light we forget but that sustains us. "You will also declare a thing, And it will be established for you; So light will shine on your ways" (Job 22:28).

God asked Job a question. "Where were you when I laid the foundations of the earth? Tell Me, if you have understanding. Who determined its measurements? Surely you know! Or who stretched the line upon it? To what were its foundations fastened? Or who laid its cornerstone, When the morning stars sang together, And all the sons of God shouted for joy?" (Job 38:4–7).

Jesus was there with His Father and the Holy Spirit on the first day of Creation. "In the beginning was the Word, and the Word was with God, and the Word was God. All things were made through Him, and without Him nothing was made that was made. In Him was life, and the life was the light of men. And the light shines in darkness, and the darkness did not comprehend it" (John 1:1–5).

God's Creation Ladder

> "God is the foundation of everything. All true science is in harmony with His works; all true education leads to obedience to His government. Science opens new wonders to our view; she soars high, and explores new depths; but she brings nothing from her research that conflicts with divine revelation. Ignorance may seek to support false views of God by appeals to science, but the book of nature and the written word shed light upon each other."
>
> *Patriarchs and Prophets,* p. 115

Each time we experience the daily change from light to darkness and darkness to light, I am reminded of my Creator. I want to know more about the Word John wrote about. So, let us go to day two of Creation week.

Creation: Day Two

After He created light, air and water were the next essentials for life that God spoke into existence. "Then God said, 'Let there be a firmament in the midst of the waters, and let it divide the waters from the waters.' Thus God made the firmament, and divided the waters, which were under the firmament from the waters which were above the firmament; and it was so. And God called the firmament Heaven. So the evening and the morning were the second day" (Gen. 1:6–8).

He formed the atmosphere by separating the water into two parts: oceanic and subterranean water and atmospheric water. The sky was now ready for the lights He would put in it as well as for the birds. "Who stretch out the heavens like a curtain.... You who laid the foundations of the earth...." (Ps. 104:2, 5).

Let's move up to the third round on the Creation ladder, so we can see what God does after there is air, water, and a sky.

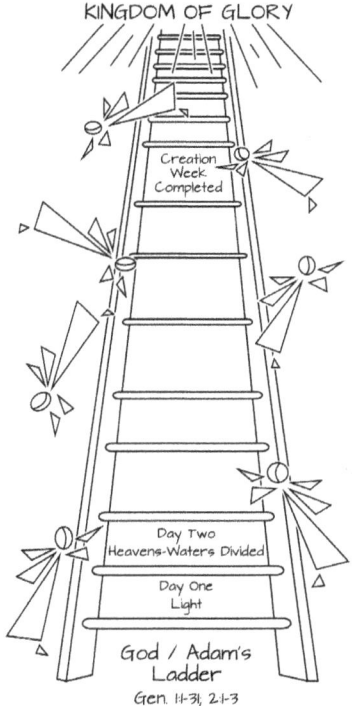

Creation: Day Three

The next thing needed was dry land in which to grow grass for the animals and herbs and fruit for the humans.

> Then God said, 'Let the waters under the heavens be gathered together into one place, and let the dry land appear'; and it was so. And God called the dry land Earth, and the gathering together of the waters He called Seas. And God saw that it was good. Then God said, 'Let the earth bring forth grass, the herb that yields seed, and the fruit tree that yields fruit according to its kind, whose seed is in itself, on the earth'; and it was so. And the earth brought forth grass, the herb that yields seed

according to its kind, and the tree that yields fruit, whose seed is in itself according to its kind. And God saw that it was good. So the evening and the morning were the third day. (Gen. 1:9–13)

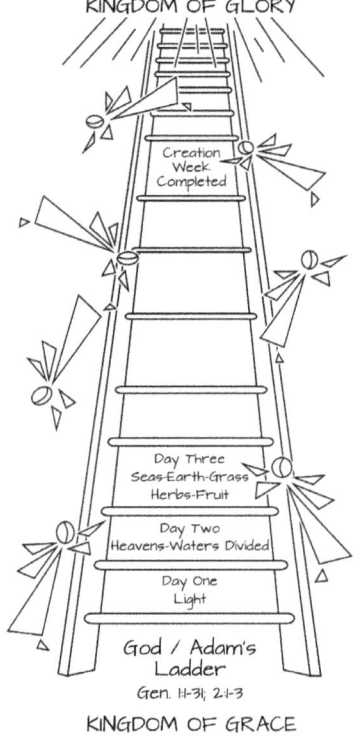

At that time God's plan watered the entire land surface using subterranean waters. This involved springs or mist, or both. There was no rain until later–when God brought judgment in Noah's day, and the earth was flooded to destroy sinful people and cleanse the earth. During Creation week, He separated the water from the earth and made the seas. The grass, herbs, and fruit trees needed water, and the dew and mist provided it. This became the Garden of Eden. Everything that God made was beautiful. Each thing was to sustain life and contribute to the happiness of humanity. God gave specific instructions for the diet of the animals and humankind, which He would create on the sixth day.

> "Everything that God had made was the perfection of beauty, and nothing seemed wanting that could contribute to the happiness of the holy pair; yet the Creator gave them still another token of His love, by preparing a garden especially for their home. In this garden were trees of every variety, many of them laden with fragrant and delicious fruit."
>
> *Patriarchs and Prophets,* pp. 46, 47

God told them how they should use the plants and trees He created. He had a purpose for everything He made. "And God said, 'See, I have given you every herb that yields seed which is on the face of all the earth, and every tree whose fruit yields seed; to you it shall be for food. Also, to every beast of the earth, to every bird of the air, and to everything that creeps on the earth, in which there is life, I have given every green herb for food'; and it was so" (Gen. 1:29, 30).

Mankind was to eat the grain from the herbs and the fruit and nuts from the trees. I am certain that I would be healthier if I had stayed with this vegan diet.

With three days of Creation completed, God was now ready to create lights with the specific purpose of sustaining the growth of the grass, herbs, and trees He had created on this day, the third day of Creation.

Let's go to day four now and discover what He chose to furnish the heavens.

CREATION: DAY FOUR

God was very organized in the way He presented Creation. He began with a planet that had no form and was void. The first three days He formed what had no form, and during the next three days, He filled what had been void.

> Then God said, 'Let there be lights in the firmament of the heavens to divide the day from the night; and let them be for signs and seasons, and for days and years; and let them be for lights in the firmament of the heavens to give light on the earth'; and it was so. Then God made two great lights: the greater light to rule the day, and the lesser light to rule the night. He made the stars also. God set them in the firmament of the heavens to give light on the earth, and to rule over the day and over the night, and to divide the light from the darkness. And God saw that it was good. So the evening and the morning were the fourth day. (Gen. 1:14–19)

The spiritual light created on day one was complimented on day four with natural lights: two great lights, the sun and moon, and the stars also. He had a purpose for each of them. They were created to be lights in the heavens, give light on the earth, divide the day from the night, and help distinguish signs, seasons, days, and years.

The psalmist recognized Creation week and gave thanksgiving to God for His enduring mercy.

> Oh, give thanks to the LORD, for He is good! ... To Him who alone does great wonders, For His mercy endures forever. To Him who by wisdom made the heavens, For His mercy endures forever; To Him who laid out the earth above the waters, For His mercy endures forever; To Him who made great lights, For His mercy endures forever–The sun to rule by day, For His mercy endures forever; The moon and stars to rule by night, For His mercy endures forever. (Ps. 136:1, 4–9)

The sun was necessary for the growth of the plants and trees God had created on the third day. Humanity and the cattle were to be created later, and neither could exist without the light of the sun.

Tim Sharp, reference editor for SPACE.com, reports that the sun is the largest and most massive object in the solar system. It is about 93 million miles from earth. The sun's light and heat takes about eight minutes to reach us, which means that the distance from the sun to earth is eight light minutes. The core of the sun's gravitational attraction produces immense pressure, and temperatures can reach up to 10,000 degrees. God distributes that heat according to His purpose, for it is still under His control. He has even made the sun stand still when needed to help His faithful people.

> Then Joshua spoke to the LORD in the day when the LORD delivered up the Amorites before the children of Israel, and he said in the sight of Israel: 'Sun, stand still over Gibeon; And Moon, in the Valley of Aijalon.' So the sun stood still, And the moon stopped, Till the people had revenge upon their enemies.... So the sun stood still in the midst of heaven, and did not hasten to go down for about a whole day. (Josh. 10:12, 13)

Before the evening fell, God's promise to Joshua had been fulfilled. The entire host of the enemy had been given into his hand. Long were the events of that day to remain in the memory of Israel. 'There was no day like that before it or after it, that Jehovah hearkened unto the voice of a man: for the LORD fought for Israel....' The Spirit of God inspired Joshua's prayer, that evidence might again be given of the power of Israel's God. Hence the request did not show presumption on the part of the great leader. Joshua had received the promise that God would surely overthrow these enemies of Israel, yet he put forth as earnest effort as though success depended upon the armies of Israel alone. He did all that human energy could do, and then he cried in faith for divine aid. The secret of success is the union of divine power with human effort. Those who achieve the greatest results are those who rely most implicitly upon the Almighty Arm. The man who commanded, 'Sun, stand thou still upon Gibeon; and thou, Moon, in the valley of Ajalon,' is the man who for hours lay prostrate upon the earth in prayer in the camp of Gilgal. The men of prayer are the men of power. This mighty miracle testifies that the creation is under the control of the Creator. Satan seeks to conceal from men the divine agency in the physical world—to keep out of sight the unwearied working of the first great cause. In this miracle all who exalt nature above the God of nature stand rebuked. (*Patriarchs and Prophets*, pp. 508, 509)

When God sent Isaiah to tell Hezekiah he would soon die, Hezekiah's prayer to God to extend his life was answered. God gave him a sign that what He said was true, and He extended his life fifteen years.

"And this is the sign to you from the LORD, that the LORD will do this thing which He has spoken: 'Behold, I will bring the shadow on the sundial, which has gone down with the sun on the sundial of Ahaz, ten degrees backward.' So the sun returned ten degrees on the dial by which it had gone down" (Isa. 38:7, 8).

God controls the moon also. It is the natural satellite of the earth, averaging in distance from the earth at around 230,600 miles. It has a diameter of about 2,000 miles, a mass approximately one-eightieth that of the earth, and an average period of revolution around the earth of twenty-seven days, seven hours, and forty-four minutes. The months and seasons are thus determined by using the moon, and the reflection of the moon gives light to the earth at night, as well as the stars.

On a clear night, the sky is illuminated with the twinkling stars. Long before Global Positioning Systems, mariners were ingenious, accurate, and keenly aware of their need to use the stars for navigation. The North Star was the reference point upon which the other calculations depended. The evening stars lead us to consider the wonders of our great Creator God. "The heavens declare the glory of God; And the firmament shows His handiwork" (Ps. 19:1).

Bible prophecy tells us that a time will come when the sun, moon, and stars will not give light. "And I will show wonders in the heavens and in the earth: Blood and fire and pillars of smoke. The sun shall be turned into darkness, And the moon into blood, Before the coming of the great and awesome day of the LORD" (Joel 2:31).

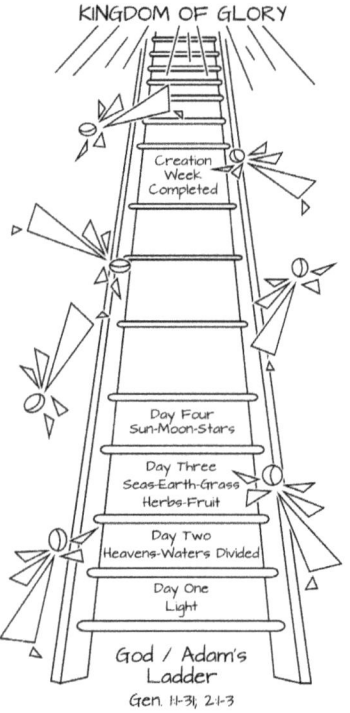

Jesus repeats these words when He speaks of signs of His second coming, and they have already occurred to some degree. "Immediately

God's Creation Ladder

after the tribulation of those days the sun will be darkened, and the moon will not give its light; the stars will fall from heaven, and the powers of the heavens will be shaken" (Matt. 24:29).

> "May 19, 1780, stands in history as 'The Dark Day.' Since the time of Moses no period of darkness of equal density, extent, and duration, has ever been recorded. The description of this event, as given by eyewitnesses, is but an echo of the words of the Lord, recorded by the prophet Joel, twenty-five hundred years previous to their fulfillment."
>
> *The Great Controversy*, p. 308

God left nothing to chance, and all is still under His control. Bible examples prove that God still controls the sun, moon, and stars.

As I studied my Bible and observed nature, I could see that the idea of combining Creation week and evolution was not possible. I had to choose between the two philosophies, and fortunately, it was not difficult for me to choose. God created and holds the world in place, in spite of Satan's interference.

Before the created objects had needs, God ensured that those needs would be met just as they were needed. Let's go to day five now and see what God has in store for us.

CREATION: DAY FIVE

The waters and the skies were ready to be filled with living things, so God continued creation by speaking them into existence.

> Then God said, 'Let the waters abound with an abundance of living creatures, and let birds fly above the earth across the face of the firmament of the heavens.' So God created great sea creatures and every living thing that moves, with which the waters abounded, according to their kind, and every winged bird according to its kind. And God saw that it was good. And God blessed them saying, 'Be fruitful and multiply, and fill the waters in the seas, and let birds multiply on the earth.' So the evening and the morning were the fifth day. (Gen. 1:20–23)

The water creatures of all kinds, as well as the birds, were all vegetarians. God also gave instructions later to the humans. He would later decide which fish and birds would be considered clean and could be eaten for food and which would be scavengers. The scavengers were created to help keep a clean world.

"These you may eat of all that are in the water: whatever in the water has fins and scales, whether in the seas or in the rivers–that you may eat.... Whatever in the water does not have fins or scales–that shall be an abomination to you" (Lev. 11:9, 12). "All clean birds you may eat" (Deut. 14:11).

God has special care over the birds of the air and the fowl on the ground, and we can learn from them. He compares Himself to the wings of a bird or some other fowl carrying and covering us with His wings.

"As an eagle stirs up its nest, Hovers over its young, Spreading out its wings, taking them up, Carrying them on its wings, So the LORD alone led him ..." (Deut. 32:11, 12).

"You have seen what I did to the Egyptians, and how I bore you on eagle's wings and brought you to myself" (Exod. 19:4).

There are trees on the hill above the road that I walk for exercise when the weather permits. Many eagles build their nests in these trees. Below the road is the lake where the eagles get their fish for food. When I see the eagles, I am reminded of this promise: "But those who wait on the LORD Shall renew their strength; They shall mount up with wings like eagles, They shall run and not be weary, They shall walk and not faint" (Isa. 40:31).

I appreciate the promise to renew my strength God has made despite my old age. God specified which foods we should eat. The diet God had originally prescribed would have kept Adam and Eve happy, with no knowledge of evil. It was important that they keep their bodies in a healthy condition. They were to care for their bodies, and God chose food for the test they must pass. Unfortunately, they failed. Today, He asks this question of us: "… Do you not know that your body is the temple of the Holy Spirit who is in you, whom you have from God, and you are not your own?" (1 Cor. 6:19).

As I grew older and began to have health problems, I tried to learn all I could about what might be causing my body to deteriorate. God did not leave us to wonder about the best diet to have a healthy body. He gave specific instructions of what we should eat.

> "In choosing man's food in Eden, the Lord showed what was the best diet; in the choice made for Israel He taught the same lesson. He brought the Israelites out of Egypt and undertook their training, that they might be a people for His own possession. Through them He desired to bless and teach the world. He provided them with the food best adapted for this purpose, not flesh, but manna, 'the bread of heaven.' It was only because of their discontent and their murmuring for the fleshpots of Egypt that animal food was granted them, and this only for a short time. Its use brought disease and death to thousands. Yet the restriction to a nonflesh diet was never heartily accepted. It continued to be the cause of discontent and murmuring, open or secret, and it was not made permanent. Upon their settlement in Canaan, the Israelites were permitted the use of animal food, but under careful restrictions which tended to lessen the evil results. The use of swine's flesh was prohibited, as also of other animals and of birds and fish whose flesh were pronounced unclean. Of the meats permitted, the eating of the fat and the blood was strictly forbidden. Only such animals could be used for food as were in good condition. No creature that was torn, that had died of itself, or from which the blood had not been carefully drained, could be used as food. By departing from the plan divinely appointed for their diet, the Israelites suffered great loss."
>
> *The Ministry of Healing*, pp. 311, 312

Now I know that what I eat determines in part how I feel. But it is too late for me to have the perfect body God gave Eve because of Adam's sin. But by their sin, they spoiled the opportunity for humans thereafter to live forever as they could have. Adam and Eve's sin made it impossible for me to have immortality, unless I am living when Jesus returns.

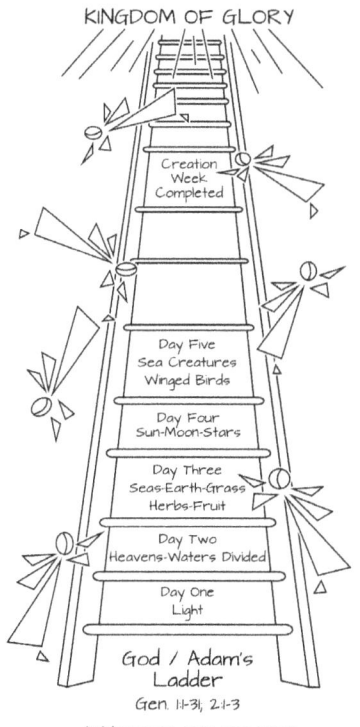

> Our bodies are Christ's purchased possession, and we are not at liberty do with them as we please. All who understand the laws of health should realize their obligation to obey these laws which God has established in their being....We must individually answer to God for our habits and practices. Therefore the question with us is not, 'What is the world's practice?' but, 'How shall I as an individual treat the habitation that God has given me?' (*The Ministry of Healing*, p. 310)

When Jesus was on earth, He was so concerned with those who were not accepting Him that he cried out in agony: "O Jerusalem, Jerusalem, the one who kills the prophets and stones those who are sent to her! How often I wanted to gather your children together, as a hen gathers her brood under her wings, but you were not willing!" (Luke 13:34).

Everything God created was with a purpose. We need to praise Him more for His Creation and providence. The psalmist was full of praise.

> Bless the LORD, O my soul! O LORD my God, You are very great: You are clothed with honor and majesty, Who cover Yourself with light as with a garment ... He sends the springs into the valleys; They flow among the hills. They give drink to every beast of the field ... By them the birds of the heaven have their home; They sing among the branches ... The cedars of Lebanon which He planted, Where the birds make their nests; The stork has her home in the fir trees. (Ps. 104:1–17)

With these praises, we can learn a lot about Creation. We can see God by observing nature, the work of His hands.

> "The distinction between articles of food as clean and unclean was not a merely ceremonial and arbitrary regulation, but was based upon sanitary principles.... There are few who realize as they should how much their habits of diet have to do with their health, their character, their usefulness in this world, and their eternal destiny. The appetite should ever be in subjection to the moral and intellectual powers. The body should be servant to the mind, and not the mind to the body."
>
> *Patriarchs and Prophets*, p. 562

I believe that God has put in all of us a certain amount of creative power. I saw it in my girls when they were small. We had a creek running behind our house, and they spent many hours making "mud pies" and other creative designs with the muddy clay. Then they would put them on boards to dry in the sun. As they got older, they made cookies, knit sweaters, and dresses. Nelle, the older daughter, now does interior designing and taught pottery classes, as well as career counseling. The younger, Jane, has made quilts and all kinds of crafty decorations for Christmas, among other things. Later, she became an administrative assistant who worked with engineers locating appropriate property on which to build cell towers. The boys both are creative in woodworking, designing, and building. Vern, the older, followed his dad's footsteps and built houses. Our youngest child, Carey, also is skilled in building as well as being a college dean of architecture. He goes on mission posts to help with building projects. Their dad and I freely admit that they have all surpassed our skills. We taught them all we knew, and they had the advantage of professional training. I am thankful they have all been successful in their pursuits. I also believe that God hears and answers the prayers of parents for His blessings on their lives.

God is about to complete His work of creating a perfect world. Day six is the next round on our Creation ladder.

CREATION: DAY SIX

The earth is now ready to accommodate the animals and humankind. All their needs have been prepared in advance.

> Then God said, 'Let the earth bring forth the living creature according to its kind; cattle and creeping thing and beast of the earth, each according to its kind'; and it was so. And God made the beast of the earth according to its kind, cattle according to its kind, and everything that creeps on the earth according to its kind. And God saw that it was good. Then God said, 'Let Us make man in Our image, according to Our likeness; let them have dominion over the fish of the sea, over the birds of the air, and over the cattle, over all the earth and over every creeping thing that creeps on the earth.' So God created man in His own image; in the image of God He created him; male and female He created them. Then God blessed them, and God said to them, 'Be fruitful and multiply; fill the earth and subdue it; have dominion over the fish of the sea, over the birds of the air, and over every living thing that moves on the earth.' And God said, 'See, I have given you every herb that yields seed which is on the face of all the earth, and every tree whose fruit yields seed; to you it shall be for food. Also, to every beast of the earth, to every bird of the air, and to everything that creeps on the earth, in which there is life, I have given every green herb for food'; And it was so. Then God saw everything that He had made, and indeed it was very good. So the evening and the morning were the sixth day." (Gen. 1:24–31)

Many times when I have finished a project I have stood back and admired my work. So it is easy for me to imagine God looking down on planet earth and realizing "it was very good."

He had made provisions for every possible need humanity would have. Everything was perfect.

Adam and Eve were created in the image of God, so they were perfect in every way.

> Man was formed in the likeness of God. His nature was in harmony with the will of God. His mind was capable of comprehending divine things. His affections were pure; his appetites and passions were under the control of reason. He was holy and happy in bearing the image of God and in

God's Creation Ladder

perfect obedience to His will. As man came forth from the hand of his Creator, he was of lofty stature and perfect symmetry. His countenance bore the ruddy tint of health, and glowed with the light of life and joy. (*Reflecting Christ*, p. 135)

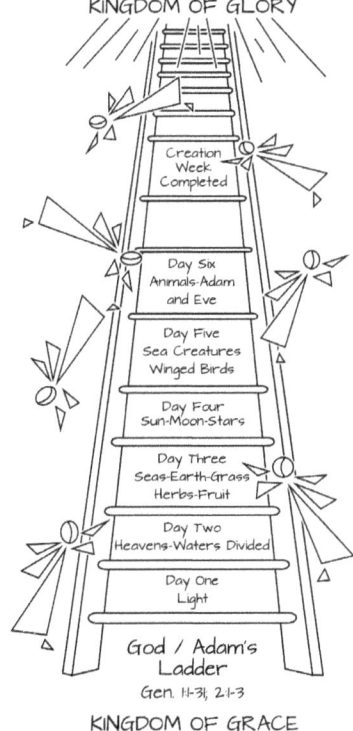

They were not created simply to look at their beautiful surroundings but to take care of them. God had given them dominion over those things created before they were. We also need labor as Christ gave us His example.

> The greater part of our Savior's life on earth was spent in patient toil in the carpenter's shop at Nazareth. Ministering angels attended the Lord of life as He walked side by side with peasants and laborers, unrecognized and unhonored. He was as faithfully fulfilling His mission while working at His humble trade as when He healed the sick or walked upon the storm-tossed waves of Galilee. So in the humblest duties and lowliest positions of life, we may walk and work with Jesus. (*Steps to Christ*, pp. 81, 82)

They were also to care for their own bodies by eating the food He specified that they should eat. There was only one tree that God told them not to eat of and that was the tree of knowledge of good and evil. If they ate the fruit from it, they would die. And sadly, they eventually ate of it. They failed God's test. And, sad to say, this is where their problems, and ours, began; Eve ate of the tree of knowledge, and then she gave some of the fruit to Adam.

> The tree of knowledge, which stood near the tree of life in the midst of the garden, was to be a test of the obedience, faith, and love of our first parents. While permitted to eat freely of every other tree, they were forbidden to taste of this, on pain of death.... They were to enjoy communion with God and with holy angels; but before they could be rendered eternally secure, their loyalty must be tested.... Obedience, perfect and perpetual, was the condition of eternal happiness. On this condition he was to have access to the tree of life. (*Patriarchs and Prophets*, pp. 48, 49)

This was the first act of disobedience, and life would never be the same on this earth again. Humanity would be born in sin with no hope of eternal life unless God intervened. We must know how it happened. We also must know that God requires perfect obedience, and He has provided the way for us through His Son, and our Savior, Jesus Christ.

> Now the serpent was more cunning than any beast of the field which the LORD God had made. And he said to the woman, 'Has God indeed said, 'You shall not eat of every tree of the garden?' And the

woman said to the serpent, 'We may eat the fruit of the trees of the garden; but of the fruit of the tree which is in the midst of the garden, God has said 'You shall not eat it, nor shall you touch it, lest you die.' Then the serpent said to the woman, 'You will not surely die. For God knows that in the day you eat of it your eyes will be opened, and you will be like God knowing good and evil.' So when the woman saw that the tree was good for food, that it was pleasant to the eyes, and a tree desirable to make one wise, she took of its fruit and ate. She also gave to her husband with her, and he ate. Then the eyes of both of them were opened, and they knew that they were naked; and they sewed fig leaves together and made themselves coverings. (Gen. 3:1–7)

God had a reason for telling Adam which foods he should eat. He was very specific. God has a reason for everything He tells us to do or not to do. This was not an arbitrary command.

They had no need to eat from the tree of knowledge of good and evil; God had told them what they needed to know. If we focus our eyes on what God has forbidden, we will become evil.

Bus God has promised that through Christ's death, we can have eternal life. God always keeps His word.

Therefore, just as through one man sin entered the world, and death through sin, and thus death spread to all men, because all have sinned.... Therefore, as through one man's offense judgment came to all men, resulting in condemnation, even so through one Man's righteous act the free gift came to all men, resulting in justification of life. For as by one man's disobedience many were made sinners, so also by one Man's obedience many will be made righteous. (Rom. 5:12, 18, 19)

> "In the place where sin abounded, God's grace much more abounds. The earth itself, the very field that Satan claims as his, is to be not only ransomed but exalted. Our little world, under the curse of sin the one dark blot in His glorious creation, will be honored above all other worlds in the universe of God."
>
> *The Desire of Ages*, p. 26

We have such a gracious, loving God, that even after they sinned, He made provisions for returning to claim His own.

So the LORD God said to the serpent: 'Because you have done this, You are cursed more than all the cattle, And more than every beast of the field; On your belly you shall go, And you shall eat dust All the days of your life. And I will put enmity Between you and the woman, And between your seed and her Seed; He shall bruise your head, and you shall bruise His heel.' To the woman He said: 'I will greatly multiply your sorrow and your conception; In pain you shall bring forth children; Your desire shall be for your husband, And he shall rule over you.' Then to Adam He said, 'Because you have heeded the voice of your wife, And have eaten from the tree

God's Creation Ladder

of which I commanded you, saying, 'You shall not eat of it:' Cursed is the ground for your sake; In toil you shall eat of it All the days of your life. Both thorns and thistles it shall bring forth for you, And you shall eat the herb of the field. In the sweat of your face you shall eat bread Till you return to the ground, For out of it you were taken; For dust you are, And to dust you shall return.' (Gen. 3:14–19)

As a result of Eve's sin, we women have pain when we give birth to our children. As the mother of four children, I can verify that. However, I believe my mother could even more than I because she had a difficult time when I was born. She almost died and had to be hospitalized after I was born at home. While a friend and neighbor of my mother took care of me for several weeks, I feel as though I must have missed that bonding that needs to develop between a mother and her child. Even after she came home and I was with her, my oldest sister, along with a hired helper, mostly took care of me until I was about four years old.

When she was no longer able to live alone and was living with me, we talked about the time when I was young. I asked her why she did not teach me the meaning of the Bible quotations she often recited. Her reply was "I don't know–I guess I just jerked you up." Words I have never forgotten! But God is loving and merciful, and I am so thankful she survived, for she was the one person I always knew loved me, until I met my husband. Then I knew there were two!

> "All men have been bought with this infinite price. By pouring the whole treasury of heaven into this world, by giving us in Christ all heaven, God has purchased the will, the affections, the mind, the soul, of every human being. Whether believers or unbelievers, all men are the Lord's property."
>
> *Christ's Object Lessons*, p. 426

Not only did God care about our habits of work and eating, He made known that we needed to have relationships with others. He said it was not good for man to be alone, so He created Eve—some say that was the crowning glory of His work of creation! They were husband and wife. "The Lord God ... made ... a woman, and He brought her unto the man.... Therefore a man shall leave his father and his mother and be joined to his wife, and they shall become one flesh" (Gen. 2:22–24).

They had daily communion with God. This was His plan for eternity.

> The Garden of Eden was a representation of what God desired the whole earth to become, and it was His purpose that, as the human family increased in numbers, they should establish other homes and schools like the one He had given. Thus in course of time the whole earth might be occupied with homes and schools where the words and the works of God should be studied, and where the students should thus be fitted more and more fully to reflect, throughout endless ages, the light of the knowledge of His glory. (*Education*, p. 22)

Now God's work of creating a perfect world was finished, but there was one day still left in our week, according to the calendar, so let's go up to day seven now.

CREATION: DAY SEVEN

The first six days God made things and people as well as the institution of marriage. After He finished creating all the elements necessary for the happiness of humanity, He rested. It was then that He made the Sabbath day for man. "Thus the heavens and the earth, and all the host of them, were finished. And on the seventh day God ended His work which He had done, And He rested on the seventh day from all His work which He had done. Then God blessed the seventh day and sanctified it, because in it He rested from all His work which God had created and made" (Gen. 2:1–3).

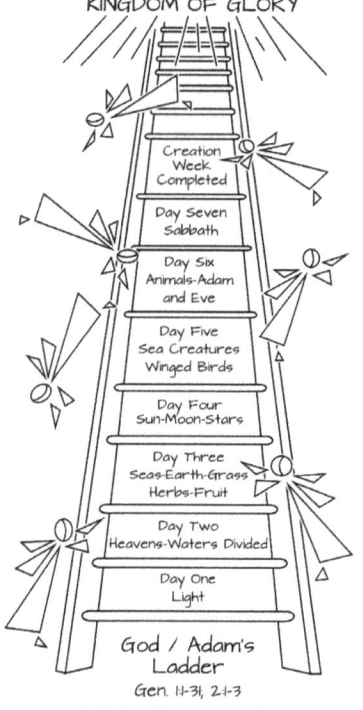

Adam and Eve were not tired; they did not need to rest. They were just formed on the sixth day. But God had worked six days, and He rested on the seventh day from all His work.

He saw that everything was "very good." He gave them the opportunity to rest with Him and get to know Him; He wanted to give them the chance to commune with Him.

He made the Sabbath for humankind today. He wants us to come to His garden each Sabbath, His garden of prayer, His house of worship, where we can praise Him for all He has done for us. He gave us a place of peace and quiet, where we can shut out the demands of the other six days.

> Remember the Sabbath day, to keep it holy. Six days you shall labor and do all your work, but the seventh day is the Sabbath of the LORD your God. In it you shall do no work: you, nor your son, nor your daughter, nor your male servant, nor your female servant, nor your cattle, nor your stranger who is within your gates. For in six days the LORD made the heavens and the earth, the sea, and all that is in them, and rested the seventh day. Therefore the LORD blessed the Sabbath day and hallowed it. (Exod. 20:8–11)

God made the Sabbath for man to enjoy time in worship and communion with Him. "And He said to them, 'The Sabbath was made for man, and not man for the Sabbath. Therefore the Son of Man is also Lord of the Sabbath" (Mark 2:27).

Adam and Even had only been in existence less than one full day before God gave them the Sabbath. God wanted to share His rest with them.

> God saw that a Sabbath was essential for man, even in Paradise. He needed to lay aside his own interests and pursuits for one day of the seven, that he might more fully contemplate the works of God and

meditate upon His power and goodness. He needed a Sabbath to remind him more vividly of God and to awaken gratitude because all that he enjoyed and possessed came from the beneficent hand of the Creator. (*Patriarchs and Prophets*, p. 48)

We discussed the Sabbath at length on God's Ten Commandment ladder; however, it was so important that Moses repeated all the commandments given in Exodus in his own words within the book of Deuteronomy. The wording is just a little different, but he explains more fully why they should keep the Sabbath.

> Observe the Sabbath day, to keep it holy, as the LORD your God commanded you. Six days you shall labor and do all your work, but the seventh day is the Sabbath of the LORD your God. In it you shall do no work; you, nor your son, nor your daughter, nor your male servant, nor your ox, nor your donkey, nor any of your cattle, nor your stranger who is within your gates, that your male servant and your female servant may rest as well as you. And remember that you were a slave in the land of Egypt, and the LORD your God brought you out from there by a mighty hand and by outstretched arm; therefore the LORD your God commanded you to keep the Sabbath day. (Deut. 5:12–15)

Moses wanted the children of Israel to remember how God had saved them from the slavery in Egypt, so they would be free to worship Him. I learned that God must have first place in my life, not because of duty or any other motivation, but because He loves me, and I love Him because of that.

> "Jehovah, the eternal, self-existent, uncreated One, Himself the Source and Sustainer of all, is alone entitled to supreme reverence and worship. Man is forbidden to give to any other object the first place in his affections or his service. Whatever we cherish that tends to lessen our love for God or to interfere with the service due Him, of that do we make a god."
>
> *Patriarchs and Prophets*, p. 305

Israel had sinned by committing idolatry again and again, and Moses was attempting to remind them that the Sabbath was a safeguard to keep them from sin.

> Before entering the Promised Land, the Israelites were admonished by Moses to 'keep the Sabbath day to sanctify it.' Deuteronomy 5:12. The Lord designed that by a faithful observance of the Sabbath command, Israel should continually be reminded of their accountability to Him as their Creator and their Redeemer. While they should keep the Sabbath in the proper spirit, idolatry could not exist; but should the claims of this precept of the Decalogue be set aside as no longer binding, the Creator would be forgotten and men would worship other gods. 'I gave them My Sabbaths,' God declared, 'to be a sign between Me and them, that they might know that I am the Lord that sanctify them.' Yet 'they despised My judgments, and walked not in My statutes, but polluted My Sabbaths: for their heart went after their idols.' And in His appeal to them to return to Him, He called their attention anew to the importance of keeping the Sabbath holy. 'I am the Lord your God,' He said;

'walk in My statutes, and keep My judgments, and do them; and hallow My Sabbaths; and they shall be a sign between Me and you, that ye may know that I am the Lord your God.' Ezekiel 20:12, 16, 19, 20. (*Prophets and Kings*, pp. 181, 182)

When God spoke, He always spoke the truth, and now we have the truth recorded in the Bible. When He was asked, "What is truth?" He replied "Thy word is truth" (see John 17:17). The Sabbath commandment is a vital part of that truth. We can depend on all of God's words to be the truth.

And what does that truth do for us? "Truth is an active, working principle, molding heart and life so that there is a constant upward movement.... The glory of God revealed above the ladder can be appreciated only by the progressive climber, who is ever attracted higher, to nobler aims which Christ reveals. All the faculties of mind and body must be enlisted" (*Mind, Character, and Personality*, vol. 2, p. 784).

Unfortunately, we may think we have kept His commandments; however, we have not taken care of God's creation like He planned. That was to be humanity's job, and, as they did this, they were to continually grow and develop. "... let them have dominion over the fish of the sea, over the birds of the air, and over the cattle, over all the earth and over every creeping thing that creeps on the earth" (Gen. 1:26).

> When Adam came from the Creator's hand, he bore, in his physical, mental, and spiritual nature, a likeness to his Maker. 'God created man in His own image' (Genesis 1:27), and it was His purpose that the longer man lived the more fully he should reveal this image—the more fully reflect the glory of the Creator. All his faculties were capable of development; their capacity and vigor were continually to increase. (*Education*, p. 15)

God's creation was marred by sin, but He already had a plan in operation to meet the need: the sacrifice of His Son, Jesus, to atone for our sins. Hebrews contains breath-taking passages that confirm that the One who made us also gave His life to save us. "God, who at various times and in various ways spoke in time past to the fathers by the prophets, has in these last days spoken to us by His Son, whom He has appointed heir of all things, through whom also He made the worlds" (Heb. 1:1, 2).

> "As regards this world, God's work of creation is completed. For "the works were finished from the foundation of the world." Hebrews 4:3. But His energy is still exerted in upholding the objects of His creation. It is not because the mechanism that has once been set in motion continues to act by its own inherent energy that the pulse beats and breath follows breath; but every breath, every pulsation of the heart, is an evidence of the all-pervading care of Him in whom 'we live, and move, and have our being.' Acts 17:28"
>
> *Patriarchs and Prophets*, p. 115

God's work of creating the world and filling it with all good things was finished. Then He gave us the Sabbath day for rest, worship, and having fellowship with others. "Not forsaking the assembling of ourselves together, as is the manner of some, but exhorting one another, and so much the more as you see the Day approaching" (Heb. 10:25).

The events that are going on all around the world are fulfilling God's warning that the earth is about to be destroyed. But through the perfect life that Jesus lived, we have the choice of surviving these calamities and being ready to go to our heavenly home when He returns. He does nothing without giving His people adequate warnings, and He has already sent the last one. Though we have walked through each day of Creation week, we still need to know about our re-creation day, which means we must turn to the three angels' messages.

THREE ANGELS MESSAGES: RE-CREATION

God has never wanted us to forget how He created us and His plan for our salvation, so He sent angels with a message reminding us to worship God as our Creator. I like to think of it as our re-creation when we follow these three angel's messages. For, if we do, we are assured of a home in heaven. He told us in the first commandment not to worship other gods. Now, through John, He related that the time for His judgment had come and what the consequences are if we do not keep His commandments. He wants us all to be re-created in His image before coming again.

> Then I saw another angel flying in the midst of heaven, having the everlasting gospel to preach to those who dwell on the earth–to every nation, tribe, tongue, and people–saying with a loud voice, 'Fear God and give glory to Him, for the hour of His judgment has come; and worship Him who made heaven and earth, the sea and springs of water.' And another angel followed, saying 'Babylon is fallen, is fallen, that great city, because she has made all nations drink of the wine of her wrath of her fornication.' Then a third angel followed them, saying with a loud voice, 'If anyone worships the beast and his image, and receives his mark on his forehead or on his hand, he himself shall also drink of the wine of the wrath of God, which is poured out full strength into the cup of His indignation. And he shall be tormented with fire and brimstone in the presence of the holy angels and in the presence of the Lamb. And the smoke of their torment ascends forever and ever; and they have no rest day or night, who worship the beast and his image, and whoever receives the mark of his name.' Here is the patience of the saints; here are those who keep the commandments of God and the faith of Jesus. (Rev. 14:6–12)

These words of warning are meant to "wake us up" to the work we are to be doing at the present time. Jesus paid the penalty for our sins by His death when His blood was shed for our salvation. However, He did not "do it all." That is, He has work for us to do that no one can do for us. We must have that total surrender to Him, so the Holy Spirit will do the work through us. Remember, as I said before "Of myself I can do nothing" (see John 5:30).

> I will praise You with uprightness of heart, When I learn Your righteous judgments. I will keep Your statutes; Oh, do not forsake me utterly! How can a young man cleanse his way? By taking heed according to Your word. With my whole heart I have sought You; Oh, let me not wander from Your commandments! Your word I have hidden in my heart, That I might not sin against You. Blessed are You, O LORD! Teach me Your statutes. (Ps. 119:7–12)

When I learned that God's commandments were really ten promises, I was like David and asked God to teach me the real meaning. He has assured me that, through the power of the Holy Spirit, they can be kept. "Every promise in God's word is ours. "By every word that proceedeth out of the mouth of God" are we to live. When assailed by temptation, look not to circumstances or to the weakness of self, but to the power of the word. All its strength is yours" (*The Desire of Ages*, p. 123).

I will let Mrs. White explain further for you regarding how we should worship God as Creator and know that we will be judged. We will be saved by God's grace and judged according to our works.

> Fearful is the issue to which the world is to be brought. The powers of earth, uniting to war against the commandments of God, will decree that 'all, both small and great, rich and poor, free and bond' (Revelation 13:16), shall conform to the customs of the church by the observance of the false sabbath. All who refuse compliance will be visited with civil penalties, and it will finally be declared that they are deserving of death. On the other hand, the law of God enjoining the Creator's rest day demands obedience and threatens wrath against all who transgress its precepts. With the issue thus clearly brought before him, whoever shall trample upon God's law to obey a human enactment receives the mark of the beast; he accepts the sign of allegiance to the power which he chooses to obey instead of God. (*The Great Controversy*, p. 604)

If we follow this message, we are assured that angels will be there to bring our work to fruition, but we must share our knowledge of and experience with the gospel to others.

"To prepare a people to stand in the day of God, a great work of reform was to be accomplished. God saw that many of His professed people were not building for eternity, and in His mercy He was about to send a message of warning to arouse them from their stupor and lead them to make ready for the coming of the Lord. This warning is brought to view in Revelation 14. Here is a threefold message represented as proclaimed by heavenly beings and immediately followed by the coming of the Son of man to reap 'the harvest of the earth.' The first of these warnings announces the approaching judgment. The prophet beheld an angel flying 'in the midst of heaven, having the everlasting gospel to preach unto them that dwell on the earth, and to every nation, and kindred, and tongue, and people, saying with a loud voice, Fear God, and give glory to Him; for the hour of His judgment is come: and worship Him that made heaven, and earth, and the sea, and the fountains of waters.' Revelation 14:6, 7. This message is declared to be a part of 'the everlasting gospel.' The work of preaching the gospel has not been committed to angels, but has been entrusted to men. Holy angels have been employed in directing this work, they have in charge the great movements for the salvation of men; but the actual proclamation of the gospel is performed by the servants of Christ upon the earth."

The Great Controversy, pp. 311, 312

God has assured us that He has a place in heaven prepared for those who choose to do His will. It is those who share this everlasting gospel with others who will be ready to meet Jesus when He comes. And while we work and wait, we are not to be anxious or fearful. We can believe the Word of God.

> Let not your heart be troubled; you believe in God, believe also in Me. In my Father's house are many mansions; if it were not so, I would have told you. I go to prepare a place for you. And if I go and prepare a place for you, I will come again and receive you to Myself; that where I am, there you may be also. And where I go you know, and the way you know.... I am the way, the truth, and the life. No one comes to the Father except through me. (John 14:1–6)

I don't know exactly what heaven will be like, but from the small glimpses I have read about, I know I will like it. "But as it is written: 'Eye has not seen, nor ear heard, Nor have entered into the heart of man The things which God has prepared For those who love Him" (1 Cor. 2:9).

God is a loving God, and even those who have chosen not to "fear God and give glory to Him " will not be subjected to eternally burning in hell (see Rev. 14:7). But they will be burned like stubble and be no more. Living in the Palouse wheat farming section of the United States has made this clear to me. After the farmers have harvested their wheat, they burn the stubble to clear the soil. There is no evidence left that there was wheat there, so it will be with the wicked.

> "For behold, the day is coming, Burning like an oven, And all the proud, yes, all who do wickedly will be stubble. And the day which is coming shall burn them up," Says the LORD of hosts, "That will leave them neither root nor branch. But to you who fear My name The Sun of Righteousness shall arise With healing on His wings; And you shall go out And grow fat like stall-fed calves. You shall trample the wicked, For they shall be ashes under the soles of your feet On the day that I do this," Says the LORD of hosts. "Remember the Law of Moses, My servant, Which I commanded him in Horeb for all Israel, With the statutes and judgments." (Mal. 4:1–4)

"Fearful is the issue to which the world is to be brought. The powers of earth, uniting to war against the commandments of God, will decree that 'all, both small and great, rich and poor, free and bond' (Revelation 13:16), shall conform to the customs of the church by the observance of the false sabbath. All who refuse compliance will be visited with civil penalties, and it will finally be declared that they are deserving of death. On the other hand, the law of God enjoining the Creator's rest day demands obedience and threatens wrath against all who transgress its precepts. With the issue thus clearly brought before him, whoever shall trample upon God's law to obey a human enactment receives the mark of the beast; he accepts the sign of allegiance to the power which he chooses to obey instead of God."

The Great Controversy, p. 604

These three angel's messages are bringing the world to a test. We must understand what it says, for God's word never fails. We need to recognize that He loves us so much that He has given us a warning message so that we will know what is ahead of us. Worshipping God as our Creator and keeping the seventh day Sabbath holy is the test that will be brought upon us.

God has made very clear His requirements. The choice is ours. I have made my choice to "fear God and give glory to Him" (see Rev. 14:7). Jacob's ladder has given me much insight into the ways of the Lord, but I know all His ways are "past finding out" (see Rom. 11:33). The next and final ladder is meant for those living in "these last days." It is meant to reveal the significance of the sanctuary in heaven as it was revealed to John and recorded in the book of Revelation. The psalmist says, "Your way, O God, is in the sanctuary; Who is so great a God as our God?" (Ps. 77:13).

Let us go with John through the sanctuary now, so we can learn more about "His way."

Chapter Seven
MOSES/JOHN'S LADDER: THE SANCTUARY

God chose Moses to give the Creation week record we have just covered so that it could be preserved in written form. He also chose Moses to teach us about the sanctuary He was going to make. Then I learned that there are two sanctuaries I needed to learn about.

First, He revealed the earthly sanctuary through Moses. God gave Moses explicit instructions about the materials he would need to collect. God also told him exactly how to build a sanctuary that would guide Israel as they traveled through the treacherous territory on their way to the land He promised to Abraham, Isaac, and Jacob. It was to be a portable replica of the sanctuary in heaven. It was a place where God could dwell as He went with them on the journey from slavery in Egypt to the Promised Land.

Then, after Christ died, John, in a vision, was given a view of the sanctuary in heaven. Every part of the sanctuary had a special meaning for me. God said to Moses, "And let them make Me a sanctuary, that I may dwell among them" (Exod. 25:8).

John wrote "The Revelation of Jesus Christ, which God gave Him to show His servants—things which must shortly take place. And He sent and signified it by His angel to His servant John, who bore witness to the word of God, and to the testimony of Jesus Christ, to all things he saw" (Rev. 1:1, 2). And the psalmist said, "Your way, O God, is in the sanctuary; Who is so great a God as our God?" (Ps. 77:13).

In Old Testament times, God told Israel that He had a plan to save them—Jesus would someday die to save them. He told them all about redemption. But they continued to disobey; they needed more. So He chose to let them experience His plan through their senses. He gave Moses the pattern and commanded His people to build a sanctuary—a place where He could come and dwell with them. The relationship God had with Moses was to be extended to Israel as a nation.

> "God commanded Moses for Israel, 'Let them make Me a sanctuary; that I may dwell among them' (Exodus 25:8), and He abode in the sanctuary, in the midst of His people. Through all their weary wandering in the desert, the symbol of His presence was with them. So Christ set up His tabernacle in the midst of our human encampment. He pitched His tent by the side of the tents of men, that He might dwell among us, and make us familiar with His divine character and life."
>
> *The Desire of Ages*, p. 23

The sanctuary teachings are probably the most neglected of all God's Word. I knew nothing about it until just a few years ago when I began seriously studying my Bible. It represents the story of salvation as we move from area to area, which are represented on the steps of Jacob's ladder that reach to heaven. God gave John visions to reveal to us those parts, which were hard to understand.

> "This revelation was given for the guidance and comfort of the church throughout the Christian dispensation.... In the Revelation are portrayed the deep things of God. The very name given to its inspired pages, 'the Revelation,' contradicts the statement that this is a sealed book. A revelation is something revealed. The Lord Himself revealed to His servant the mysteries contained in this book, and He designs that they shall be open to the study of all. Its truths are addressed to those living in the last days of this earth's history, as well as to those living in the days of John.... Let none think, because they cannot explain the meaning of every symbol in the Revelation, that it is useless for them to search this book in an effort to know the meaning of the truth it contains.... Those whose hearts are open to the reception of truth will be enabled to understand its teachings, and will be granted the blessing promised to those who 'hear the words of this prophecy, and keep those things which are written therein.' In the Revelation all the books of the Bible meet and end. Here is the complement of the book of Daniel. One is a prophecy; the other a revelation. The book that was sealed is not the Revelation, but that portion of the prophecy of Daniel relating to the last days. The angel commanded, 'But thou, O Daniel, shut up the words, and seal the book, even to the time of the end.' Daniel 12:4"
>
> *The Acts of the Apostles*, pp. 583-585

When our daughter, Jane, was in grade school, her Bible teacher gave the children their choice of projects to complete. Jane chose to make a model of the sanctuary. Like many students do, she failed to tell us about the project until the night before it was due. It was impossible for her to build it by herself in such a short time, so we all helped. We found the description God gave Moses for building the earthly sanctuary, and we all began to work. Vern Jr. helped his dad with the woodwork, Jane overlaid the wood with gold paint, and Nelle and I helped her make the curtains out of some blue satin brocade from my remnant box. Her teacher was impressed, and she got a top grade. Of course she didn't tell her teacher how much help she had received, but I believe he probably knew.

I doubt if Jane really understood what each piece of furniture represented, or even the shedding of the blood of the animals on the altar. I didn't. Her dad knew, but he never shared his knowledge of the Bible unless I asked a specific question, and unfortunately, many times I didn't know enough to ask. He shared with the children by reading Bible stories to them while I finished my evening chores and listened. He loved us deeply.

What a wonderful opportunity we missed to study the meaning of the sanctuary and discuss it as a family. As I think of the experience now and see the signs that indicate how near Christ's second coming is, I realize how long

I procrastinated before I began to study my Bible in a meaningful way. Now it is my desire to know more about Jesus all the time.

It has been difficult for me to understand what the sanctuary was all about because it involves time prophecies given to Daniel in visions. These prophecies were interpreted by John, also in the form of visions, in Revelation. The prophecies in these two books guided me in my discovery of the meaning of the sanctuary—it is God's plan for our salvation.

It contains the precise instructions for us today as we await Christ's return. History has revealed that the prophecies of Daniel have been fulfilled as wars between nations resulted in the defeat of one kingdom and the rule of another. According to Daniel's prophecy, we are living in the last days.

> "Prophecy has traced the rise and fall of the world's great empires—Babylon, Medo-Persia, Greece, and Rome. With each of these, as with nations of less power, history repeated itself. Each had its period of test, each failed, its glory faded, its power departed, and its place was occupied by another. While the nations rejected God's principles, and in this rejection wrought their own ruin, it was still manifest that the divine, overruling purpose was working through all their movements."
>
> *Education*, p. 177

King Nebuchadnezzar had a dream and demanded that the wise men interpret it for him. By the time Daniel was called in, not only could the king's own wise men not figure out its meaning, but the king himself had forgotten his dream! God miraculously gave Daniel the dream and its interpretation.

> You, O king, were watching; and behold, a great image! This great image, whose splendor was excellent, stood before you; and its form was awesome. This image's head was of fine gold, its chest and arms of silver, its belly and thighs of bronze, its legs of iron, its feet partly of iron and partly of clay. You watched while a stone was cut out without hands, which struck the image on its feet of iron and clay, and broke them in pieces. Then the iron, the clay, the bronze, the silver, and the gold were crushed together, and became like chaff from the summer threshing floors; the wind carried them away so that no trace of them was found. And the stone that struck the image became a great mountain and filled the whole earth. This is the dream. Now we will tell the interpretation of it before the king. You, O king, are a king of kings. For the God of heaven has given you a kingdom, power, strength, and glory; and wherever the children of men dwell, or the beasts of the field and the birds of the heaven, He has given them into your hand, and has made you ruler over them all—you are this head of gold. But after you shall arise another kingdom inferior to yours; then another, a third kingdom of bronze, which shall rule over all the earth. And the fourth kingdom shall be as strong as iron, inasmuch as iron breaks in pieces and shatters everything; and like iron that crushes, that kingdom will break in pieces and crush all the others. Whereas you saw the feet and toes, partly of potter's clay and partly of iron, the kingdom shall be

divided; yet the strength of the iron shall be in it, just as you saw the iron mixed with ceramic clay. And as the toes of the feet were partly of iron and partly of clay, so the kingdom shall be partly strong and partly fragile. As you saw iron mixed with ceramic clay they will mingle with the seed of men; but they will not adhere to one another, just as iron does not mix with clay. And in the days of these kings the God of heaven will set up a kingdom which shall never be destroyed; and the kingdom shall not be left to other people; It shall break in pieces and consume all these kingdoms, and it shall stand forever. Inasmuch as you saw that the stone was cut out of the mountain without hands, and that it broke in pieces the iron, the bronze, the clay, the silver, and the gold—the great God has made known to the king what will come to pass after this. The dream is certain, and its interpretation sure. (Dan. 2:31–45)

Nothing can destroy the kingdom built by God and founded upon the Rock, which is Jesus Christ.

> "'Other foundation can no man lay than that is laid, which is Jesus Christ.' 1 Corinthians 3:11. 'Upon this rock,' said Jesus, 'I will build My church.' In the presence of God, and all the heavenly intelligences, in the presence of the unseen army of hell, Christ founded His church upon the living Rock. That Rock is Himself,—His own body, for us broken and bruised. Against the church built upon this foundation, the gates of hell shall not prevail."
>
> *The Desire of Ages*, p. 413

Many books have been written about both Daniel and Revelation; God gives the prophecy to Daniel, and it is interpreted to John in visions.

I shall only share what I have learned from Moses and John regarding the sanctuary. The sanctuary was opened to John in vision while he was a prisoner on the island of Patmos. He had been exiled because of his faith. We can ascend our model of Jacob's ladder to reach the kingdom of God's glory through John's vision. Jesus promised John "... To him who overcomes I will give to eat from the tree of life, which is in the midst of the Paradise of God" (Rev. 2:7). "... He who overcomes shall not be hurt by the second death" (Rev. 2:11.

"He who overcomes shall inherit all things, and I will be his God and he shall be My Son. But the cowardly, unbelieving, abominable, murderers, sexually immoral, sorcerers, idolaters, and all liars shall have their part in the lake which burns with fire and brimstone, which is the second death" (Rev. 21:7, 8). "To him who overcomes I will grant to sit with Me on My throne, as I also overcame and sat down with My Father on His throne" (Rev. 3:21).

Ellen White has always shown me how important Daniel's prophecies are to my life and yours. Nothing is more important than studying God's Word.

> As we near the close of this world's history, the prophecies recorded in Daniel demand our special attention, as they relate to the very time in which we are living. With them should be linked the teachings of the last book of the New Testament Scriptures. Satan has led many to believe that the prophetic portions of the writings of Daniel and of John the Revelator cannot be understood.

But the promise is plain that special blessings will accompany the study of these prophecies. 'The wise shall understand' ([Daniel 12] verse 10), was spoken of the visions of Daniel that were to be unsealed in the latter days; and of the revelation that Christ gave to His servant John for the guidance of God's people all through the centuries, the promise is, 'Blessed is he that readeth, and they that hear the words of this prophecy, and keep those things which are written therein.' Revelation 1:3. From the rise and fall of nations as made plain in the books of Daniel and Revelation, we need to learn how worthless is mere outward and worldly glory. Babylon, with all its power and magnificence, the like of which our world has never since beheld,—power and magnificence which to the people of that day seemed so stable and enduring,—how completely has it passed away.... And so perishes all that has not God for its foundation. Only that which is bound up with His purpose, and expresses His character, can endure. His principles are the only steadfast things our world knows. A careful study of the working out of God's purposes in the history of nations and in the revelation of things to come, will help us to estimate at their true value things seen and things unseen, and to learn what is the true aim of life" (*Prophets and Kings*, pp. 547, 548).

It is only as we have become meek that we will be allowed to enter the sanctuary. The meek will inherit the earth after being judged worthy through our belief in our Savior, Jesus Christ.

> "The meek 'shall inherit the earth.' It was through the desire for self-exaltation that sin entered into the world, and our first parents lost the dominion over this fair earth, their kingdom. It is through self-abnegation that Christ redeems what was lost. And He says we are to overcome as He did."
>
> *Thoughts from the Mount of Blessings*, p. 17

We have already learned about the meek as we ascended Jesus' ladder. Now I needed to know how I could reach the throne of God and sit down with Jesus. John revealed the vision he had. "After these things I looked, and behold, a door standing open in heaven.... Immediately I was in the Spirit; and behold, a throne set in heaven, and One sat on the throne" (Rev. 4:1, 2).

John goes on to describe what God revealed to him, but we must first be concerned about the steps we must take to enter that throne room. After that, we will see what is there. However, before relaying God's plan for the tabernacle, Moses reinforced the sanctity of the Sabbath, the cornerstone of this relationship. Here we see the importance of keeping God's law, as it takes precedence over life itself.

"Then Moses gathered all the congregation of the children of Israel together, and said to them, 'These are the words which the LORD has commanded you to do: Work shall be done for six days, but the seventh day shall be a holy day for you, a Sabbath of rest to the LORD ...'" (Exod. 35:1, 2).

Despite being involved with building the sanctuary, the people would not be working on the Sabbath, the day of worship. The importance of worship on Sabbath was above everything else. Worship is based upon God's law, so breaking it in order to build the tabernacle, would be sin. The sanctuary was designed by God for worship. In light of this we can learn how we should approach worship today.

The first step to worship for the ancient Israelites was to reflect on what their sins had caused and bring them to repentance. True conversion and transformation still begins with repentance and a complete realization of who we are before God. There is awe and joy in this process, not superficial emotionalism. To celebrate through the clapping of hands, dancing, and rejoicing in this context seems like a contradiction to reverence. Deep soul searching as we approach God would be more consistent with the sanctuary model of worship. The Seventh-day Adventist church is unique in its understanding of the sanctuary message, and this sets us apart as we consider our approach to worship.

> "Although God dwells not in temples made with hands, yet He honors with His presence the assemblies of His people. He has promised that when they come together to seek Him, to acknowledge their sins, and to pray for one another, He will meet with them by His Spirit. But those who assemble to worship Him should put away every evil thing. Unless they worship Him in spirit and truth and in the beauty of holiness, their coming together will be of no avail."
>
> *Prophets and Kings*, p. 50

Everything about the sanctuary opened their eyes to some part of what salvation meant. No one was to be a spectator; everyone was actively involved. Everything about the sanctuary illustrated something real—a part of the plan for our salvation. It is God's plan of restoring His people back to His image. It is a movement; there is a starting place and an ending place. So, let's begin our journey on the ladder now and realize the simplicity of salvation. These are the instructions God gave to Moses to build a replica of the sanctuary which is in heaven. "Then the LORD spoke to Moses, saying: 'Speak to the children of Israel, that they bring Me an offering. From everyone who gives it willingly with his heart you shall take My offering" (Exod. 25:1, 2).

> "For the building of the sanctuary great and expensive preparations were necessary; a large amount of the most precious and costly material was required; yet the Lord accepted only freewill offerings.... Devotion to God and a spirit of sacrifice were the first requisites in preparing a dwelling place for the Most High."
>
> *Patriarchs and Prophets*, p. 343

And this is the offering which you shall take from them: gold, silver, and bronze; blue, purple, and scarlet thread, fine linen, and goats' hair; ram skins dyed red, badger skins, and acacia wood; oil for the light, and spices for the anointing oil, and for the sweet incense; onyx stones, and stones to be set in the ephod and in the breastplate. And let them make Me a sanctuary, that I may dwell among them. According to all that I show you, that is, the pattern of the tabernacle and the pattern of all its furnishings, just so you shall make it. (Exod. 25:3–9)

Jesus is waiting to take us through the sanctuary to prepare us for His coming when we, in fact, will go with Him to our heavenly home. So let's begin our journey to the throne room.

AREA OUTSIDE THE COURTYARD

The sanctuary, courtyard, and the tents and surrounding area are a miniature of the plan of salvation. The area outside of the courtyard represents the world of sin in which we live.

The sins that were being committed are identified for us.

I say then: Walk in the Spirit, and you shall not fulfill the lust of the flesh.... Now the works of the flesh are evident, which are: adultery, fornication, uncleanness, lewdness, idolatry, sorcery, hatred, contentions, jealousies, outbursts of wrath, selfish ambitions, dissentions, heresies, envy, murders, drunkenness, revelries, and the like; of which I tell you beforehand, just as I also told you in time past, that those who practice such things will not inherit the kingdom of God. (Gal. 5:16–21)

This outside area is where the tents were arranged according to tribe. It was about half a mile from the courtyard. When a person sinned, he or she would take a lamb, which represented Christ, while it was still in its first year with no defects and take it to the courtyard. Of course, this was in view of their friends and neighbors. It must have been a humbling experience. Getting rid of sin in our lives is always a humbling experience, but that is what God requires.

I knew that I needed to leave behind my pride and selfishness, and I had learned that I must depend on the Holy Spirit to do it for me. "God resists the proud, but gives grace to the humble.... Humble yourselves in the sight of the Lord, and He will lift you up" (James 4:6, 10).

> "The followers of Christ are to separate themselves from sinners, choosing their society only when there is opportunity to do them good. We cannot be too decided in shunning the company of those who exert an influence to draw us away from God. While we pray, 'Lead us not into temptation,' we are to shun temptation, so far as possible."
>
> *Patriarchs and Prophets*, p. 459

Paul tells us who it is we are to separate ourselves from—those in the church who are sinning even though they know better. The area outside the courtyard could be considered the church.

I wrote to you in my epistle not to keep company with sexually immoral people. Yet I certainly did not mean with the sexually immoral people of this world, or with the covetous, or extortioners, or idolaters, since then you would need to go out of the world. But now I have written to you not to keep company with anyone named a brother, who is sexually immoral, or covetous, or an idolater, or a reviler, or a drunkard, or an extortioner—not even to eat with such a person. For what have I to do with judging those who are outside? Do you not judge those who are inside? But those who are outside God judges. Therefore 'put away from yourselves the evil person.' (1 Cor. 5:9–13)

Joel gives warning to God's ministers of their need to repent. "Gird yourselves and lament, you priests; Wail, you who minister before the altar; Come, lie all night in sackcloth,

You who minister to my God.... Alas for the day! For the day of the LORD is at hand; It shall come as destruction from the Almighty" (Joel 1:13, 15).

Joel sees the nearness of the return of Christ and implores those who are loyal to Him to repent. Even the priests and rulers are included.

Just as Noah preached repentance and pleaded with men and women to come into the ark and be saved before the flood, which covered the earth and destroyed all except those in the ark, God is showing us the way into the sanctuary for our salvation. He gives us the freedom to choose—He never forces. Either we choose to respond to His call to repent and receive eternal life with Jesus, or we refuse to enter the sanctuary with Him and receive eternal death. We decide our own destiny.

God always sends a warning message before He allows His people to be affected, and He always fulfills His word. He wants us to realize that we need repentance and reformation.

Through the inspiration of Paul, we read these words "Let this mind be in you which was also in Christ Jesus" (Phil. 2:5).

It is the new covenant God made with His people—He wants His people to surrender their minds to Jesus.

> "But this is the covenant that I will make with the house of Israel after those days, says the LORD: I will put My law in their minds, and write it on their hearts; and I will be their God, and they shall be My people. No more shall every man teach his neighbor, and every man his brother, saying, 'Know the LORD,' for they all know Me, from the least of them to the greatest of them, says the Lord. For I will forgive their iniquity, and their sin I will remember no more."
>
> Jer. 31:33, 34

Jesus invites us to come in. "Behold, I stand at the door and knock. If anyone hears My voice and opens the door, I will come in to him and dine with him, and he with Me. To him who overcomes I will grant to sit with Me on My throne, as I also overcame and sat down with My Father on His throne" (Rev. 3:20, 21).

By taking the lamb, the sinner is just beginning his journey to the foot of the cross. Remember the sanctuary is a movement. It is a process—the process of sanctification. Now let's move to the next step on Moses' and John's ladder and enter the courtyard of the sanctuary.

The Courtyard

The sinner now enters the courtyard with his lamb. He is surrounded with hangings made of fine woven linen and pillars of bronze with hooks and bands of silver. When he goes through the gate, he is no longer in view of onlookers.

For the gate of the court there shall be a screen twenty cubits long, woven of blue, purple, and scarlet thread, and fine woven linen, made by a weaver. It shall have four pillars and four sockets. All the pillars around the court shall have bands of silver; their hooks shall be of silver and their sockets of bronze. The length of the court shall be one hundred cubits, the width fifty throughout, and the height five cubits, made of fine woven linen, and its sockets of bronze. All the utensils of the tabernacle for all its service, all its pegs, and all the pegs of the court, shall be of bronze. (Exod. 27:16–19)

The earthly priests began their daily work in the courtyard of the sanctuary. They entered reverently, chanting or singing praises to God. The praise honored God and prepared the way for Him to work in the salvation of the people.

"Enter into His gates with thanksgiving, And into His courts with praise. Be thankful to Him, and bless His name. For the LORD is good; His mercy is everlasting, And His truth endures to all generations" (Ps. 100:4, 5).

> "Music forms a part of God's worship in the courts above, and we should endeavor, in our songs of praise, to approach as nearly as possible to the harmony of the heavenly choirs. The proper training of the voice is an important feature in education and should not be neglected. Singing. as a part of religious service, is as much an act of worship as is prayer. The heart must feel the spirit of the song to give it right expression."
> *Patriarchs and Prophets*, p. 594

I often sing my prayers. I told you about this when I sang my prayer of surrender and laid "All on the Altar." Directly beyond the gate into the sanctuary is the altar of sacrifice where the sinner who has brought his lamb meets the priest.

> "Christ's death proves God's great love for man. It is our pledge of salvation. To remove the cross from the Christian would be like blotting the sun from the sky. The cross brings us near to God, reconciling us to Him. With the relenting compassion of a father's love, Jehovah looks upon the suffering that His Son endured in order to save the race from eternal death, and accepts us in the Beloved. Without the cross, man could have no union with the Father. On it depends our every hope. From it shines the light of the Saviour's love, and when at the foot of the cross the sinner looks up to the One who died to save him, he may rejoice with fullness of joy, for his sins are pardoned. Kneeling in faith at the cross, he has reached the highest place to which man can attain. Through the cross we learn that the heavenly Father loves us with a love that is infinite. Can we wonder that Paul exclaimed, 'God forbid that I should glory, save in the cross of our Lord Jesus Christ"? Galatians 6:14. It is our privilege also to glory in the cross, our privilege to give ourselves wholly to Him who gave Himself for us. Then, with the light that streams from Calvary shining in our faces, we may go forth to reveal this light to those in darkness."
>
> *The Acts of the Apostles*, pp. 209, 210

As Paul said, we have nothing of ourselves to glory in, but as we take our next step up the ladder, we shall glory in how we are lifted up.

THE ALTAR OF SACRIFICE

Passing through the gate into the courtyard, there is the first piece of furniture–the bronze altar where the animal was sacrificed and burned as a sin offering. It was located just beyond the gate. It stood at the entrance to the tabernacle, and it represented the need of the sinner to be cleansed from sin before entering the presence of God.

God's instructions to Moses were:

> You shall make an altar of acacia wood, five cubits long and five cubits wide–the altar shall be square–and its height shall be three cubits. You shall make its horns on its four corners; its horns shall be of one piece with it. And you shall overlay it with bronze. Also you shall make its pans to receive its ashes, and its shovels and its basins and its forks and its firepans; you shall make all the utensils of bronze. You shall make a grate for it, a network of bronze; and on the network you shall make four bronze rings at its four corners. You shall put it under the

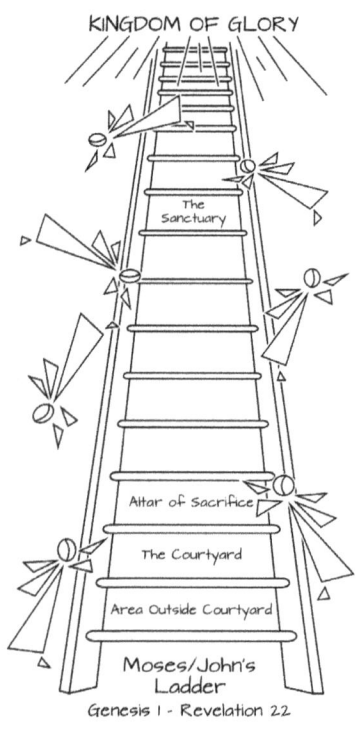

rim of the altar beneath, that the network may be midway up the altar. And you shall make poles for the altar, poles of acacia wood, and overlay them with bronze. The poles shall be put in the rings, and the poles shall be on the two sides of the altar to bear it. You shall make it hollow with boards; as it was shown you on the mountain, so shall they make it. (Exod. 27:1–8)

The horns of the altar represented strength and power. David recognized these horns as powerful, and he made mention of what had made him great. "The LORD is my rock and my fortress and my deliverer; My God, my strength, in whom I will trust; My shield and the horn of my salvation, my stronghold" (Ps. 18:2).

> "The sincere, contrite soul is precious in the sight of God. He places His own signet upon men, not by their rank, not by their wealth, not by their intellectual greatness, but by their oneness with Christ. The Lord of glory is satisfied with those who are meek and lowly in heart. 'Thou hast also given me,' said David, 'the shield of Thy salvation: ... and Thy gentleness'—as an element in the human character—'hath made me great.' Psalm 18:35"
>
> *The Desire of Ages*, p. 437

Forgiveness can only be accomplished through the blood of the Lamb. The real sacrifice for all sin was accomplished at the cross of Calvary. "The next day John saw Jesus coming toward him, and said 'Behold! The Lamb of God who takes away the sin of the world!'" (John 1:29).

It is at the altar that the sinner confesses his sins, is forgiven, and is freed from guilt. "If we confess our sins, He is faithful and just to forgive us our sins and to cleanse us from all unrighteousness" (1 John 1:9).

In the sanctuary once the sinner has confessed and the lamb is slain, he can leave with confidence that God has forgiven him, and he can claim the promise of God, which was given through Paul. "I have been crucified with Christ; it is no longer I who live, but Christ lives in me; and the life which I now live in the flesh I live by faith in the Son of God, who loved me and gave Himself for me" (Gal. 2:20).

Earlier, Jacob had this experience.

> "Jacob prevailed because he was persevering and determined. His victory is an evidence of the power of importunate prayer. All who will lay hold of God's promise, as he did, and be as earnest and persevering as he was will succeed as he succeeded. Those who are unwilling to deny self, to agonize before God, to pray long and earnestly for His blessing, will not obtain it. Wrestling with God—how few know what it is! How few have ever had their souls drawn out after God with intensity of desire until every power is on the stretch. When waves of despair which no language can express sweep over the suppliant, how few cling with unyielding faith to the promises of God."
>
> *The Great Controversy*, p. 621

The blood of the animals sacrificed pointed to Jesus, whose blood would be shed on the cross. He put an end to the need to sacrifice animals in the earthly sanctuary. The blood Jesus shed covers us in the heavenly sanctuary. What a sacrifice God made for us in giving His Son to die for our sins.

"For God so loved the world that He gave His only begotten Son, that whoever believes in Him should not perish but have everlasting life. For God did not send His Son into the world to condemn the world, but that the world through Him might be saved" (John 3:16, 17).

There are times when the blood of humans can save the life of another by transfusion, but God is speaking of eternal life in our heavenly home.

Our son, Vern Jr., who was drafted into the military during the Vietnam War, told us very little of what he went through while he was there. But two things he said remain in my memory. He was in the medics and did his best to save the lives of wounded soldiers. He saw more than anyone needs to see of blood flowing from a fellow soldier whose life was ebbing away. He recalled that many times he gave his own blood for the transfusion, and it seemed like every time he gave his blood, the soldier died. He did what he could, and I believe that he might see some of those soldiers rise from their graves to be taken to heaven because Jesus gave His blood for them.

He did another thing that lifted the spirits of the wounded, as well as his own. He had always spent time observing God's creatures in nature, and he had set up aquariums with tropical fish at home, so he could observe and enjoy them. He had seen the tropical fish swimming in the river near the base hospital, so he built an aquarium, stocked it with plants and fish from the river, and put it where the wounded had something to enjoy watching. Both he and the wounded were blessed by the endeavor, and we were so proud of him.

Seeing all the blood-shed and death took its toll, but God is good. He has given him a wife who shares his interests. She also enjoys observing nature and is very creative. She is like one of my own daughters to me. I can say the same thing about both of my son's wives. How blessed I am!

The offerings that were to be sacrificed on the altar of the sanctuary were to be "without blemish" (see Deut. 17:1). Later, these instructions were disregarded, and Malachi has to warn the priests about neglecting God. At that time, lame, blind, and sick animals were accepted by the priests and sacrificed for the people. God responds by saying,

> You offer defiled food on My altar, But say, 'In what way have we defiled You? By saying, 'The table of the LORD is contemptible.' And when you offer the blind as a sacrifice, Is it not evil? And when you offer the lame and sick, Is it not evil? Offer it then to your governor! Would he be pleased with you? Would he accept you favorably? Says the LORD of hosts. (Mal. 1:7, 8)

God reminded the priests of their responsibility before God and His people. They were to provide "true instruction" and walk with God "in peace and righteousness" for the lips of the priests are to preserve knowledge (see Mal. 2:1–9).

"The law of truth was in his mouth, And injustice was not found on his lips. He walked with Me in peace and equity, And turned many away from iniquity. For the lips of a priest should keep knowledge, And people should seek the law from his mouth; For he is the messenger of the LORD of hosts" (Mal. 2:6, 7).

The priests were to uphold the rites and instructions of the sacrificial system before the Israelites until the Lamb these sacrifices pointed to would come. There are grave lessons for pastors and leaders in our churches to ever lift up God's instructions regarding true worship before our people. How tempting it is for us today to become lax in our responsibilities. God desires obedience in respect to His ordinances, so let us approach Him with awe and reverence. He emphasized that the offerings were to be the best they had, perfect in God's sight.

As I look back, I think of one time when I made a decision for Jane that did not meet that requirement. Each of the children had a ewe, which had lambs each spring, and our church had an "investment program," which encouraged us to invest something to the Lord, so we could watch it increase in value and have a good offering to give. We gave Jane's sick lamb as an investment for God to bless, keep alive, and grow to be ready for the market when that time came. But the lamb died in spite of all our attempts to keep it alive. Now I realize we should have given one of the healthy lambs. I learned a lesson, and I have dedicated part of the increase on all that I own to God.

I cringe when I think of the honor I was proud to accept as a result of a paper Jane wrote for a class at school. The assignment was to write why they had the "best mother." She wrote of how I helped her try to save the life of her lamb, and she even mentioned how I sat by the fire all night with the lamb to keep him warm. Of course he was dying, so saving him was impossible, except through a miracle of God. He is the only one who gives life, and He chose not to do so. I often wonder if there are other times I don't remember, so I ask, and God forgives.

"In Him we have redemption through His blood, the forgiveness of sins, according to the riches of His grace" (Eph. 1:7).

Moses saw to it that God's instructions were followed exactly as God had given them. It would be a place for Him to dwell while they continued their journey to the Promised Land. God will dwell in our hearts if we allow Him.

Just beyond the altar of sacrifice was the laver. Let's move up to the fourth step on the ladder and learn about the purpose of the laver.

THE LAVER

Moses gave the detailed instructions from God to the artisans who constructed the laver.

And the artisans were skilled enough to follow those directions precisely. "He made the laver of bronze and its base of bronze, from the bronze mirrors of the serving women who assembled at the door of the tabernacle of meeting" (Exod. 38:8).

The bronze came from the mirrors women used to look at themselves to be sure they looked nice and that everything was perfectly arranged. They had to be careful not to allow vanity to creep into their hearts. The laver represents baptism. Baptism means death to our old ways and selfish

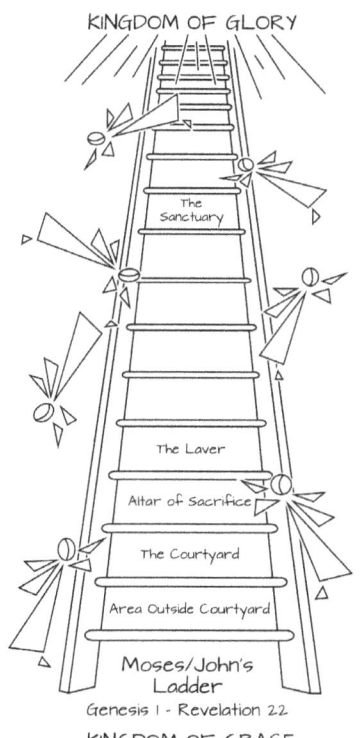

thoughts. You are buried under the water to represent a death—the death of your sinfulness. But when you come back up out of the water, you are resurrected as a new creature in Christ Jesus. All vanity is gone.

John the Baptist baptized others in the Jordan River before Jesus came to him for baptism. When Jesus came, he was humbled. "Then Jesus came from Galilee to John at the Jordan to be baptized by him. And John tried to prevent Him, saying, 'I need to be baptized by You, and are You coming to me?' But Jesus answered and said to him, 'Permit it to be so now, for thus it is fitting for us to fulfill all righteousness.' Then he allowed Him" (Matt. 3:13–15).

My first baptism was a total emotional experience. The second was after I learned the truth about the Sabbath; I was baptized along with my husband, and though I felt I was on the right path, I still knew nothing about the sanctuary. But God never gives up on us if we follow the light that is given to us. "Who may ascend into the hill of the LORD? Or who may stand in His holy place? He who has clean hands and a pure heart, Who has not lifted up his soul to an idol, Nor sworn deceitfully. He shall receive blessing from the LORD, And righteousness from the God of his salvation. This is Jacob [spiritual Israel], the generation of those who seek Him, Who seek Your face" (Ps. 24:3–6).

By allowing His meekness to guide me, I believe He will continue to lead me.

> "The meek are guided by the Lord, because they are teachable, willing to be instructed. They have a sincere desire to know and to do the will of God.... But His promise is only to those who are willing to follow the Lord wholly. God does not force the will of any; hence He cannot lead those who are too proud to be taught, who are bent upon having their own way."
>
> *Patriarchs and Prophets*, p. 384

The Bible account says that Jesus took a basin (a portable laver) and a towel and began to wash the disciples' feet. Peter objected.

> After that He poured water into a basin and began to wash the disciples' feet, and to wipe them with the towel with which He was girded. Then He came to Simon Peter. And Peter said to Him, 'Lord, are You washing my feet?' Jesus answered and said to him, 'What I am doing you do not understand now, but you will know after this.' Peter said to Him, 'You shall never wash my feet!' Jesus answered him, 'If I do not wash you, you have no part with Me.' Simon Peter said to Him, 'Lord, not my feet only, but also my hands and my head!' (John 13:5–9)

David also asked God to cleanse him when he repented of his sin with Bathsheba. "Purge me with hyssop, and I shall be clean; Wash me, and I shall be whiter than snow" (Ps. 51:7).

Like Peter and David, I want to be washed inside and out until I am "whiter than snow!"

> Do not listen to the enemy's suggestion to stay away from Christ until you have made yourself better; until you are good enough to come to God. If you wait until then, you will never come. When Satan

Moses/John's Ladder: The Sanctuary

points to your filthy garments, repeat the promise of Jesus. 'Him that cometh to Me, I will in no wise cast out." John 6:37. Tell the enemy that the blood of Jesus Christ cleanses from all sin. Make the prayer of David your own.... (*Christ's Object Lessons*, pp. 205, 206)

The laver also provided water for washing the feet and hands of the priest before he offered the burnt offering or entered to minister in the Holy Place.

After the priests had been cleansed at the laver, they entered the Holy Place in the sanctuary where there were three pieces of furniture. On the left was the gold lampstand. On the right was the table of showbread. Directly in front was the altar of incense. The Holy Place represents the walk we must have when we've made a commitment to serve Jesus. It stands for sanctification.

It took a lot of Bible study for God's followers who believed in the imminent return of Jesus to realize that the door into the heavenly Holy Place was opened in 1844, according to Daniel's prophecy. They had formerly misinterpreted the prophecy to mean that Jesus would come to take those who believed His Word to heaven, and that would be the end of this world. What a disappointment!

Let us move now into the Holy Place of the sanctuary and learn about the three articles of furniture that are there. I will share what I learned about the gold lampstand first.

THE GOLD LAMPSTAND

The lampstand in the earthly sanctuary was fed by holy oil. It lit up the entire sanctuary with a light that was never allowed to go out. Moses gives a beautiful description of this symbolic light.

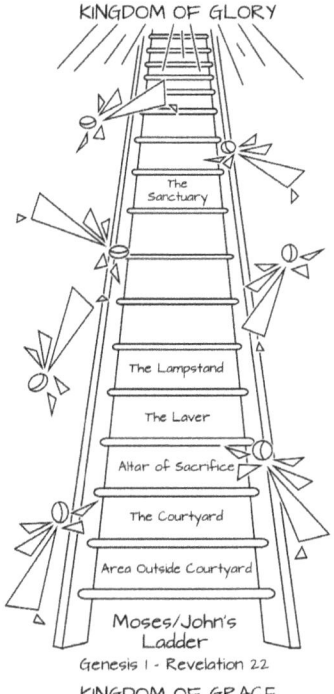

> You shall also make a lampstand of pure gold; the lampstand shall be of hammered work. Its shaft, its branches, its bowls, its ornamental knobs, and flowers shall be of one piece. And six branches shall come out of its sides; three branches of the lampstand out of one side, and three branches of the lampstand out of the other side. Three bowls shall be made like almond blossoms on one branch, with an ornamental knob and a flower, and three bowls made like almond blossoms on the other branch, with an ornamental knob and a flower—and so for the six branches that come out of the lampstand. On the lampstand itself four bowls shall be made like almond blossoms, each with its ornamental knob and flower. And there shall be a knob under the first two branches of the same, a knob under the second two branches of the same, and a knob under the third two branches of the same, according to the six branches that extend from the lampstand. Their knobs and their branches shall be of one piece; all of it shall be one hammered piece of pure gold. You shall make seven lamps for it, and they shall arrange

its lamps so that they give light in front of it. And its wick-trimmers and their trays shall be of pure gold. It shall be made of a talent of pure gold, with all these utensils. And see to it that you make them according to the pattern which was shown you on the mountain. (Exod. 25:31–40)

The olive oil for the seven-branched candlestick was to be beaten and pounded with a mortar, which produced clear and pure oil not achievable with a mill stone. The olive oil represented the purity and eternal vigilance of the Holy Spirit.

After we have been emptied of sin and self at the laver, we are ready to be filled with the Spirit. It is God's precious gift to us.

> "The Holy Spirit is the highest of all gifts that He could solicit from His Father for the exaltation of His people. The Spirit was to be given as a regenerating agent, and without this the sacrifice of Christ would have been of no avail. The power of evil had been strengthening for centuries, and the submission of men to this satanic captivity was amazing. Sin could be resisted and overcome only through the mighty agency of the Third Person of the Godhead, who would come with no modified energy, but in the fullness of divine power. It is the Spirit that makes effectual what has been wrought out by the world's Redeemer. It is by the Spirit that the heart is made pure. Through the Spirit the believer becomes a partaker of the divine nature. Christ has given His Spirit as a divine power to overcome all hereditary and cultivated tendencies to evil, and to impress His own character upon His church.... The very image of God is to be reproduced in humanity."
>
> *The Desire of Ages*, p. 671

We should have experienced this when we were re-created on the Creation ladder, and when we learned about meekness on Jesus' ladder. I learned that I can go to God each morning, recognizing that I have no power of my own to be like Jesus, and He will give me just what I need morning-by-morning. The Israelites were to be an extension of His light to the world. They were to be the guardians of God's Word which was "to be a lamp unto your feet" (see Ps. 119:105).

> "Moses made the earthly, 'according to the fashion that he had seen.' Paul declares that 'the tabernacle, and all the vessels of the ministry,' when completed, were 'the patterns of things in the heavens.' Acts 7:44; Hebrews 9:21, 23. And John says that he saw the sanctuary in heaven. That sanctuary, in which Jesus ministers in our behalf, is the great original, of which the sanctuary built by Moses was a copy."
>
> *Patriarchs and Prophets*, p. 357

"The lamps in the earthly sanctuary were to burn continually. So the Christian is ever to let the Spirit of God rule in his life, and thus shed its light abroad" (Steven N. Haskell, *The Cross and Its Shadow*, p. 52). "Command the children of Israel that they bring to you pure oil of pressed olives for the light, to make the lamps burn continuously" (Lev. 24:2).

"None but the high priest could perform the sacred work of lighting the lamps in the earthly sanctuary; he trimmed and lighted them each morning and evening" (Steven N. Haskell, *The Cross and Its Shadow*, p. 52). "Aaron shall burn on it sweet incense every morning; when he tends the lamps, he shall burn incense on it. And when Aaron lights the lamps at twilight, he shall burn incense on it, a perpetual incense before the Lord throughout your generations" (Exod. 30:7, 8).

"So none, but our High Priest, who was 'tempted in all points like as we are' [Hebrews 4:15], can give us the help we need" (Steven N. Haskell, *The Cross and Its Shadow*, p. 52).

The gold lampstand, or candlestick, was made out of one talent of gold. Perhaps this is significant, for we all are given at least one talent—that talent is time. This is the one talent we have in common with everyone else. I mentioned how we value time when I revealed my graduate research. Among the five areas measured, time was deemed the least important. However, the way we use our time is an important factor in determining our salvation. We are to give our time to God. For when we made the commitment to follow Him, we said that we were no longer going to honor ourselves but instead had totally given ourselves to following Christ. When we give ourselves unreservedly, He lights our pathway so we have a clearer understanding of His will and how we are to use our time to His glory.

Jesus is the light of the world. This light that burned with olive oil also represented the Holy Spirit, who gives us light as we read God's Word. The main function of the Holy Spirit is to convict us of sin, righteousness, and judgment. The Holy Spirit works on our conscience. We learn to hear God's voice speaking to us through the Word. And we must respond willingly just as the Israelites did when they gave the materials needed to build the sanctuary. Their willingness is repeated five times in Exodus 35.

- "... Whoever is of a willing heart, let him bring it as an offering to the LORD ..." (verse five).
- "Then everyone came whose heart was stirred, and everyone whose spirit was willing, and they brought the Lord's offering for the work of the tabernacle of meeting ..." (verse twenty-one).
- "They came, both men and women, as many as had a willing heart ..." (verse twenty-two).
- "And all the women whose hearts stirred with wisdom spun yarn of goat's hair" (verse twenty-six).
- "... All the men and women whose hearts were willing to bring material for all ..." (verse twenty-nine).

Despite establishing the importance of His law, God's worship is based upon freedom of choice. A willing spirit is the fruit of a thankful heart, which is the true spirit of worship. Obedience to God's law and a thankful heart is at the foundation of the worship established with the building of the sanctuary.

> "It was the golden oil emptied by the heavenly messengers into the golden tubes, to be conducted from the golden bowl into the lamps of the sanctuary, that produced a continuous bright and shining light. It is the love of God continually transferred to man that enables him to impart light. Into the hearts of all who are united to God by faith the golden oil of love flows freely, to shine out again in good works, in real, heartfelt service for God."
>
> *Christ's Object Lessons,* pp. 418, 419

The gifts brought by the people were the fruit of the condition of their heart. The beauty of the precious gifts of gold, bronze, and rare stones were to serve as a reminder of the beauty of the relationship between God and his people. The symbolism implied within the tabernacle would establish God's relationship not only with Israel, but with the entire human race. The Holy Spirit is given without measure only to those who ask in sincerity of heart and are willing to serve in God's appointed way. There must be a total dedication without fear of what might happen. Having "fear of the Lord" is a prerequisite as described by Isaiah.

> The Spirit of the Lord shall rest upon Him, The Spirit of wisdom and understanding, The Spirit of counsel and might, The Spirit of knowledge and of the fear of the Lord. His delight is in the fear of the LORD, and He shall not judge by the sight of His eyes, Nor decide by the hearing of His ears; But with righteousness He shall judge the poor, And decide with equity for the meek of the earth.... (Isa. 11:2–4)

Isaiah mentioned "fear of the Lord" twice in this description of those who have the "Spirit of the Lord" upon them. I wondered just what the "fear of the Lord" meant in this context. I already wrote about overcoming my fear. Now I have found that "fear of the Lord" is described many times in scripture.

- "The fear of the Lord is the beginning of wisdom ..." (Ps. 111:10).
- "And by the fear of the LORD one departs from evil" (Prov. 16:6).
- "The fear of the Lord prolongs days" (Prov. 10:27).
- "The fear of the Lord is a fountain of life" (Prov. 14:27).
- "The fear of the Lord is clean, enduring forever ..." (Ps. 19:9).
- "The fear of the Lord leads to life" (Prov. 19:23).
- "By humility and the fear of the Lord are riches and honor and life" (Prov. 22:4).
- "The fear of the Lord is to hate evil" (Prov. 8:13).

I learned that the fear of the Lord is an important ingredient in living a righteous life. It seemed to be a prerequisite for other aspects of the Holy Spirit that Isaiah listed.. I concluded that this kind of fear was a type of reverence or awe. Then my attention was called to texts in the New Testament which brought new light on the subject for me. It tells what "fear of the Lord" really is. "Who, in the days of His flesh, when He had offered up prayers and supplications, with vehement cries and tears to Him who was able to save Him from death, and was heard because of His godly fear" (Heb. 5:7).

The King James Bible renders "godly fear" as "reverent submission." This was easier to understand. Then I found a quotation which helped me understand even further:

"But the life of Jesus was a life of constant trust, sustained by continual communion; and His service for heaven and earth was without failure or faltering. As a man He supplicated the throne of God, till His humanity was charged with a heavenly current that connected humanity with divinity. Receiving life from God, He imparted life to men" (*Education*, pp. 80, 81).

Jesus desired to do His Father's will, and it was His delight. This is my desire also. "I desire to do Your will, O my God, And Your law is within my heart" (Ps. 40:8). "For I have come down from heaven, not to do My own will, but the will of Him who sent Me" (John 6:38). "And He who sent Me is with Me. The Father has not left Me alone, for I always do those things that please Him" (John 8:29).

Can I expect the Spirit to work in my life in the same way He did in Jesus? I believe I can. But I cannot comprehend the Word of the Lord without the Spirit to enlighten my mind. The light shines to the degree in which we take the Word and risk our all upon it; and as we come into difficulties while following the instructions given through these prophets, the Lord sends messages of strength and encouragement through the living Prophet, Jesus, to enable us to press forward to victory. I realize that this is where I must be willing to submit to His infilling of the Holy Spirit. Then will I be able to produce the fruit of the Spirit, which was the journey of Paul's ladder in chapter four.

> "Warn every soul that is in danger. Leave none to deceive themselves. Call sin by its right name. Declare what God has said in regard to lying, Sabbathbreaking, stealing, idolatry, and every other evil."
>
> *The Desire of Ages*, p. 806

I must remember how Moses described the golden candlesticks for the earthly sanctuary and how John saw them in the heavenly sanctuary:

- Exodus 40:24—There was a golden candlestick in the first apartment of earthly sanctuary.
- Revelation 1:12—John saw the seven golden candlesticks in heaven.
- Exodus 25:37—There were seven lamps upon the candlestick.
- Revelation 4:2, 5—John saw seven lamps of fire before the throne of God in heaven.
- Exodus 30:7, 8—The high priest trimmed and lighted the lamps in the earthly sanctuary. Revelation 1:12–18—John saw Christ, our High Priest, in the midst of the candlesticks.
- Leviticus 24:2—The lamps were burned continually, always shedding forth light.
- John 1:9—The Holy Spirit lightens every soul that comes into the world.

I choose to accept and pray for His infilling of light.

The table of showbread is the next piece of furniture in the sanctuary, so let's go there and learn about the bread on the table.

THE TABLE OF SHOWBREAD

The constant light of the lampstand in the earthly sanctuary revealed a golden table. God told Moses:

> You shall also make a table of acacia wood; two cubits shall be its length, a cubit its width, and a cubit and a half its height. And you shall overlay it with pure gold, and make a molding of gold all around. You shall make for it a frame of a handbreadth all around, and you shall make a gold molding for the frame all around. And you shall make for it four rings of gold, and put the rings on the four corners that are at its four legs. The rings shall be close to the frame, as holders for the poles to bear the table. And you shall make the poles of acacia wood, and overlay them with gold, that the table may be carried with them. You shall make its dishes, its pans, its pitchers, and its bowls for pouring. You shall make them of pure gold. And you shall set the showbread on the table before Me always. (Exod. 25:23–30)

The table of showbread represents our spiritual food—Jesus is the bread of life—I eat and gain strength. "The table of showbread was placed on the north side of the first apartment of the sanctuary" (Steven N. Haskell, *The Cross and Its Shadow*, p. 55). The table held twelve loaves of unleavened bread, one loaf for each tribe, which were kept continually before the presence of the Lord. Each Sabbath this bread was replaced with fresh loaves. The week-old bread, still consecrated by priestly ministration, was eaten by Aaron and his sons.

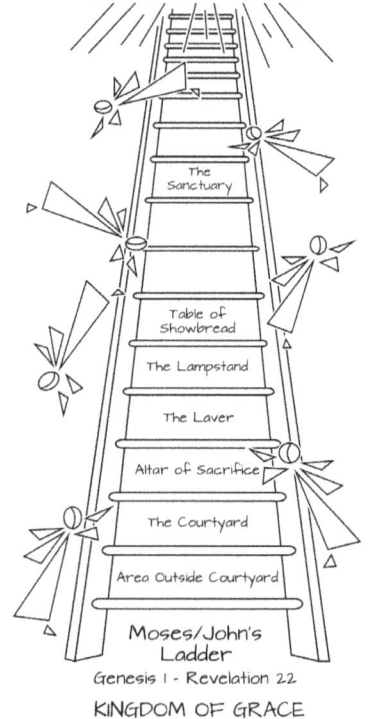

> And you shall take fine flour and bake twelve cakes with it.... You shall set them in two rows, six in a row, on the pure gold table before the LORD. And you shall put pure frankincense on each row, that it may be on the bread for a memorial, an offering made by fire to the LORD. Every Sabbath he shall set it in order before the LORD continually, being taken from the children of Israel by an everlasting covenant. And it shall be for Aaron and his sons, and they shall eat it in a holy place; for it is most holy to him from the offerings of the LORD made by fire, by a perpetual statute. (Lev. 24:5–9)

"These cakes were placed on the table hot, each Sabbath day [Leviticus 24:8; 1 Samuel 21:3–6; Matthew 12:3, 4], arranged in two rows, or piles, six in a row, with pure frankincense on each row" (Steven N. Haskell, *The Cross and Its Shadow*, p. 55).

"During the entire week the bread lay on the table. By some translators it is called 'the bread of the presence.' At the end of the week it was removed and eaten by the priests (Leviticus 24:9).

"This explains why Ahimelech the priest had no common bread on the Sabbath to give to David, as the priests were accustomed to eat the 'hallowed bread' on that day. It was not lawful to bake common bread upon the Sabbath; the command is very plain that all bread for Sabbath use in the homes should be baked upon the sixth day" (Steven N. Haskell, *The Cross and Its Shadow*, p. 55).

> And so it was, on the sixth day, that they gathered twice as much bread, two omers for each one. And all the rulers of the congregation came and told Moses. Then he said to them, 'This is what the Lord has said: 'Tomorrow is a Sabbath rest, a holy Sabbath to the LORD. Bake what you will bake today, and boil what you will boil; and lay up for yourselves all that remains, to be kept until morning.' (Exod. 16:22, 23)

"But the Lord directed that the Levites should prepare the showbread every Sabbath.... The bread was prepared on the Sabbath, and while hot was placed upon the table. The following Sabbath it was removed, and eaten by the priests on that day. The priests served 'unto the example and shadow of heavenly things;' therefore there is a heavenly lesson for us in the antitype of the showbread. It was a continual offering, ever before the Lord.. It taught that man was wholly dependent upon God for both temporal and spiritual food" (Steven N. Haskell, *The Cross and Its Shadow*, pp. 55, 56).

"Who serve the copy and shadow of the heavenly things, as Moses was divinely instructed when he was about to make the tabernacle. For He said, 'See that you make all things according to the pattern shown you on the mountain'" (Heb. 8:5).

Both alike come to us through Christ who continually intercedes for us (see Steven N. Haskell, *The Cross and Its Shadow*). "Therefore He is also able to save to the uttermost those who come to God through Him, since He always lives to make intercession for them" (Heb. 7:25).

> "Here is revealed the sanctuary of the new covenant. The sanctuary of the first covenant was pitched by man, built by Moses; this is pitched by the Lord, not by man. In that sanctuary the earthly priests performed their service; in this, Christ, our great High Priest, ministers at God's right hand. One sanctuary was on earth, the other is in heaven."
> *The Great Controversy*, p. 413

> "Though the ministration was to be removed from the earthly to the heavenly temple; though the sanctuary and our great high priest would be invisible to human sight, yet the disciples were to suffer no loss thereby.... While Jesus ministers in the sanctuary above, He is still by His Spirit the minister of the church on earth.... While He delegates His power to inferior ministers, His energizing presence is still with His church."
> *The Desire of Ages*, p. 166

Jesus gives many lessons within the table of show bread. "I am the bread of life," declared Jesus. "He who comes to me shall never hunger, and he who believes in me shall never thirst" (John 6:35).

> Then Jesus said to them, 'Most assuredly, I say to you, unless you eat the flesh of the Son of Man and drink His blood, you have no life in you. Whoever eats my flesh and drinks My blood has eternal life, and I will raise him up at the last day. For My flesh is food indeed, and My blood is drink indeed. He who eats My flesh and drinks My blood abides in Me, and I in him. As the living Father sent Me, and I live because of the Father, so he who feeds on Me will live because of Me. This is the bread that came down from heaven—not as your fathers ate the manna, and are dead. He who eats this bread will live forever. (John 6:53–58)

"To eat the flesh and drink the blood of Christ is to receive Him as a personal Saviour, believing that He forgives our sins, and that we are complete in Him. It is by beholding His love, by dwelling upon it, by drinking it in, that we are to become partakers of His nature. What food is to the body, Christ must be to the soul. Food cannot benefit us unless we eat it, unless it becomes a part of our being. So Christ is of no value to us if we do not know Him as a personal Saviour. A theoretical knowledge will do us no good. We must feed upon Him, receive Him into the heart, so that His life becomes our life, His love, His grace, must be assimilated."

The Desire of Ages, p. 389

I learned that eating daily at the table of His presence is a preparation for service and for sacrifice. We know that the bread represents the Word of God. We have to eat and see that God is good. We are what we eat, physically and spiritually. As we eat the Word of God and it is assimilated into us, it makes us new creatures in Jesus Christ. It has a changing effect on the human mind.

"The Holy Spirit comes to the soul as a Comforter. By the transforming agency of His grace, the image of God is reproduced in the disciple; he becomes a new creature. Love takes the place of hatred, and the heart receives the divine similitude. This is what it means to live "by every word that proceedeth out of the mouth of God." This is eating the Bread that comes down from heaven."

The Desire of Ages, p. 391

I was interested in a study done by the University of Montreal to measure the brain activity of Carmelite nuns while they were in a state of "mystical experience."

> Magnetic Resonance Imaging [was used to measure] the brain activity of Carmelite nuns [who were] subjectively in a state of union with God. The state was associated with significant loci of activation

in the right medial orbitofrontal cortex, right middle temporal cortex, right inferior and superior parietal lobules, right caudate, left medial prefrontal cortex, left anterior cingulated cortex, left inferior parietal lobule, left insula, left caudate, and left brainstem. Other loci of activation were seen in the extra-striate visual cortex. These results suggest that mystical experiences are mediated by several brain regions and systems (U.S. National Library of Medicine, http://www.ncbi.nlm.nih.gov/pubmed/16872743, [accessed May 14, 2013]).

Of course, one can induce changes in the brain by taking drugs, etc., and there is a form of self-hypnosis that can change the brain waves, but God wants us to feed our mind by filling it with His Word, the Bread of Life. He has told us exactly what kind of bread to eat.

> Finally, brethren, whatever things are true, whatever things are noble, whatever things are just, whatever things are pure, whatever things are lovely, whatever things are of good report, if there is any virtue and if there is anything praiseworthy—meditate on these things. The things which you learned and received and heard and saw in me, these do, and the God of peace will be with you. (Phil. 4:8, 9)

My definition of faith has helped me to realize that it can only be maintained by feeding on the Word of God. My faith depends on knowing what the Word of God says, believing what the Word of God says, expecting Him to keep His promise to do it, and depending on God to do what He says.

God told us long ago that our thinking has a decided effect on our being. "Do not eat the bread of a miser, Nor desire his delicacies; For as he thinks in his heart, so is he. 'Eat and drink!' he says to you, But his heart is not with you. The morsel you have eaten, you will vomit up, And waste your pleasant words" (Prov. 23:6–8).

> "Let your heart break for the longing it has for God, for the living God. The life of Christ has shown what humanity can do by being partaker of the divine nature. All that Christ received from God we too may have. Then ask and receive. With the persevering faith of Jacob, with the unyielding persistence of Elijah, claim for yourself all that God has promised."
>
> *Christ's Object Lessons*, p. 149

We know that we can safely read the Bible and its words have the right influence on our body. Paul gives good counsel on our thinking. "For if anyone thinks of himself to be something, when he is nothing, he deceives himself. But let each one examine his own work, and then he will have rejoicing in himself alone, and not in another. For each one shall bear his own load" (Gal. 6:3–5).

It is not God's will that Christians be vacillating and changeable. We profess Christ, and in order to bring honor to His name, we must resemble Him in both actions and character. Eating at the table makes our feelings, thoughts, and actions operate in harmony.

Paul continues in Galatians: "Let him who is taught the word share in all good things with him who teaches. Do not be deceived, God is not mocked; for whatever a man sows, that he will also reap" (Gal. 6:6, 7).

I remember my mother quoting this to my older siblings when I was too young to understand what it meant. As I began to read some inspired writings, the meaning became clear.

I must put away all evil thinking. By myself, it is impossible, but God has promised the power.

> "The relation that exists between the mind and the body is very intimate. When one is affected, the other sympathizes. The condition of the mind affects the health to a far greater degree than many realize. Many of the diseases from which men suffer are the result of mental depression. Grief, anxiety, discontent, remorse, guilt, distrust, all tend to break down the life forces and to invite decay and death. Disease is sometimes produced, and is often greatly aggravated, by the imagination. Many are lifelong invalids who might be well if they only thought so. Many imagine that every slight exposure will cause illness, and the evil effect is produced because it is expected. Many die from disease the cause of which is wholly imaginary. Courage, hope, faith, sympathy, love, promote health and prolong life. A contented mind, a cheerful spirit, is health to the body and strength to the soul. 'A merry [rejoicing] heart doeth good like a medicine.' Proverbs 17:22. In the treatment of the sick the effect of mental influence should not be overlooked. Rightly used, this influence affords one of the most effective agencies for combating disease."
>
> *The Ministry of Healing,* p. 241

> "Every seed sown produces a harvest of its kind. So it is in human life. We all need to sow the seeds of compassion, sympathy, and love; for we shall reap what we sow. Every characteristic of selfishness, self-love, self-esteem, every act of self-indulgence, will bring forth a like harvest. He who lives for self is sowing to the flesh, and of the flesh he will reap corruption."
>
> *Christ's Object Lessons,* p. 84

God has always provided bread for His people. Moses could assure the people that they would have bread and water. Just by striking a rock, God made water flow. God also provided bread in the form of manna for them as they wandered through the wilderness. "And the children of Israel ate manna forty years, until they came to an inhabited land; they ate manna until they came to the border of the land of Canaan" (Exod. 16:35).

When Elijah was fleeing for his life, God provided bread and water for him.

> Then as he lay and slept under a broom tree, suddenly an angel touched him, and said to him, 'Arise and eat.' Then he looked, and there by his head was a cake baked on coals, and a jar of water. So he ate and drank, and lay down again. And the angel of the LORD came back the second time,

and touched him, and said, 'Arise and eat, because the journey is too great for you.' So he arose, and ate and drank; and he went in the strength of that food forty day and forty nights as far as Horeb, the mountain of God.(1 Kings 19:5-8)

> "The reception of the Word, the bread from heaven, is declared to be the reception of Christ Himself. As the Word of God is received into the soul, we partake of the flesh and blood of the Son of God. As it enlightens the mind, the heart is opened still more to receive the engrafted Word, that we may grow thereby. Man is called upon to eat and masticate the Word; but unless his heart is open to the entrance of that Word, unless he drinks in the Word, unless he is taught of God, there will be a misconception, misapplication, and misinterpretation of that Word. As the blood is formed in the body by the food eaten, so Christ is formed within by the eating of the Word of God, which is His flesh and blood. He who feeds upon that Word has Christ formed within, the hope of glory. The written Word introduces to the searcher the flesh and blood of the Son of God; and through obedience to that Word, he becomes a partaker of the divine nature. As the necessity for temporal food cannot be supplied by once partaking of it, so the Word of God must be daily eaten to supply the spiritual necessities... So there is need of constantly feeding on the Word, the knowledge of which is eternal life. That Word must be our meat and drink. It is in this alone that the soul will find its nourishment and vitality. We must feast upon its precious instruction, that we may be renewed in the spirit of our mind, and grow up into Christ, our living Head"
> "Connection With Christ," *The Review and Herald*, November 23, 1897

> "Into the experience of all there come times of keen disappointment and utter discouragement—days when sorrow is the portion ...; days when troubles harass the soul, till death seems preferable to life.... Could we at such times discern with spiritual insight the meaning of God's providences we should see angels seeking to save us from ourselves, striving to plant our feet upon a foundation more firm than the everlasting hills, and new faith, new life, would spring into being."
> *Prophets and Kings*, p. 162

"God designed that His people should each Sabbath day gain a fresh experience in divine things, which would make them better fitted to meet the temptations of the week. The soul that never gains a deeper experience on the Sabbath fails to keep the Sabbath as God would have him" (Steven N. Haskell, *The Cross and Its Shadow*, p. 57).

"Moreover I also gave them My Sabbaths, to be a sign between them and Me, that they might know that I am the LORD who sanctifies them" (Ezek. 20:12).

> "Then the Sabbath is a sign of Christ's power to make us holy. And it is given to all whom Christ makes holy. As a sign of His sanctifying power, the Sabbath is given to all who through Christ become a part of the Israel of God.... And the Lord says, 'If thou turn away thy foot from the Sabbath, from doing thy pleasure on My holy day; and call the Sabbath a delight, the holy of the Lord, honorable; ... then shalt thou delight thyself in the Lord.' Isaiah 58:13, 14. To all who receive the Sabbath as a sign of Christ's creative and redeeming power, it will be a delight. Seeing Christ in it, they delight themselves in Him. The Sabbath points them to the works of creation as an evidence of His mighty power in redemption."
>
> *The Desire of Ages*, pp. 288, 289

"We may have a few minutes of quiet study of the Word on the Sabbath day when we hear the Lord speaking to us individually, but if the words are not incorporated into our lives, they give us no abiding strength. As the priests ate the bread prepared the Sabbath before, they assimilated it, and thus received strength for daily duties.

"Peter evidently understood this truth when he admonished the church to desire the sincere milk of the word that they might grow thereby and he said if they did this they would be 'a holy priesthood'" (Steven N. Haskell, *The Cross and Its Shadow*, p. 58).

> Therefore, laying aside all malice, all deceit, hypocrisy, envy, and all evil speaking, as newborn babes, desire the pure milk of the word, that you may grow thereby, if indeed you have tasted that the Lord is gracious. Coming to Him as to a living stone, rejected indeed by men, but chosen by God and precious, you also, as living stones are being built up a spiritual house, a holy priesthood, to offer up spiritual sacrifices acceptable to God through Jesus Christ. (1 Peter 2:1–5)

"Here is the secret of true Christian living. Eternal life does not come to the soul through forms and ceremonies" (Steven N. Haskell, *The Cross and Its Shadow*, p. 58). However, church services should be conducted in an orderly manner. "Let all things be done decently and in order" (1 Cor. 14:40).

> "[God] requires that order and system be observed in the conduct of church affairs today no less than in the days of old. He desires His work to be carried forward with thoroughness and exactness so that He may place upon it the seal of His approval. Christian is to be united with Christian, church with church, the human instrumentality cooperating with the divine, every agency subordinate to the Holy Spirit, and all combined in giving to the world the good tidings of the grace of God."
>
> *The Acts of the Apostles*, p. 96

Forms and ceremonies are all right in their place, but eternal life results from feeding upon the true bread that comes from the presence of God. In speaking of the church, Paul said, "For we, though many, are one bread and one body; for we all partake of that one bread" (1 Cor. 10:17).

Today, we have been given that privileged position to share God's Word, "that one bread," with the world around us. To do this we must be constantly in prayer. This is the subject on the next step we shall ascend in the sanctuary—the altar of incense.

THE ALTAR OF INCENSE

This is where I offer prayers for forgiveness. Jesus, my High Priest, intercedes for me, and the smoke ascends above the veil and into the Most Holy Place where Jesus sits on the throne by His and my Father, God.

> You shall make an altar to burn incense on; you shall make it of acacia wood. A cubit shall be its length and a cubit its width—it shall be square—and two cubits shall be its height. Its horns shall be of one piece with it. And you shall overlay its top, its sides all around, and its horns with pure gold; and you shall make for it a molding of gold all around. Two gold rings you shall make for it, under the molding on both its sides. You shall place them on its two sides, and they will be holders for the poles with which to bear it. You shall make the poles of acacia wood, and overlay them with gold. And you shall put it before the veil that is before the ark of the Testimony, before the mercy seat that is over the Testimony, where I will meet with you. (Exod. 30:1–6)

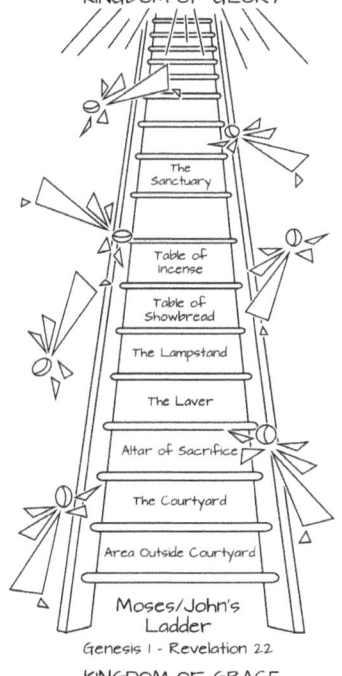

"The golden altar, or altar of incense, was before the veil in the first apartment of the sanctuary" (Steven N. Haskell, *The Cross and Its Shadow*, p. 59). The veil separated the Holy from the Most Holy Place. It had angels woven in it. These angels represented God's ministering spirits for us, and they shielded humanity from a holy God because we would cease to exist if we were to look upon a pure and holy God.

"Around the top [of the altar] was a beautiful crown of gold ... [where] holy fire was kept constantly burning, from which ascended the fragrant smoke of the incense placed upon it every morning and evening. The perfume pervaded the entire sanctuary, and was carried by the breeze far beyond the precincts of the court ... The high priest alone was to perform the sacred duty of placing incense before the Lord on the golden altar" (Ibid., pp. 59, 60).

"Aaron shall burn on it sweet incense every morning; when he tends the lamps, he shall burn incense on it. And when Aaron lights the lamps at twilight, he shall burn incense on it, a perpetual incense before the Lord throughout your generations" (Exod. 30:7, 8).

> In the offering of incense the priest was brought more directly into the presence of God than in any other act of their daily ministration.... When the priest offered incense before the Lord, he looked toward the ark; and as the cloud of incense arose, the divine glory descended upon the mercy seat

and filled the most holy place, and often so filled both apartments that the priest was obliged to retire to the door of the tabernacle. As in that typical service the priest looked by faith to the mercy seat which he could not see, so the people of God are now to direct their prayers to Christ, their great High Priest, who, unseen by human vision, is pleading in their behalf in the sanctuary above. The incense, ascending with the prayers of Israel, represents the merits and intercession of Christ, His perfect righteousness, which through faith is imputed to His people, and which can alone make the worship of sinful beings acceptable to God. (*Patriarchs and Prophets*, p. 353)

Ellen White wrote, "Moses, when directed to build the sanctuary, was 'caused to see' the heavenly model of which he was to make a 'shadow.' Revelation 8:3, 4, margin. "John, the beloved disciple, was permitted several times in vision to behold the Saviour officiating in the heavenly sanctuary. He saw a heavenly being standing at the golden altar. He beheld the incense being offered upon that holy altar. How it must have thrilled his soul when he saw that precious incense added to the poor, faltering prayers of the struggling saints here on the earth" (*The Cross and Its Shadow*, p. 60).

Sometimes I just don't know how or what to pray for. But even then, I can tell Him my concerns and pray for God's will. The Spirit will present them for me by adding the fragrant incense.

"Likewise the Spirit also helps in our weaknesses. For we do not know what we should pray for as we ought, but the Spirit Himself makes intercession for us with groaning which cannot be uttered. Now He who searches the hearts knows what the mind of the Spirit is, because He makes intercession for the saints according to the will of God" (Rom. 8:26, 27).

> "Every sincere prayer is heard in heaven. It may not be fluently expressed; but if the heart is in it, it will ascend to the sanctuary where Jesus ministers, and He will present it to the Father without one awkward, stammering word, beautiful and fragrant with the incense of His own perfection."
>
> *The Desire of Ages*, p. 667

John assures us that God hears our prayers. "Then another angel, having a golden censer, came and stood at the altar. He was given much incense, that he should offer it with the prayers of all the saints upon the golden altar which was before the throne. And the smoke of the incense, with the prayers of the saints, ascended before God from the angel's hand" (Rev. 8:3, 4).

I know that my prayers will reach the Father, and will be answered in a way that is for my best good, either in the present or in the future. The Spirit could not present the prayers of sinful mortals before a pure and holy God without adding the fragrant incense.

Not all prayers that are accepted before God are answered immediately, as it would not always be best for us; but every prayer to which the fragrance of Christ's righteousness has been added is lodged on heaven's altar, and in God's good time, they will be answered. John saw those who officiated before the throne of God holding in their hands "vials full of incense," which, he said, were "prayers of saints." "... each having a harp, and golden bowls full of incense, which are the prayers of the saints" (Rev. 5:8).

While we wait for the answer to our prayer, we can know that God has a reason. He tells us to continue to pray. "Pray without ceasing" (1 Thess. 5:17). "And we know that all things work together for good to those who love God, to those who are the called according to His purpose" (Rom. 8:28).

> "Study the history of Joseph and of Daniel. The Lord did not prevent the plottings of men who sought to do them harm; but He caused all these devices to work for good to His servants who amidst trial and conflict preserved their faith and loyalty."
>
> *The Ministry of Healing*, p. 487

"Our prayers, made fragrant by the righteousness of Christ, are presented by the Holy Spirit before the Father. To John in vision it appeared like a cloud of smoke bearing the prayers and fragrant incense up before the throne of God. The weakest saint who knows how to press his petitions to the throne of grace ... has all the treasures of heaven at his command ... The name of Jesus is often added to prayers in a meaningless way ... but every prayer of faith reaches the ear of the God of the universe" (Steven N. Haskell, *The Cross and Its Shadow*, p. 61).

I'm thankful I learned what it meant "to pray in the name of Jesus." "David understood what was typified by the incense, and prayed, 'Let my prayer be set before You as incense, The lifting up of my hands as the evening sacrifice' [Ps. 141:2]" (Ibid.).

As I learned more, we began to have morning and evening worship. My husband, Vern, read Bible stories to the children while I listened nearby making preparations for our early morning departure to school. There was competition between Nelle and Jane to see who would get to sit on either side of their dad. Many times I had the children recite their memory verses or singing a song as I drove them the twenty-five miles to school; I thought of that as worship as well. Even though this might not be what is usually thought of as morning and evening worship, it was the best I knew to do at the time, and God has honored our efforts. God is available any time of day, and Jesus is waiting to present our praise and petitions to Him. He never forgets us even though sometimes we forget our children.

Once we left our youngest son, Carey, at church. He was four years old, and we thought he had gotten in the car ahead of us with the three older children. They all sat in the back seat, and we did not look and take a head count. We just got in and drove away. In only a few minutes, we realized he was missing and went back. He was standing on the steps, waiting for us. He knew we would be back to get him.

Another time, Nelle was missing. The children were playing, and I got busy doing other things away from them. When I went to check, I could not find her. She had climbed up in the top bunk, which was Vern Jr.'s place to sleep, covered herself, and fell asleep. How my heart leapt for joy when I finally found her! But God will never forget us. He keeps our tears and prayers before Him.

> "If ever there was a time when every house should be a house of prayer, it is now. Fathers and mothers should often lift up their hearts to God in humble supplication for themselves and their children. Let the father, as priest of the household, lay upon the altar of God the morning and evening sacrifice, while the wife and children unite in prayer and praise. In such a household Jesus will love to tarry."
>
> *Patriarchs and Prophets*, p. 144

When Jesus was preparing His disciples for His separation in person from them, he assured them, "Whatsoever ye shall ask the Father in My name, he will give it you." John 16:23 The power in a name is the character of the individual that bears the name. The name of the precious Redeemer is honored, and every petition presented in that name is granted in the courts of heaven because Jesus lived a sinless life.... It is Christ's righteousness that makes our prayers accepted before the Father....

As there was no other part of the daily ministration that brought the priest so directly into the presence of God as the offering of incense; so there is no part of our religious service that brings us so close to the Master as the pouring out of our souls in earnest prayer. Anciently ... the prayer of faith entered the "holy dwelling-place" of God in heaven. 2 Chronicles 30:27

A lamb was burned upon the brazen altar in the court each morning and evening at the time the incense was renewed upon the altar. Exodus 29:38–42. The golden altar was an "altar of continual intercession," representing the prayers of God's people coming up before Him continually; while the brazen altar was an "altar of continual atonement," representing the putting away and destruction of sin, the only thing that separates us from God and prevents our prayers from being answered.

The morning and evening lamb was offered as a whole burnt-offering for the entire congregation, showing their desire to put away sin and consecrate themselves to the Lord, so that their prayers could ascend from off the altar with the fragrant incense.

In ancient Israel the people living near the temple gathered at the hour of sacrifice, and often "the whole multitude of the people were praying without at the time of incense." Luke 1:10 The habit of morning and evening prayer in the home came from this typical worship. The faithful Israelite who was far from the temple would pray with his face toward the temple where the incense was ascending each morning and evening. Josephus says the incense was offered as the sun was setting in the evening, and in the morning as it was rising....

In the heavenly sanctuary there is an inexhaustible supply of Christ's righteousness. In the type the incense was always ascending, typifying that at any time, day or night, when a struggling soul cries out for help, or gives thanks and praise for help received, his prayer is heard. In the morning, as the duties of the day seem more than human strength can bear, the burdened soul can remember that in the type a fresh supply of incense was placed on the altar each morning, and from out of the antitypical heavenly sanctuary help will come for the day to the one that claims divine help in the name of Jesus. Deuteronomy 33:25 In the evening, as we review the work of the day and find it marred by sin, there is blessed comfort, as we kneel confessing our sins, to know that in heaven the fragrant incense of Christ's righteousness will be added to our prayers; as in the cloud of incense shielded the priest, Leviticus 16:13 so Christ's righteousness will cover the mistakes of the day; and the Father, looking upon us, will behold only the spotless robe of Christ's righteousness....

No fire was to be used for burning the incense except that taken from the altar before the Lord. Nadab and Abihu, while under the influence of strong drink, offered "strange fire" before the Lord, and were slain. Leviticus 10:1–10 Their fate is an object-lesson of all who fail to appreciate the perfect righteousness of Christ, and appear before the Lord clothed in the "filthy rags" of their own righteousness. Isaiah 64:6

When the plague was smiting the hosts of Israel, Aaron the high priest, put incense on the censer and ran among the people, "and the plague was stayed." Numbers 16:46–48 ...

The horns of the golden altar were often touched with the blood of the sin-offering, thus typifying that it was Christ's death that made it possible for our prayers to be answered and for us to be clothed in His righteousness. As the fragrance of the incense was not confined to the sanctuary, but was carried in the air to the surrounding neighborhood; so in like manner, when one is clothed with Christ's righteousness, an influence will go out from him which those that come in contact with him will recognize by its fragrance as of heavenly origin. (*The Cross and its Shadow*, pp. 61-65)

We must remember that our prayers do not ascend to God alone. They bring us into the very presence of God and are joined with those of Christ, our High Priest, who fulfilled the role of the sacrificial Lamb, and now intercedes in our behalf. We need no earthly intercessor because we all have equal access to the power of the Creator of the universe who has promised that He will hear us.

"Now this is the confidence that we have in Him, that if we ask anything according to His will, He hears us. And if we know that He hears us, whatever we ask, we know that we have the petition that we have asked of Him" (1 John 5:14, 15).

"... Christ mingles with them the merits of His own life of perfect obedience. Our prayers are made fragrant by this incense. Christ has pledged Himself to intercede in our behalf, and the Father always hears the Son."

Sons and Daughters of God, p. 22

As we leave the altar of incense, let us not forget Moses and John's participation as related in the Old and New Testaments.

- Exodus 30:1–3; 40:26–The golden altar was before the veil.
- Revelation 8:3–There is a golden altar in heaven before the throne of God.
- Exodus 30:7, 8–Incense was burned on the golden altar by the high priest morning and evening.
- Revelation 8:3, 4–Much incense is added to the prayers of all saints, and they then ascend before God.
- Exodus 30:9; Leviticus 10:1–9–The one who should burn incense with strange fire was to be destroyed.
- John 3:18–He who does not believe in Jesus is condemned already and will be destroyed.

The Throne Room is the next step on our ladder, so now that we know our prayers have preceded us, we can boldly enter.

The Throne Room

Behind the veil was the Most Holy and most beautiful Place in the sanctuary. God said,

> And they shall make an ark of acacia wood; two and a half cubits shall be its length, a cubit and a half its width, and a cubit and a half its height. And you shall overlay it with pure gold, inside and out you shall overlay it, and shall make on it a molding of gold all around. You shall cast four rings of gold for it, and put them in its four corners; two rings shall be on one side, and two rings on the other side. And you shall make poles of acacia wood, and overlay them with gold. You shall put the poles into the rings on the sides of the ark, that the ark may be carried by them. The poles shall be in the rings of the ark; they shall not be taken from it. And you shall put into the ark the Testimony I will give you. You shall make a mercy seat of pure gold: two and a half cubits shall be its length and a cubit and a half its width. And you shall make two cherubim of gold; of hammered work you shall make them at the two ends of the mercy seat. Make one cherub at one end, and the other cherub at the other end; you shall make the cherubim at the two ends of it of one piece with the mercy seat. And the cherubim shall stretch out their wings above, covering the mercy seat with their wings, and they shall face one another; the faces of the cherubim shall be toward the mercy seat. You shall put the mercy seat on top of the ark, and in the ark you shall put the Testimony that

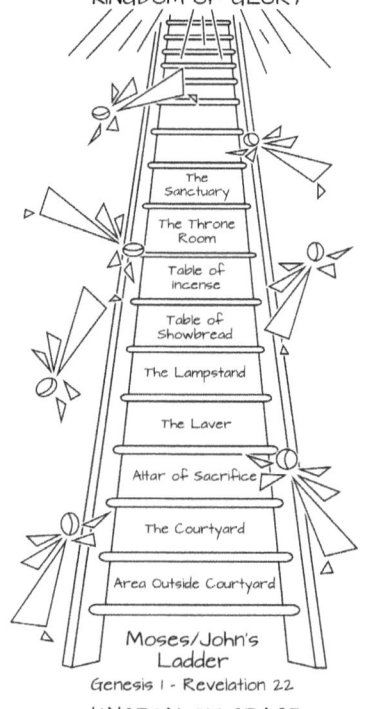

I will give you. And there I will meet with you, and I will speak with you from above the mercy seat, from between the two cherubim which are on the ark of the Testimony, about everything which I will give you in commandment to the children of Israel. (Exod. 25:10–22)

I learned that God is seated on His throne. Only the high priest—God's chosen mediator—could pass through the veil and enter this sacred dwelling once a year on the Day of Atonement. His job was to sprinkle the blood of the Lord's goat before and upon the mercy seat to atone for the sins of those who had broken the law within the ark.. The Ark was made to hold the tablets on which God wrote the commandments, a jar of manna, and Aaron's rod that budded. Three visions were given to depict God's throne: two in the Old Testament by Ezekiel and Daniel, and one in the New Testament by John.

Ezekiel recorded his vision:

> A voice came from above the firmament that was over their heads; whenever they stood, they let down their wings. And above the firmament over their heads was the likeness of a throne, in appearance like a sapphire stone; on the likeness of the throne was a likeness with the appearance of a man high above. Also from the appearance of His waist and upward I saw, as it were, the color of amber with the appearance of fire all around within it; and from the appearance of His waist and downward I saw, as it were, the appearance of fire with brightness all around. Like the appearance of a rainbow in a cloud on a rainy day, so was the appearance of the brightness all around it. This was the appearance of the likeness of the glory of the LORD. (Ezek. 1:25–28)

> "The rainbow of promise encircling the throne on high is an everlasting testimony.... It testifies to the universe that God will never forsake His children in the struggle with evil. It is an assurance to us of strength and protection as long as the throne itself shall endure."
> *The Ministry of Healing*, p. 94

> "...And the rainbow encircling the throne on high is also a token to God's children of His covenant of peace. As the bow in the cloud results from the union of sunshine and shower, so the bow above God's throne represents the union of His mercy and His justice."
> *Education*, p. 115

I remembered that after the flood God gave Noah the sign of the rainbow. As a child I believed the myth that there was a pot of gold at the end of the rainbow, and I wished that I could find it. But there was no way that I could go that far. Now, I know that there is a "pot of gold" waiting for me when I get to see Jesus in the heavenly sanctuary and the glittering golden ark; I will have reached the end of the rainbow and receive the gift of eternal life.

Daniel's description gives us further insight: "I watched till thrones were put in place, And the Ancient of Days was seated; His garment was white as snow, And the hair of His head was like pure wool. His throne was a fiery flame, its wheels a burning fire; A fiery stream issued And came forth from before Him. A thousand thousands ministered to Him; Ten thousand times ten thousand stood before Him. The court was seated, And the books were opened" (Dan. 7:9, 10).

More recently, John was given a more complete vision of the sanctuary. He emphasized that God created all things.

> After these things I looked, and behold, a door standing open in heaven. And the first voice which I heard was like a trumpet speaking with me, saying, 'Come up here, and I will show you things which must take place after this.' Immediately I was in the Spirit; and behold, a throne set in heaven, and One sat on the throne. And He who sat there was like a jasper and a sardius stone in appearance; and there was a rainbow around the throne, in appearance like an emerald. Around the throne were twenty-four elders sitting, clothed in white robes; and they had crowns of gold on their heads. And from the throne proceeded lightnings, thunderings, and voices. Seven lamps of fire were burning before the throne, which are the seven Spirits of God. Before the throne there was a sea of glass, like crystal. And in the midst of the throne, and around the throne, were four living creatures full of eyes in front and in back. The first living creature was like a lion, the second living creature like a calf, the third living creature had a face like a man, and the fourth living creature was like a flying eagle. The four living creatures, each having six wings, were full of eyes around and within. And they do not rest day or night, saying: 'Holy, holy, holy, Lord God Almighty, Who was and is and is to come!' Whenever the living creatures give glory and honor and thanks to Him who sits on the throne, who lives forever and ever, the twenty-four elders fall down before Him who sits on the throne and worship Him who lives forever and ever, and cast their crowns before the throne, saying: 'You are worthy, O Lord, To receive glory and honor and power; For You created all things, And by Your will they exist and were created. (Rev. 4:1–11)

"The ark in the tabernacle on earth contained the two tables of stone, upon which were inscribed the precepts of the law of God. The ark was merely a receptacle for the tables of the law, and the presence of these divine precepts gave to it its value and sacredness. When the temple of God was opened in heaven, the ark of his testament was seen. Within the holy of holies, in the sanctuary in Heaven, the divine law is sacredly enshrined—the law that was spoken by God himself amid the thunders of Sinai, and written with his own finger on the tables of stone."

The Great Controversy, p. 433, 43

Judgment takes place in the throne room. In chapter six, I quoted the "the three angels' messages" (see Rev. 14:6–12). I learned that this is "God's judgment hour message" (see Rev. 14:7). And I want to be one who will participate in that judgment of those who are not in heaven with me, so I can understand why they are not there. My greatest desire is to be ready for that day when the saved will participate. There will be many names that will be brought up so that we will fully understand why they are not there, and it will take a thousand years to complete. Even if loved ones are missing, we will realize why.

God gave John the vision revealing all of the sanctuary messages. I shall emphasize the judgment scenes because we all will have to face our Creator and account for how we have lived. "...For we shall all stand before the judgment seat of Christ" (Rom. 14:10).

> "Thus was presented to the prophet's vision the great and solemn day when the characters and the lives of men should pass in review before the Judge of all the earth, and to every man should be rendered 'according to his works.' The Ancient of Days is God the Father.... And holy angels as ministers and witnesses, in number 'ten thousand times ten thousand, and thousands of thousands,' attend this great tribunal."
>
> *The Great Controversy*, p. 479

Daniel revealed when this time of judgment would begin. "And he said to me, 'For two thousand three hundred days; then the sanctuary shall be cleansed'" (Dan. 8:14).

Bible scholars studied these prophesies diligently, and in 1844 God revealed to them that the cleansing of the sanctuary was not Christ's second coming, as they formerly believed, but that it was the beginning of God's judgment.

> "'The temple of God was opened in heaven, and there was seen in His temple the ark of His testament.' Revelation 11:19 ... this apartment was opened only upon the great Day of Atonement for the cleansing of the sanctuary. Therefore the announcement that the temple of God was opened in heaven and the ark of His testament was seen points to the opening of the most holy place of the heavenly sanctuary in 1844 as Christ entered there to perform the closing work of the atonement. Those who by faith followed their great High Priest as He entered upon His ministry in the most holy place, beheld the ark of His testament. As they had studied the subject of the sanctuary they had come to understand the Savior's change of ministration, and they saw that He was now officiating before the ark of God, pleading His blood in behalf of sinners."
>
> *The Great Controversy*, p. 433

We do not know when we will be judged any more than we know when Jesus will return. However, we do know that it is going on now as John wrote. And before Jesus returns, He has already decided who He will take to heaven with Him. Those who are taken to heaven and participate in the judgment of the wicked will have no interference from Satan. They shall live and reign with Christ for 1,000 years between the resurrection of the saved and the resurrection of those who refused to obey God's law.

> ... The dragon, that serpent of old, who is the Devil and Satan, and bound him there for a thousand years ... And I saw thrones, and they sat on them, and the judgment was committed to them. Then I saw the souls of those ... who had not worshiped the beast or his image, and had not received his mark on their foreheads or on their hands. And they lived and reigned with Christ for a thousand years. (Rev. 20:2–4)

The righteous will be raised from graves and taken to heaven along with the righteous still alive; the wicked will be slain by the brightness of His coming. I've written about His second coming already, so we know that "every eye shall see Him" (Rev. 1:7). This is the first resurrection—when the righteous are raised from the grave and taken to heaven. But there will also be a second resurrection—when the wicked are raised after the judgment is completed.

> "During the thousand years between the first and second resurrection the judgment of the wicked takes place.... John in the Revelation says: 'I saw thrones, and they sat upon them, and judgment was given unto them'.... It is at the time that, as foretold by Paul, 'the saints shall judge the world.' 1Corinthians 6:2. In union with Christ they judge the wicked, comparing their acts with the statute book, the Bible, and deciding every case according to the deeds done in the body."
>
> *The Great Controversy*, pp. 660, 661

It is important for the redeemed from earth to understand God's dealings with those whom they knew while they lived on earth. They must know for sure that God has been just. After the judgment of the wicked is finished by the righteous who are in heaven, the wicked will be raised to life.

> "At the close of the thousand years the second resurrection will take place. Then the wicked will be raised from the dead and appear before God for the execution of 'the judgment written.' Thus the Revelator, after describing the resurrection of the righteous, says, 'The rest of the dead lived not again until the thousand years were finished.' [Revelation 20:5; Isaiah 24:22]"
>
> *The Great Controversy*, p. 661

Seeing how detailed God was in the instructions to Moses, it made me realize that He is the same way with us in the affairs of our everyday life. He expects us to obey His Word, the Bible. It gives us directions to follow in every step of our life, and with our prayers, sprinkled with incense, we know God hears and will answer in His timing.

He knew my heart, and as I look back on my experiences, I know that God led me all the way. Now that I am nearing the end of my life, I am assured that He will lead me the rest of the way. I continually pray in the name of Jesus at the table of incense, and as the incense takes my prayers through the veil and before the mercy seat, I am confident that His robe of righteousness covers me.

"That mercy-seat, with the cloud of glory, the visible representation of God's presence, and its covering cherubim, is a figure, or 'shadow,' of the throne of the great God, who proclaims His name as 'merciful and gracious, longsuffering, and abundant in goodness and truth' [Exod. 34:5–7]" (Steven N. Haskell, *The Cross and Its Shadow*, p. 46).

> "In the temple in heaven, the dwelling place of God, His throne is established in righteousness and judgment. In the most holy place is His law, the great rule of right by which all mankind are tested. The ark that enshrines the tables of the law is covered with the mercy seat, before which Christ pleads His blood in the sinner's behalf. Thus is represented the union of justice and mercy in the plan of human redemption. This union infinite wisdom alone could devise and infinite power accomplish; it is a union that fills all heaven with wonder and adoration. The cherubim of the earthly sanctuary, looking reverently down upon the mercy seat, represent the interest with which the heavenly host contemplate the work of redemption. This is the mystery of mercy into which angels desire to look—that God can be just while He justifies the repenting sinner and renews His association with the fallen race; that Christ could stoop to raise unnumbered multitudes from the abyss of ruin and clothe them with the spotless garments of His own righteousness to unite with angels who have never fallen and to dwell forever in the presence of God."
>
> *The Great Controversy*, p. 415

Now the Lord descended in the cloud and stood with him there, and proclaimed the name of the Lord. And the Lord passed before him and proclaimed, 'The LORD, the LORD God, merciful and gracious, longsuffering, and abounding in goodness and truth, keeping mercy for thousands, forgiving iniquity and transgression and sin, by no means clearing the guilty, visiting the iniquity of the fathers upon the children and the children's children to the third and fourth generation. (Exod. 34:5–7)

"These golden cherubim with outstretched wings were a representation of the covering cherubim that surround the throne of God in heaven. [Ezek. 28:14]" (Steven N. Haskell, *The Cross and Its Shadow*, p. 47).

When the living cherubim are mentioned in the Bible, they seem to be guardians of holiness, often associated with God's throne and the closest creatures in His presence. In Genesis, we are told that because of sin, the cherubim protected the eastern entrance of the Garden of Eden. "So He drove out the man; and He placed cherubim at the east of the garden of Eden, and a flaming sword which turned every way, to guard the way to the tree of life" (Gen. 3:23).

Now they must guard and separate holiness from un-holiness, the sacred from the profane. No profane hands were allowed to touch the ark when it was moved. Uzzah was killed for reaching forth his hand to steady it when the oxen that were pulling it stumbled: "And when they came to Nachon's threshing floor, Uzzah put out his hand to the ark of God and took hold of it, for the oxen stumbled. Then the anger of the Lord was aroused against Uzzah, and God struck him there for his error; and he died there by the ark of God" (2 Sam. 6:6, 7).

> "Upon Uzzah rested the greater sin of presumption. Transgression of God's law had lessened his sense of its sacredness, and with unconfessed sins upon him he had, in face of the divine prohibition, presumed to touch the symbol of God's presence. God can accept no partial obedience, no lax way of treating His commandments. By the judgment upon Uzzah, He designed to impress upon all Israel the importance of giving strict heed to His requirements."
>
> *Patriarchs and Prophets*, p. 706

In John's book of revelations, we see the cherubim again proclaiming God's holiness as He sits upon the heavenly throne preparing for the final judgment and restoration of God's kingdom. The cherubim's presence in the sanctuary indicated God's throne and judgment seat where He would forgive sins and restore His kingdom on earth.

> "[God] does not ask if we are worthy of His love, but He pours upon us the riches of His love, to make us worthy. He is not vindictive. He seeks not to punish, but to redeem. Even the severity which He manifests through His providences is manifested for the salvation of the wayward.... It is true that God 'will by no means clear the guilty' (Exodus 34:7), but He would take away the guilt."
>
> *Thoughts from the Mount of Blessings*, p. 22

"Within the Ark was the Lord's own copy of that holy law given to mankind in the beginning.... [If there had been no law, He] could never have driven our first parents from the garden of Eden [Gen. 3:23] on account of their sin, if they had been ignorant of His holy law. How God proclaimed His law to our first parents He never revealed in His Holy Book; but when it was necessary again to make His law known to His people, after their long servitude in Egypt, He had the account of that awe-inspiring event recorded" (Steven N. Haskell, *The Cross and Its Shadow*, p. 46). He spoke the words in their hearing and recorded them on two tables of stone. After breaking the first tablets, Moses returned for another copy, which he put in the ark.

"There can be no government without law. The very suggestion of a kingdom is always connected with law. There could be no judgment without a law as a standard of judgment. God declares that 'as many as have sinned in the law shall be judged by the law' [Rom. 2:12]" (Steven N. Haskell, *The Cross and Its Shadow*, p. 48).

> "Not one command has been annulled, not a jot or tittle has been changed. Those principles that were made known to man in Paradise as the great law of life will exist unchanged in Paradise restored. When Eden shall bloom on earth again, God's law of love will be obeyed by all beneath the sun."
>
> *Thoughts from the Mount of Blessings*, pp. 50, 51

> "Since it is impossible for God, consistently with His justice and mercy, to save the sinner in his sins, He deprives him of the existence which his transgressions have forfeited and of which he has proved himself unworthy. Says the inspired writer: 'Yet a little while, and the wicked shall not be: yea, thou shalt diligently consider his place, and it shall not be'.... Covered with infamy, they sink into hopeless, eternal oblivion. Thus will be made an end of sin, with all the woe and ruin which have resulted from it."
>
> *The Great Controversy*, pp. 544, 545

> "In the temple in heaven, the dwelling place of God, His throne is established in righteousness and judgment. In the most holy place is His law, the great rule of right by which all mankind are tested. The ark that enshrines the tables of the law is covered with the mercy seat, before which Christ pleads His blood in the sinner's behalf. Thus is represented the union of justice and mercy in the plan of human redemption."
>
> *The Great Controversy*, p. 415

"The Lord has made known His salvation; His righteousness He has revealed in the sight of the nations. He has remembered His mercy and His faithfulness to the house of Israel; All the ends of the earth have seen the salvation of our God" (Ps. 98:2, 3).

It was God's plan that His people in every generation be educated as to the plan of salvation that He had provided for them. God still desires to abide with His people today and gives us instruction through His Word. Like the artisans working in the making of the sanctuary, we are given knowledge and wisdom to do His work on this earth. Our worship involves reciprocity through obedience and following God's biblical specifications. God's people bring gifts with thankful hearts through tithes and offerings, a vital part of worship. And finally, we become the venue to spread God's love to others. His presence must be felt in our midst as He abides in the throne of our hearts. But in spite of all God's efforts, some choose to be lost. The wicked who are raised after the thousand years of judgment have made their choice. God has to destroy them to put an end to sin.

"Behold, I stand at the door and knock. If anyone hears My voice and opens the door, I will come in to him and dine with him, and he with Me. To him who overcomes I will grant to sit with Me on My throne, as I also overcame and sat down with My Father on His throne" (Rev. 3:20).

We have already discussed the three angels' message somewhat in chapter six, and God made it clear that now is the time to give this message to the world. The angels are sent from the throne room to John with messages regarding seven churches, seven seals, the sealing of the twelve tribes, seven trumpets, and the importance of the ark of God. Both Moses and John are very clear about the earthly and the heavenly sanctuaries.

- Exodus 26:33–The ark was placed in the Most Holy Place.

- Revelation 11:19–The ark of His covenant was seen in the heavenly sanctuary.
- Exodus 25:21, 22–God's visible presence was manifested above the mercy seat.
- Hebrews 4:16–"Let us therefore come boldly to the throne grace, that we may obtain mercy...."

While I wait for His appearance, I want to be part of His temple here on earth–I want to be one of those stones He speaks about in the Bible.

> "In the temple there is not one misshapen stone. Each is perfect, and in the diversity there is unity, making a complete whole. One thing is sure, every stone is a living stone, a stone that emits light. Now is the time for the stones taken from the quarry of the world to be brought into the workshop of God, and hewed, squared, and polished, that they may shine."
>
> *Reflecting Christ*, p. 273

All God's stones are not the same; there is diversity in the gifts God has given each of us. I choose to use my gifts to produce the fruit that is manifest by His Spirit. I want to be polished so that I will fit into the space between the stones surrounding me. God has promised to keep me from stumbling, but if I do fall, He will pick me up and put me back on the ladder. Then I will be prepared to live on the earth made new as God has promised. Until then, I shall keep learning and waiting. Our journey has taken us through the sanctuary, and I can now say the same as my husband did before he died: "The next thing I know, I will see Jesus." But there is still more! Let's go one more step beyond Jacob's ladder of faith.

BEYOND JACOB'S LADDER

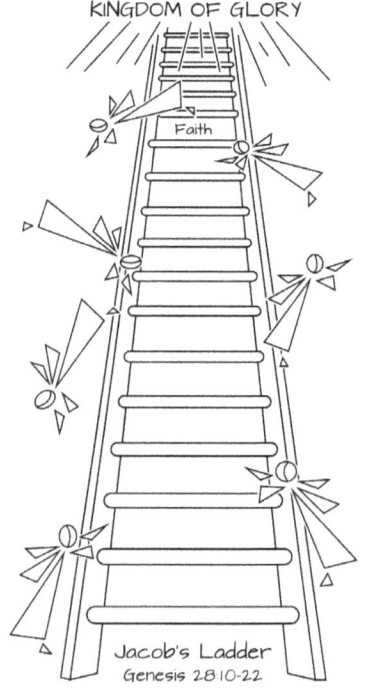

Because of his faith, Jacob became Israel. In order for us to receive the promises God promised to Jacob, we must also have faith. Then we can go beyond Jacob's ladder and receive the reward God has promised just as God's servants did in the beginning. "By faith Abel ... By faith Enoch ... By faith Noah ... By faith Abraham ... By faith Sarah ... By faith Isaac ... By faith Jacob ... By faith Joseph ... By faith Moses ..." (Heb. 11:4–23). "But without faith it is impossible to please Him, for he who comes to God must believe that He is, and that He is a rewarder of those who diligently seek Him" (Heb. 11:6).

While those who have been redeemed will spend 1,000 years with God in the Most Holy Place, the earth will lie desolate. It will be left in ruins by the great earthquake when Jesus came to take them to heaven. Satan has no one to tempt.

"Behold, the LORD makes the earth empty and makes it waste, Distorts its surface And scatters abroad its inhabitants.... The land shall be entirely emptied and utterly plundered, For the LORD has spoken this word.... The earth is also defiled under its inhabitants, Because they have transgressed the laws, Changed the ordinance, Broken the everlasting covenant" (Isa. 24:1, 3, 5).

Isaiah makes the reason clear, and John tells me that I must accept Jesus as my Savior in order to be ready to go beyond the sanctuary. All who desire to go beyond the sanctuary must believe in Him. But still today, many reject His call. "He came to His own, and His own did not receive Him" (John 1:11).

Now John describes what he saw in vision. "Now I saw a new heaven and earth, for the first heaven and the first earth had passed away. Also there was no more sea. Then I, John, saw the holy city, New Jerusalem, coming down out of heaven from God, prepared as a bride adorned for her husband" (Rev. 21:1, 2).

We will have escaped the second death. "And He said to me, 'It is done! I am the Alpha and the Omega, the Beginning and the End. I will give of the fountain of the water of life freely to him who thirsts. He who overcomes shall inherit all things, and I will be his God and he shall be my Son" (Rev. 21:6–8).

Satan has spent 6,000 years doing his work of devastation. Now, he is finished.

> For a thousand years, Satan will wander to and fro in the desolate earth to behold the results of his rebellion against the law of God. During this time his sufferings are intense. Since his fall his life of unceasing activity has banished reflection; but he is now deprived of his power and left to contemplate the part which he has acted since first he rebelled against the government of heaven, and to look forward with trembling and terror to the dreadful future when he must suffer for all the evil that he has done and be punished for the sins that he has caused to be committed. To God's people the captivity of Satan will bring gladness and rejoicing. (*The Great Controversy*, p. 660)

Now God's original purpose for creating the earth is fulfilled. "For thus says the LORD, Who created the heavens, Who is God, Who formed the earth and made it, Who has established it, Who did not create it in vain, Who formed it to be inhabited: 'I am the LORD, and there is no other'" (Isa. 45:18).

"According to the teaching of the Holy Scriptures, the only city that will endure is the city whose builder and maker is God. With the eye of faith man may behold the threshold of heaven, flushed with God's living glory. Through His ministering servants the Lord Jesus is calling upon men to strive with sanctified ambition to secure the immortal inheritance. He urges them to lay up treasure beside the throne of God."

Prophets and Kings, p. 274

Those who go beyond see the New Jerusalem. "For he waited for the city which has foundations, whose builder and maker is God" (Heb. 11:10).

We see what we have not been able to comprehend before–God's original glory. We will finally receive our inheritance. "... God is not ashamed to be called their God, for He has prepared a city for them" (Heb. 11:16).

"Human language is inadequate to describe the reward of the righteous. It will be known only to those who behold it. No finite mind can comprehend the glory of the Paradise of God" (*The Great Controversy*, p. 675).

Jesus' encouragement while He was with the disciples is fulfilled. "Let not your heart be troubled; you believe in God, believe also in Me. In My Father's house are many mansions; if it were not so, I would have told you. I go to prepare a place for you. And if I go and prepare a place for you I will come again and receive you to Myself; that where I am, there you may be also" (John 14:1–3).

I am now about to understand the promise that if we follow Him by faith, He will be our God and we will be His people. "And I heard a loud voice from heaven saying, 'Behold, the tabernacle of God is with men, and He will dwell with them, and they shall be His people. God Himself will be with them and be their God. And God will wipe away every tear from their eyes; there shall be no more death, nor sorrow, nor crying. There shall be no more pain, for the former things have passed away'" (Rev. 21:3–5).

We can only imagine these things being reality. "But as it is written; 'Eye has not seen, nor ear heard, Nor have entered into the hearts of man The things which God has prepared for those who love Him'" (1 Cor. 2:9).

> The Holy City, the New Jerusalem, which is the capital and representative of the kingdom, is called 'the bride, the Lamb's wife. Said the angel to John: 'Come hither, I will show thee the bride, the Lamb's wife'.... 'He carried me away in the spirit,' says the prophet, 'and showed me that great city, the holy Jerusalem, descending out of heaven from God.' Revelation 21: 9, 10. (*The Great Controversy*, p. 426)

> "There is no disappointment, no sorrow, no sin, no one who shall say, 'I am sick;' there are no burial trains, no mourning, no death, no partings, no broken hearts; but Jesus is there, peace is there."
> *Thoughts from the Mount of Blessings*, p. 17

"Into the city of God there will enter nothing that defiles. All who are to be dwellers there will here have become pure in heart. In one who is learning of Jesus, there will be manifest a growing distaste for careless manners, unseemly language, and coarse thought. When Christ abides in the heart, there will be purity and refinement of thought and manner" (*Thoughts from the Mount of Blessings*, pp. 24, 25).

All will be peaceful, and God will live with us throughout eternity. But Satan must be destroyed. We will see the earth in ruins and a desperate Satan whose followers have just been resurrected. He will make one last attempt to overthrow God's people, and his followers will still believe it is possible. But God intervenes. "And anyone not found written in the Book of Life was cast into the lake of fire" (Rev. 20:15).

> "The fire that consumes the wicked purifies the earth. Every trace of the curse is swept away. No eternally burning hell will keep before the ransomed the fearful consequences of sin. One reminder alone remains: Our Redeemer will ever bear the marks of His crucifixion. Upon His wounded head, upon His side, His hands and feet, are the only traces of the cruel work that sin has wrought."
>
> *The Great Controversy*, p. 674

Satan is consumed by fire along with the earth that he took over and ruined. All the other worlds have viewed this, and God's character has finally been vindicated. John gives a beautiful description of what God revealed to him about the new earth.

> And He showed me a pure river of water of life, clear as crystal, proceeding from the throne of God and of the Lamb. In the middle of its street, and on either side of the river, was the tree of life, which bore twelve fruits, each tree yielding its fruit every month. The leaves of the tree were for the healing of the nations. And there shall be no more curse, but the throne of God and of the Lamb shall be in it, and His servants shall serve Him. They shall see His face, and His name shall be on their foreheads. There shall be no night there: They need no lamp nor light of the sun, for the Lord God gives them light. And they shall reign forever and ever. (Rev. 22:1–5)

We will be living in the presence of God.

> "In the City of God 'there shall be no night.' None will need or desire repose. There will be no weariness in doing the will of God and offering praise to His name. We shall ever feel the freshness of the morning and shall ever be far from its close.... The light of the sun will be superseded by a radiance which is not painfully dazzling, yet which immeasurably surpasses the brightness of our noontide.... The redeemed walk in the sunless glory of perpetual day."
>
> *The Great Controversy,* p. 676

God originally said, "... 'Let there be light'; and there was light" (Gen. 1:3).

> Far above the city, upon a foundation of burnished gold, is a throne, high and lifted up. Upon the throne sits the Son of God, and around Him are the subjects of His kingdom. The power and majesty of Christ no language can describe, no pen portray. The glory of the Eternal Father is enshrouding His Son. The brightness of His presence fills the City of God, and flows out beyond the gates, flooding the whole earth with its radiance. (*The Great Controversy*, p. 665)

Again we are reminded of the glorious light that appeared on the first day of creation–the light of God's glory. We have now made it full circle from Eden created to Eden restored. We are told many other things about life on this new earth.

> They shall build houses and inhabit them; They shall plant vineyards and eat their fruit. They shall not build and another inhabit; They shall not plant and another eat; For as the days of a tree, so shall be the days of My people, And My elect shall long enjoy the work of their hands ... 'The wolf and the lamb shall feed together, The lion shall eat straw like the ox, And dust shall be the serpent's food. They shall not hurt nor destroy in all My holy mountain,' Says the LORD. (Isa. 65:21, 22, 25)

I hope that my house will be next to my family and friends I have known here, all in the presence of Jesus and the angels.

> God's greatest gift is Christ, whose life is ours, given for us. He died for us, and was raised for us, that we might come forth from the tomb to a glorious companionship with heavenly angels, to meet our loved ones and to recognize their faces, for the Christlikeness does not destroy their image, but transforms it into his glorious image. Every saint connected in family relationship here will know each other there. (*Selected Messages,* vol. 3, p. 316)

Ellen White was given some visions of what the new earth would be like, but she said she would not be able to describe it in a way we could understand because of its magnificence. "Human language is inadequate to describe the reward of the righteous. It will be known only to those who behold it. No finite mind can comprehend the glory of the Paradise of God" (*The Great Controversy,* p. 675).

However, she was able to convey enough to give us a little glimpse of what it is like, and she describes the joy of parents who are reunited with their children.

> We see a retinue of angels on either side of the gate, and as we pass in, Jesus speaks, 'Come, ye blessed of My Father, inherit the kingdom that is prepared for you from the foundation of the world.' Here He tells you to be a partaker of His joy, and what is that? It is the joy of seeing of the travail of your soul, fathers. It is the joy of seeing that your efforts, mothers, are rewarded. Here are your children; the crown of life is upon their heads.... (*Child Guidance,* pp. 567, 568)

What joy that will be for parents whose children have died before them and for those who may have thought their children were not saved.

"How many toil unselfishly and unweariedly for those who pass beyond their reach and knowledge! Parents and teachers lie down in their last sleep, their lifework seeming to have been wrought in vain; they know not that their faithfulness has unsealed springs of blessings that can never cease to flow; only by faith they see the children they have trained become a benediction and an inspiration to their fellow men, and the influence repeat itself a thousandfold."

Education, p. 306

What more could anyone ask than to live forever on the new earth with the family they lived with before Jesus came to rescue them? But we must remember the prerequisites. If we would be among those who will live on the new earth, we must first live in worshipful service to God while we are on this sin-filled earth. There will be music there and a song that only those who were redeemed from the earth will be able to sing. Not even the angels can sing it. It is a song of experience.

"They sing the song of Moses, the servant of God, and the song of the Lamb, saying: 'Great and marvelous are Your works, Lord God Almighty! Just and true are Your ways, O King of the Saints! Who shall not fear You, O Lord, and glorify Your name? For You alone are holy,

For all nations shall come and worship before you, For Your Judgments have been manifested'" (Rev. 15:3, 4).

God gave me a song of commitment years ago, and I have never forgotten. I still sing it. But to be able to sing the song of the redeemed—how glorious that will be! Let that be the desire of our hearts as we continue on the steps of Jacob's ladder and await Christ's return to take us to our heavenly home.

"He who testifies to these things says, 'Surely I am coming quickly.' Amen. Even so, come, Lord Jesus! The grace of our Lord Jesus Christ be with you all. Amen" (Rev. 22:20, 21). Knowing that the grace of Jesus is with me, I shall continue to wait patiently and remember how God has led me all the way through Jacob's ladder, which represents Christ, our Redeemer and Friend.

Epilogue

My journey on the ladders has been long, and I have been blessed by having faith. And through faith, I have learned to love. Through the experience, I have learned that love is the greatest thing.

Love to God: "You shall love the Lord, your God with all your heart, with all your soul, and with all your strength" (Deut. 6:5).

Love to my children: "As a father pities (loves) his children, So the Lord pities those who fear Him" (Ps. 103:13).

Love to all those with whom I come in contact: "This is My commandment, that you love one another as I have loved you" (John 15:12).

> "Love to man is the earthward manifestation of the love of God. It was to implant this love, to make us children of one family, that the King of glory became one with us. And when His parting words are fulfilled, 'Love one another, as I have loved you' (John 15:12): when we love the world as He has loved it, then for us His mission is accomplished. We are fitted for heaven; for we have heaven in our hearts."
>
> *The Desire of Ages*, p. 641

I have reached the top round on seven ladders and am thankful for the experience. But there is always more to learn. We make a big mistake when we treat our Christian experience like an achievement instead of a relationship that involves an ongoing process of learning and growth. I shall be learning throughout all eternity. In the words of Paul, you can't just point to the past and say you've arrived. The Christian experience is more than that. When you serve an infinite God, the potential for growth is also unlimited!

"Brethren, I do not count myself to have apprehended; but one thing I do, forgetting those things which are behind and reaching forward to those things which are ahead, I press toward the goal for the prize of the upward call of God in Christ Jesus" (Phil. 3:13, 14).

Jacob's ladder taught me that Jesus is the ladder, and He will keep me on it unless I choose to get off. Jacob's victory was the knowledge I needed. It is the evidence that made me realize that all who claim God's promises as he did and pray long and perseveringly will succeed as he did.

> "And the years of eternity, as they roll, will bring richer and still more revelations of God and of Christ. As knowledge is progressive, so will love, reverence, and happiness increase."
>
> *The Great Controversy*, p. 678

Epilogue

Peter's ladder taught me the steps that we must add to the faith, which God gave us as a gift: virtue/power/grace, knowledge, self-control, perseverance and patience, godliness, brotherly kindness and love. We are to become partakers of "the divine nature." I am still trying to understand love and how I can show that love to others more fully.

God's ladder taught me the Ten Commandments, and that those laws exemplify His character as well as the life Jesus lived among men. I cannot keep them by myself, but if I choose, the Holy Spirit will dwell within me and observe them for me.

Jesus' ladder taught me the blessings He has in store for me; however, He warned me that if I accept those blessings, I can expect to be reviled and persecuted. Yet, through it all, He promised He will never leave me nor forsake me.

Paul's ladder taught me to add to the love I discovered on Peter's ladder, and the joy I found on Jesus' ladder. He also encouraged me to have peace, patience, kindness, goodness, faithfulness, gentleness, and self-control. He called these character traits the "fruit of the Spirit," and if I choose, the Holy Spirit will grow those fruit in me as evidence that I know what His Commandments are.

God's Creation Ladder taught me that God, the Father, His Son, Jesus, and the Holy Spirit were all involved in Creation. They created the heaven and the earth and everything in them in six literal days, in the order needed for the survival of the living creations. Then He rested on the seventh day, and He made it holy. He instructed humanity to rest on the Sabbath in memory of His Creation, and He included that as a requirement of the Ten Commandments. He sent three angels to remind us to worship God as our Creator and give glory to Him because we are now in the time of the judgment.

John's ladder taught me that we are very near the end of time and that we should be proclaiming the third angel's message. He also made me see that Jesus is in the sanctuary with His Father making intercession for us and in the act of judging the world, and that Jesus will return to take those to their heavenly home very soon. God will cleanse the earth and make it new for us to dwell in forever, without sin ever entering again.

It has been an interesting journey, and my spiritual life has grown with the experience. Even though it is harder for me to remember what I read now, God has promised to bring to my memory those things I might need if I am called to give an account for my faith. "Now when they bring you to the synagogues and magistrates and authorities, do not worry about how or what you should answer, or what you should say. For the Holy Spirit will teach you in that very hour what you ought to say" (Luke 12:11, 12).

Since I found my working definition of faith—knowing what the Word says; believing what the Word says; expecting the Word to do what it says; and depending on the Word to do what it says—I am confident that my salvation is sure. My faith will not save me, but it is my faith in the faithfulness of Jesus that brings forth the works that show that I am being saved by God's grace. I have spent much time reading my Bible and other inspirational books to develop a relationship with Jesus. I know that I am saved by grace, through the faithfulness of Jesus. And even though my faith may be small, I have His promises, and God's Word is sure. "... Assuredly, I say to you, if you have faith as a mustard seed, you will say to this mountain, 'Move from here to there,' and it will move; and nothing will be impossible for you. However, this kind does not go out except by prayer and fasting'" (Matt. 17:20, 21).

I have spent time in prayer and fasting, and I have never forgotten the one verse my mother always ended her letters with after I was married. She never scolded me for entering into marriage with a man she thought was not best for me because of the difference in our ages. The verse helped me through many trials: "I can do all things through Christ who strengthens me" (Phil. 4:13).

Even though I did not know it, Jesus was doing work that I took credit for in my selfish pride. I thought I did the things that helped me through my trials. Now I know who provided the power that was doing the work. And yet, I now know that I do have something to do, which will determine my salvation. I must choose to surrender my will daily and continue to study, pray, obey, and keep God's Word fresh in my mind. I have been chosen, and I have chosen. "Therefore, my beloved, as you have always obeyed, not as in my presence only, but now much more in my absence, work out your own salvation with fear and trembling; for it is God who works in you both to will and to do for His good pleasure" (Phil. 2: 12, 13).

I would like to have had an experience like Samuel, but I failed to hear God's voice until I was older. I am thankful that He does all things according to His timing. It is never too late.

> (Now Samuel did not yet know the LORD, nor was the word of the LORD yet revealed to him.) And the LORD called Samuel again the third time. So he arose and went to Eli, and said, 'Here I am, for you did call me.' Then Eli perceived that the LORD had called the boy. Therefore Eli said to Samuel, 'Go, lie down; and it shall be, if He calls you, that you must say, 'Speak, LORD, for Your servant hears!'… So Samuel grew, and the LORD was with him and let none of his words fall to the ground. (1 Sam. 3:7–9, 19)

Even if I should forget all these things I have learned during my older years, I am confident that I can rely on my innocent childhood faith. I believe that God's Word is true; He loves me; I belong to Him. I can never forget the song I learned as a child. I believe knowing it is what carried me through all those years when I did not understand His plan of salvation. He waited until I was ready before He revealed more.

I believe the Bible is the inspired Word of God and reveals my purpose in life. "All Scripture is given by inspiration of God, and is profitable for doctrine, for reproof, for correction, for instruction in righteousness, that the man of God many be complete, thoroughly equipped for every good work" (2 Tim. 3:16, 17).

I believe that Jesus is the eternal, self-existent God and is not a created being. Even though He is fully God, He took upon Himself the form of a man to live and die for our sins. I believe that the penalty for my sins was paid on the cross of Calvary by Jesus' death. "For the wages of sin is death, but the gift of God is eternal life in Christ Jesus our Lord" (Rom. 6:23).

By believing in Jesus Christ and accepting the grace of His shed blood, I have received the gift of eternal life. I love Jesus for His sacrificial death. I know that I am not saved by my works, but because I am being saved, I choose to obey His commandments. "Not of works, lest any man should boast" (Eph. 2:9). "If you love Me, keep My commandments" (John 14:15).

I believe prophecy reveals that Jesus is coming again in God's timing. "He who testifies to these things says, 'Surely I am coming quickly.' Amen. Even so, come, Lord Jesus" (Rev. 22:20).

Epilogue

> "Then they that have kept God's commandments shall breathe in immortal vigor beneath the tree of life, and through unending ages the inhabitants of sinless worlds shall behold, in that garden of delight, a sample of the perfect work of God's creation, untouched by the curse of sin—a sample of what the whole earth would have become, had man but fulfilled the Creator's glorious plan."
>
> *Patriarchs and Prophets*, p. 62

I am truly thankful that the Holy Spirit made me aware of how Jacob's ladder could lead me from the kingdom of grace, which we experience on earth, to the top of the ladder where we will see the glory of God face-to-face. I long to see Jesus and my loved ones in the land promised to Jacob. Then we shall have free access again to the tree of life.

I shall never forget Jacob's ladder and how God spoke to Jacob and later wrestled with him to test his loyalty. He passed the test, was forgiven, and was given a new name. "As an evidence that Jacob had been forgiven, his name was changed from one that was a reminder of his sin, to one that commemorated his victory" (*Patriarchs and Prophets*, p. 198).

My belief in Christ's death on the cross for my sins is His test for me. For if I believe His Word and live by the power of the Holy Spirit, I know I shall pass the test as Jacob did.

"Then [Jacob] dreamed and behold, a ladder was set up on the earth, And its top reached to heaven; And there the angels of God were ascending and descending on it. And behold, the Lord stood above it and said: 'I am the LORD God of Abraham your father and the God of Isaac; The land on which you lie I will give to you and your descendants" (Gen. 28:12, 13).

> "The ladder represented Christ, who had opened the communication between earth and heaven. In Christ's humiliation He descended to the very depths of human woe in sympathy and pity for fallen man, which was represented to Jacob by one end of the ladder resting upon the earth, while the top of the ladder, reaching unto heaven, represents the divine power of Christ grasping the Infinite and thus linking earth to heaven and finite man to the infinite God. Through Christ the communication is opened between God and man. Angels may pass to and fro from heaven to earth with messages of love to fallen man, and to minister unto those who shall be heirs of salvation. It is through Christ alone that the heavenly messengers minister to men."
>
> *Confrontation*, p. 46

Just as God spoke to Jacob in a dream, He speaks to us by His words written in the Bible. "In the beginning was the Word, and the Word was with God, And the Word was God" (John 1:1). My prayer for all who read this book is that they get on the bottom round of faith and go to the top of Jacob's ladder, depending on Jesus each step of the way. Then we will all be ready and waiting for Jesus' return to take us through the gate to be with Him forever.

"He who testifies to these things says,
'Surely I am coming quickly.'
Amen.
Even so, come Lord Jesus!
The grace of our Lord Jesus Christ be with you all.
Amen"
(Rev. 22:20, 21).

We invite you to view the complete
selection of titles we publish at:

www.TEACHServices.com

Scan with your mobile
device to go directly
to our website.

Please write or email us your praises, reactions, or
thoughts about this or any other book we publish at:

P.O. Box 954
Ringgold, GA 30736

info@TEACHServices.com

TEACH Services, Inc., titles may be purchased in bulk for educational, business,
fund-raising, or sales promotional use.
For information, please e-mail:

BulkSales@TEACHServices.com

Finally, if you are interested in seeing
your own book in print, please contact us at

publishing@TEACHServices.com

We would be happy to review your manuscript for free.

www.ingramcontent.com/pod-product-compliance
Lightning Source LLC
Chambersburg PA
CBHW080449170426
43196CB00016B/2733